The Age of Charlemagne

George James

Published 2017 by Didactic Press

CONTENTS

HISTORICAL INTRODUCTION.

One of the noblest possessions of the Roman Empire was the province of ancient Gaul. Much blood and treasure had been expended in its conquest; infinite wisdom, moderation, and vigour had been displayed in the means taken to attach it to the dominion of the Caesars; and the passing of several centuries had strongly cemented the union, and incorporated the conquered with their conquerors. Unwieldy bulk, enfeebling luxury, intestine divisions, and universal corruption soon, however, began to draw down the impending destruction upon the head of the imperial city. Attack after attack, invasion following invasion, left her still weaker under each succeeding monarch; province after province was wrested from her sway, till at length Odoacer, chief of the Scyrri, raised his standard in Italy; Romulus Augustulus yielded the empty symbols of an authority he did not possess; and the Roman Empire was no more.

Previous to this period, however, Gaul had been in fact, though not in name, separated from the falling monarchy, and portioned out among a thousand barbarous tribes. The country between the Rhone and the Alps had long been possessed by the Burgundians; the Goths held the whole territories situated between the Loire and the Pyrenees; Brittany, or Armorica, was divided between fresh colonies of Saxons and the remains of the aborigines; great part of the east of Belgium was in the hands of the Franks; and the Roman legions that were still left to maintain the almost nominal possession of Gaul, cooped up in a narrow space, and threatened daily by active and warlike enemies, thought of nothing but casting off the control of their enfeebled country, and finding strength in independence.

In the meantime the larger cities were filled with a mixed population, consisting partly of the Roman colonists, partly of the ancient Gauls, partly of their savage conquerors. Some few, indeed, either by accident or courageous resistance, had escaped the fury of the invaders and remained free, while all around them had been subdued; some had been sacked and left desolate; and some, having been ceded by the falling emperors themselves to the Goths, or to any other of the tribes in temporary alliance with Rome, had passed more mildly under the sway of the barbarians, and enjoyed as much protection as could be afforded in times so disastrous.

Such was the general aspect of the province a little previous to the final overthrow of the Roman Empire. But those were days of change, when nothing was fixed; and the nation which ruled today, tomorrow had passed away, and was unknown; and all that continued with unaltered force was ravage, disorder, and destruction.

Each of the savage tribes of the north, in its passage to more fertile regions, had expended its first fury on the plains of Gaul, and had contributed to sweep away letters, and institutions, and arts.

"Innumerable nations of barbarians", says St. Jerome, in his letter to Aggerunchia, "took possession of the whole of Gaul. The Quadi, the Vandals, the Sarmatians, the Alani, the Gepidae, the Herculi, Saxons, Burgundians, Germans, and Pannonians—horrible republic!—ravaged the whole country between the Alps, the Pyrenees, the ocean, and the Rhine. Assur was with them. Mayence, formerly a famous city, was taken and sacked, and thousands of its inhabitants massacred. Worms was ruined by a long siege; the people of the powerful cities of Rheims, Amiens, and Arras, the Morini, situated in the far parts of Belgium, and the inhabitants of Tournay, Spires, and Strasburg, were transported into Germany. Aquitaine, the Lyonaise, and the Narbonaise were entirely devastated, except some few of the towns; and these the steel smote without, while famine desolated them within".

The Goths, the Vandals, and the Huns added, one after the other, a fresh load to the mountain of calamities piled up on unhappy Gaul; and often left scattered colonies behind, still to devour the land, and to carry on the work of barbarism so signally begun.

With such a picture before our eyes, it is scarcely possible to conceive the existence of anything like a state of society regulated, even in the slightest degree, by fixed principles. In what relationship, could man live with man, when all ties were broken, and when the discordant elements of the population offered a chaos of different nations, languages, manners, and ideas, precluding the possibility even of that simple form of government common among savage nations? In the fields and plains, then, it is probable that the whole was chaotic confusion, and that for a long time all rule was at an end, except that rule which it is the object of every law to correct,— the rule of the strong over the weak.

Within the larger cities, however, two or three principles of security still existed. In those towns which had resisted the barbarians, it seems that the institutions of Rome yet remained almost entire; and that, though the inhabitants were cut off from the source of their laws, the necessity of combination for the general defence maintained at least some internal regularity and order. The extent to which the Roman law was preserved during the middle ages is a question of great difficulty, and one on which I am not called to enter at large in this place, more especially as the subject has been argued ably elsewhere. That it was preserved in a considerable degree is evident from the continual reference made to it by all the barbarian codes; and the cause of the permanence of the municipal institutions of Rome, while all other principles of government were swept away, may probably be discovered in the popular and independent character of the civic constitution throughout the whole empire.

This independent civic constitution originated in Italy itself; but being extended more or less to all the provinces by the emperors, it was especially perfected in Gaul; and it is worthwhile to examine what was really the municipal government of a Gallic city under the sway of Rome, in order to form some opinion of the conservative influence which those institutions still exercised in the midst of the convulsions which rent the empire at its fall.

The model of each provincial city was Rome itself; and as the institutions of the great capital varied by the progress of time, so the forms of local administration changed. The general assemblies of the people were the original source of power; in them the laws were at first enacted, and a popular council or senate chosen, which gradually took the whole authority into its own hands. The name of this municipal council was, in the early days of the empire, *Ordo Decurionum*; but at length it was termed simply Curia; and its members were called *decurions*, or *curiales*. Sometimes, also, they received the name of senators, although this would seem to have been an appellation of courtesy.

The internal management of the affairs of the city, combining both the legislative and the executive authority, was the chief function of the *Curia*; but, in Italy itself, the magisterial jurisdiction was intrusted to an officer sometimes called duumvir, sometimes quatuorvir, or magistratus, who was chosen by the decurions from their own body, though the imperial governors, and often the retiring magistrate, exercised great influence in the election. In the provinces, however, no such magistrate existed, except in a few cases; and the presidency of the council was intrusted to the eldest decurion, while the magisterial functions were exercised by the whole as a body. Thus, at the time of the barbarian invasions, a popular power and an individual government was found in each of the cities, independent of the state. Its conservative influence was great while suffered to exist, and it was easily renewable when casually overturned by any passing torrent of barbarians.

These, in general, contented themselves with plunder and massacre, and neither strove for nor desired a lengthened possession of the places they captured. Even those cities which were taken by the Vandals and the Huns were generally abandoned by them as soon as they were pillaged; so that such of the inhabitants as had effected their escape to any place of refuge came back when the desolating force had passed by, and possibly resumed their habits as well as their dwellings.

Such was the case when the city of Rheims was besieged and taken by the barbarians. Satisfied with their plunder, and by no means disposed to remain stationary in any one spot, the body of Vandals by which it had been subdued speedily left the city, which afforded them no further object for their rapacity; and the inhabitants who had fled to the mountains returned, taking care to ascribe their deliverance from their cruel enemies to a miraculous interposition of Heaven.

There was another power also which acted to preserve the seeds of order in the cities, to bind at least a portion of the population together by strong and indissoluble ties, and to maintain one species of authority while every other authority was at an end,—I mean the Christian religion, and the power cast into the hands of the church by an influencing feeling totally apart from the frail and falling institutions of humanity whereby it was surrounded.

Christianity had then been long preached in Gaul; and, in spite of the barbarous ignorance which obscured it, and the dark superstitions with which it was mingled, its innate principles of union, benevolence, and peace were felt where every other good feeling was overwhelmed, and tended potently to preserve order in the midst of a thousand causes of disorganization. Perhaps even the very blind and enthusiastic superstition of the Christians of that age, the multitude of miracles which they supposed themselves capable of performing, and the many wonderful interpositions of Heaven which they reported in their own favour, was not without its use, both in commanding respect for the only chastening principle that yet remained, and in preparing the minds of the semi-barbarous Romans, and of the deeper savages with whom they were now mingled, for a religion the least superstitious in its own nature of any doctrine that ever was promulgated on earth.

Far is it from my object to countenance deceit, or even policy, in any matter of religion—a matter which neither requires nor admits of prop or guidance from mortal man. But still, it is the business of the historian not only to state events but to examine their causes, and to trace their effects; and it appears to me an indisputable fact, that the superstition with which the vivid imagination of a barbarous people clothed the simplest and purest of doctrines served to assimilate it to their own minds, and to ensure easier reception to principles calculated in the end to elevate, to purify, and to correct. In a worldly point of view it did much more: it added an imaginary dignity in the eyes of the people to the real dignity of devotion and a holy life; and by making the clergy respected and reverenced, it called those who were great and powerful, not only to embrace the faith, but, on interested motives, to solicit those stations in the church which added to their consideration with their countrymen, in an age when the multitude of followers and adherents was the only means of safety. Thus we find the various bishoprics of Gaul as strenuously solicited and intrigued for in the fourth, fifth, and sixth centuries as any mundane honour of our latter days, and the writers of those ages, in general, state ail the great dignitaries of their church to have sprung from families which they qualify as possessing senatorial rank, or great wealth and possessions.

It is true, that to counterbalance in the eyes of the worldly any advantages which the higher stations of the church might possess, there were to be thrown into the opposite scale frequent persecutions, tortures, and even martyrdom; but it must be remembered that such a fate rarely fell on any but the more zealous, who made themselves prominent by their enthusiasm, and like elevated points in a thunder-storm, drew down the fire upon themselves by their very pre-eminence. To these, however, their zeal was a sufficient support. They coveted the name of martyr; and it is probable that the heroic constancy with which they bore the most excruciating suffering did more to strengthen and confirm the faithful, and to convert all who possessed that nobler fire of the mind which is so easily exalted into enthusiasm, than the prospect even of honours, dignity, and power did to attract the worldly and interested.

Thus spread the Christian religion through a great part of Gaul; and the power given by it to the bishops, the remains of the municipal senates established by the Romans, together with the few and simple laws of the barbarians, formed the whole guarantee of order, of property, and of life, in that day,—a frail tenure by which to hold both existence and tranquillity, it is true; but still it was some check upon man's unruly passions—some barrier in the way of absolute anarchy.

The laws of the barbarians just mentioned were of course very different, according to the habits and degree of civilization of the various nations which had formed them. In most cases they were simply traditionary, and frequently depended in all points on the will of the chief by whom the tribe was led. An exception, however, to this want of regular written institutions is to be found in the case of the Burgundians, who seem to have been influenced by more settled habits than the rest of the invaders of Gaul. They first set the example of establishing written laws. This undertaking—one of the greatest steps in the progress of civilization—was begun, if not completed, by Gondebald, King of Burgundy, who, somewhere about the year 500, caused to be published part of the *loi Gombette*, as it is now called, about a century after the compilation of the Theodosian, and about thirty years prior to the Justinian code.

Remarkable in itself as the first of the barbarous codes of law, this composition is still more so in two other points of view. In the first place, the very cause of its institution, as stated by Gregory of Tours, shows, in a melancholy degree, to what a pitch of degradation the great overthrower of all dynasties had already reduced the mighty Romans,—the conquerors and oppressors of the world.

"Gondibert", says the historian, "having recovered his dominion over all that part of the country now called Burgundy, he therein instituted milder laws, that the Romans might not be oppressed!". Two centuries before, who had dared to oppress a Roman? In the second place, this code is not a little curious as fixing the origin of judicial combats; for here do we find, for the first time, that barbarous and unjust mode of judgment authorized as a law. Among a people whose manners, wishes, arts, and knowledge were all referable in some way to the idea of attack and defence, whose acquisitions had been made by the sword, and by the sword alone could be maintained, it was not wonderful that strength and courage should have been ranked as virtues, and weakness and cowardice should have been in themselves looked upon as crimes; but when to this was added a firm belief in the immediate and apparent interposition of Heaven in all human affairs, the trial by battle was the natural result both of national feelings and religious impressions.

Long before the fall of the western empire, as I have already stated, the doctrines of Christianity had been promulgated in Gaul, and had obtained many and powerful followers in each of the large cities. Nevertheless, over the face of the country in general, religious opinions were as various as the various nations who possessed the soil. The grand division was of course between the idolaters and the Christians; but even among the Christians themselves existed a vast and distressing schism, which neutralized the efforts of zeal, and wasted the powers which should have been applied solely to promote the great objects of Christianity, in profane contests, and most unchristian persecutions.

It is not my purpose here to examine, even cursorily, the tenets of Arius, or to trace the extension of his doctrine. Suffice it, that, though condemned by the ecumenical council of Nice, and attacked by the whole powers of the Roman church, the followers of the Arian heresy in Gaul were far superior in numbers, if not in zeal and talent, to those who adhered to the Nicene Creed. The Goths, possessing the country from the Loire to the Pyrenees, and the Burgundians, on the other side of the Rhone, were almost universally Arians, while the rest of the population of France was divided between Catholics of the Roman church, the remains of the ancient tribes of heathen Gaul, and the various nations of idolatrous Franks, who were now rapidly extending their dominions in the northern and eastern parts of Flanders.

In the choice between those who differed with them on certain doctrinal points, and those who rejected their religion altogether, the followers of the council of Nice, of course, hesitated not a moment. The universal weakness of human nature on such subjects made them look with an infinitely more favourable eye upon heathens than they did upon heretics; and consequently the progress of the Franks was hailed with gladness by all the Catholic clergy of Gaul. Cabals and intrigues of every kind were carried on to facilitate their conquests; and their coming was anticipated with joy, even in the very dominions of the Goths.

As it is to be my task, henceforward, to trace the course of the Franks, I must be permitted for a moment to look back upon their prior history as far as I find it clear and uninvolved, without, however, entering upon any of those long and laborious discussions concerning the origin of nations, which rarely do aught but exercise the writer's imagination, without proving either pleasing or instructive to the reader.

The nation of the Franks was evidently composed of many distinct tribes, and originally inhabited some district of Germany, probably not far from the Rhine. Their first settlements in Gaul took place during the military government of the Emperor Julian; but in that age they presented themselves on the Roman territory, not so much as conquerors or aggressors, as refugees, driven from their native land by a more powerful tribe.

The vigorous mind of Julian was at that time occupied in endeavouring, by every earthly means, to uphold the vast but decaying fabric of the Roman Empire, to restore to it its pristine lustre, and to renew its ancient force. The advantages of mingling with the corrupted legionaries of Rome fresh troops, whose savage strength and wild courage had not yet been in the least degree affected by the enfeebling power of luxury, did not escape him; and he permitted the tribe of Franks who had been compelled to seek refuge in the Roman territory, to settle quietly in Brabant. More prudent, however, than his successors, he took care that the barbarians whom he admitted should be too few in number to prove dangerous; and thus, though he received that tribe called the Salii, who had been driven across the Rhine by their enemies—though he attacked and slaughtered the Quadi, who pursued them —though he assigned the emigrants lands, and granted them every hospitable privilege—, he drove back the Chamavi, another tribe of the same nation, who followed, expelled the rest of the savage hordes who had already passed the Rhine, and closed the boundaries of the Roman empire against any further influx of barbarians.

After this period, we continually find the Salii serving in the Roman infantry, and remarkable for their activity as foot soldiers. Everything, indeed, leads us to suppose, that as long as the Empire existed, they were distinguished by the Romans from the other tribes of Franks, with whom the imperial generals waged a continual and devastating warfare on the confines of Gaul and Germany. It is certain, also, that on their settlement at Tessander Lo, in Brabant, the tribe of the Salii were assigned certain districts; and, as we afterward find them fighting conspicuously among the forces of the empire, it is more than probable that these lands were granted on the condition of military service,—by no means an uncommon practice among the Romans. Called upon himself to bring a certain number of men into the field, the Duke, as he is named, or chief of the Salii, to whom the territory was granted, of course portioned it out among his followers on the same condition; and the proprietor of every estate thus acquired was obliged to appear in arms at the call of his leader. Women, not being able to fulfil the warlike duties of such a tenure, were cut off from possession of the soil in the country of the Salii; and hence, probably, the motive and the origin of that part of the *Salique law* which declares that, on Salique ground, no part of the land can descend in heritage to a woman,—a law which, though apparently unjust, was only the natural consequence of the terms on which the territories were originally granted.

For many years this law, now confined in its application to royal successions, was extended nominally to all noble feoffs. Its rigour, however, was moderated; and on the occasion of lands falling by inheritance to a woman, the heiress was obliged to marry, at the will of her feudal lord, such a person as could fulfil the duties of her feoff. In the case of minors, the spirit also of the law was adhered to, and the guardian was required to serve in place of his ward, becoming, at the same time, absolute lord of the estate till such a period as the heir was able to accomplish its feudal duties in person. These modifications did not take place for many centuries after the period of which I speak; and it seems certain, that the strict terms of the Salique law, though then but a traditionary custom, were enforced in all the lands either originally granted to the Franks by the mere bounty of the emperors, or afterward wrung from the Romans as their power hurried onwards in its decline.

By what accidental difference in national character, or what superior wisdom in their institutions, it is difficult to say, but it appears that, while the greater part of the invaders of the Roman Empire contented themselves with hasty inroads, and transitory conquests, the Franks, animated by a more regular and persevering spirit, pursued slowly, but steadily, that system of territorial aggrandizement which in the end rendered them masters of all Gaul. In the year 453, we find a large body of Franks assisting the consul Aetius against Attila, at the famous Battle of Mauriacum, or Mery sur Seine, in which that great Roman completely triumphed over the Huns. The Franks here, however, appeared no longer in the inferior station of foreign auxiliaries, fighting under a Roman chief, but as great and powerful allies, led by their own king; and we find that Aetius was obliged, though strong in his own genius and the attachment of the troops he commanded, to have recourse to stratagem for the purpose of delivering himself from the presence of friends who might have become more dangerous than the enemies whom he had just defeated.

Orderic Vital, in his history of Normandy, is, I believe, the first who mentions a race of monarchs somewhat antecedent to the period of Aetius, and deduces them from Francus Duke of Sens, proceeding with Ferramond, or Pharramond, Clodius, Meroveus, and Childeric: but nothing certain is to be learned concerning any of the chiefs or kings except the two last; and it is much better to leave what is obscure in its original state of doubt, than, by recording what careless writers have invented on the subject, to perpetuate fables where truth cannot be obtained.

We are too likely, in following even the written history of remote times, to be led into error by the follies and the prejudices of the historians, especially if they themselves lived in ages of darkness and ignorance; for where we have reason to complain once of the scantiness of the facts transmitted to us, we have cause a thousand times to regret the additions that imagination has made to reality, and the distortion with which human weakness, passion, and superstition have represented events, that we have now no means of ascertaining.

Of Childeric, however, we possess at least such knowledge as can be obtained from the writings of an author who lived scarcely a century and a half after his reign; and as upon his conquests was based all that vast extension of power gained by the Franks during the succeeding reign, it may not be amiss to pause an instant upon his history.

Like most men of a very enterprising turn of mind, concerning whose lives we have an early record, he seems to have been animated by strong passions and vehement desires. These, in the ungoverned days of youth, led him into errors and debaucheries, which, by irritating and disgusting even his barbarous subjects, caused his expulsion from the throne, and had very nearly cost him his life. He fled, however, for safety to the kingdom of Thuringia; and, foreseeing that, as anger subsided, as death laid his hand upon his enemies, and as time obliterated the first sharp memory of his faults, a period might come when his people would regret him, he divided a piece of gold with a faithful attendant whom he left behind, bidding him watch the changes of popular feeling during his absence, and when the

Francs should desire his return, to send him as a sure token, the half of the broken coin.

After his departure, Aegidius the Roman Master-general of Gaul, was elected by the Franks for their king; and reigned for eight years over them, during which time the western empire hurried rapidly on towards its fall. At length, from what cause it does not appear, whether from the oppression of Aegidius, or from the intrigues of Childeric, the Franks became discontented with the government which they had established, the half of the piece of gold was transmitted to the exiled monarch, the Roman was in his turn dethroned, and Childeric once more entered into peaceable possession of his kingdom.

In the meanwhile, Aegidius retired to Soissons, where he fixed the seat of his government, and appears to have exercised an authority almost independent of Rome. But our accounts of Gaul in that day are so obscure, that it is impossible to discover with precision how far any tie still existed between the imperial general and his declining country. Certain it is, that while, indignant at the assassination of Majorian, Aegidius resisted the tyrannical authority of Ricimer, the barbarian who then commanded Italy, he acknowledged his own dependence on his country, and only rejected the fetters by which it was enthralled. But the precise degree of connexion which still remained between Rome and Gaul, and in whose name, or in what manner the master-general continued to govern the Gallic province, will probably ever be hidden from research. Nor is it more possible to ascertain, what part Childeric played in the various struggles which took place between the Romans of Gaul and the various barbarian tribes which surrounded them. Sometimes we find him joined with their friends, sometimes with their enemies, but always fighting on the victorious side, establishing his power and increasing his dominions.

The tribes of Franks who now possessed apart of Gaul were no longer confined to the Salii. Fresh bodies had poured in from Germany as the Roman power declined; and, though maintaining a strict alliance with each other, they seem to have been governed by different monarchs, till after the reign of Childeric, who was probably King of the Sicambri. Each tribe must necessarily have been but scanty in numbers, and the domains apportioned to each but small; for we find the chief town of Childeric to have been Tournay, while Cambray, Cologne, and Terouane had distinct hordes and chiefs; and it is probable that many others may have escaped my notice.

No one of these tribes, however, could have supplied a sufficient body of men to have aided the Romans in so signal a manner at the battle of Mauriacum, or to have gained such victories as we find recorded, over large bodies of Goths, Huns, and Saxons; and thence I would deduce that some general principle of union existed between them; and that the command over the whole was deferred to the king of one particular branch : which branch—as well from Meroveus having commanded on the victory over Attila, as from the continual mention of Childeric, without any notice of the other Prankish kings—I should certainly conclude to have been, by accident, if not by custom, the tribe of Sicambri.

Misfortune does not always teach wisdom; but in the case of Childeric, either adversity or years appear to have cured his follies; and from the time of his reinstatement, he seems to have turned the current of a quick and impetuous spirit to the purposes of ambition, if not of virtue. In Childeric we find the real architect of the power of the Franks in Gaul; and though it was another who united all the separated parts into the one great fabric of the French kingdom, he led the way and laid the foundation-stone.

After a reign of twenty-four years, Childeric died at Tournay. His rival,

Aegidius, had preceded him to the tomb several years, leaving a son, named Syagrius, to occupy the anomalous post which by his death became vacant,—a substitute without a principal—a viceroy deputed by no king. Gregory of Tours, indeed, calls this Syagrius King of the Romans; and as the good bishop is himself very curious in the investigation of what titles were bestowed upon the first chiefs of the Franks, it is more than probable that, in this instance, he made use of an honorary epithet that the Roman himself had assumed, when the western empire was absolutely at an end.

Childeric also left a son to succeed to his power; but, before proceeding with the following reign, which saw the conversion of the Franks to Christianity, and produced many changes in their national customs, it may be as well to state, in as few words as possible, all that is known of their religion and manners at the period of which I write.

Idolaters, like all the rest of the northern nations, the worship of the Franks was of that simple class which first presents itself to the mind of man, when finding, by the sense of his own feebleness and dependance, the necessity of adoring some object, he sees the Godhead in everything that contributes to his comfort, or supports his existence, mistaking the gifts which maintain life and happiness for the power that bestows. The forests that gave them shelter—the waters that fertilized their land—the savage beasts, the object of their chase—together with the more glorious parts of the wonderful creation, the sun, the moon, and the stars,—were all subjects for their worship, and the prototypes of their idols. Of their forms of adoration and religious ceremonies we know little, except that they offered sacrifices. Various of the customs of the Druids and the ancient Gauls have been attributed to them also; but whether correctly or not, I do not know, as I have personally met with the assertion alone, in the works of authors who wrote long after the manners of the Franks had become little more than matter for conjecture.

In regard to the degree of perfection to which they had brought various arts and manufactures, we have reason to believe that the Franks themselves, previous to their establishment in Gaul, had not proceeded farther in this branch of civilization than in any other. That, with all the tribes of the north, they were skilful and ardent huntsmen, cannot be doubted; and in the Salique law we find the protection of the chase as strictly attended to as the descent of lands, or any other case in which man is brought in relationship with man. They had also, it appears, made great progress, at an early period, in the domestication of all those useful animals whose subjection by any nation is generally considered as marking a considerable advance in civilization. The horse was in common use among them, and that no small trouble and skill was expended in rearing dogs for the field, we learn from the fact, that the penalty decreed, by the above-cited law, against any person stealing a dog which had been trained, was infinitely higher than that attached to the theft under other circumstances.

Stags, also, were domesticated among them, and were specially named in the laws for the protection of property. It is probable that, in regard to the other useful sciences, the most prominent inventions which the Romans had introduced into Gaul were eagerly adopted by the nations that followed them, though their refinements and more elegant arts were lost; and thus we find, that the Franks,—who, in all likelihood, had not proceeded farther themselves than the application of the hand-mill for grinding their corn, or, at farthest, the mill turned by some animal of draught—, immediately upon their conquest of the Gallic territory multiplied regulations for the preservation of the water-mills with which the country was plentifully supplied. Nevertheless, it may be necessary to remark, that, even previous to their having crossed the Rhine, they had advanced so wonderfully in agriculture, that Claudian declares it was not possible to distinguish, by the aspect of the land, which was the Roman, which the barbarian bank of that river. The only circumstance which could lead us to suppose that, at a period previous to the fall of the Roman Empire, the Franks had made any considerable progress in other arts, was the discovery of a tomb at Tournay, in the year 1653, which various circumstances indicated as the burial-place of Childeric, of whose history we have given a slight sketch. Besides a quantity of the bones of horses— probably sacrificed on the death of the king—a great many ornaments of gold were found, together with various medals, a style, the figure of a bull's head, and several other things manufactured in gold, as well as a number of rings, on some of which appeared the effigy of Childeric, with the inscription, in Latin: *Childericus Rex*. The remains also of a tunic, a sword, and part of an axe were discovered, as well as some tablets, on which, I believe, no writing was to be traced. The most curious, however, of the objects contained in this tomb were a multitude of bees, wrought in gold, some with eyes, and some without,—a symbol of empire which Childeric had probably derived from the Romans. To the same source also is to be attributed that degree of progress in several manufactures which was exhibited in the various objects discovered.

It is not likely, however small was the portion of energy which remained with the Romans of Gaul, that Aegidius should have reigned as king for nearly eight years over the Franks, without endeavouring to communicate to them,—if but in ostentation—, the arts and inventions of his native country; nor is it more probable that the Franks should remain, for many generations, in near alliance and continual contact with a polished nation like the Romans, without acquiring some knowledge of their more necessary manufactures; though their mental improvements they neglected, and their refined arts they despised. Thus, it would seem that when the Franks first came in contact with the Romans, they were mere barbarians, living by the chase, dwelling in huts, and governed by a military chief; but, gradually, the proximity of luxurious civilization, the service of some of their tribes in the Roman armies, the alliances, and even the wars, of some others with the empire, changed their manners and improved their arts. They grew dwellers in cities, their kings became hereditary, customs were fixed into laws, and, without losing their warlike and enterprising spirit, they received all such of the Roman inventions and manufactures as were consistent with the character of a young, conquering, and yet unsettled people.

Such was the state of the Frankish nation at the death of Childeric, in the year 481. To him succeeded his son Clovis, at the age of fifteen, endowed with all those qualities of mind and body necessary to the leader of a warlike nation, in a barbarous age,—strong, bold, hardy, determined, with an ambitious spirit calculated to rise in times of change am conquest, and at that precise period of life when the fire of enterprise burns most brightly in the human breast.

Chief of a tribe of Franks probably superior to the others in power, and distinguished by its monarchs having led the whole confederacy with success for many years, Clovis was further assured of support from his fellow-kings—at least inasmuch as the ties of kindred could assure it among barbarians—from the circumstance of each of the other chiefs being related to himself in a nearer or more remote degree. The first five years of his reign he seems to have spent in tranquillity, consolidating his power, habituating himself to dominion, and strengthening and securing his own possessions before he attacked those of others. At the end of that period his active life commenced, and he prepared for the series of conquests which rendered him the master of the whole of Gaul.

Whether hereditary enmity prompted him, or the more politic consideration of destroying at once a foreign power in the heart of dominions which, beyond all doubt, he designed, from a very early period, to annex to his own, we have no means of ascertaining; but the first aggression of the young monarch of the Franks was directed against Syagrius and the Romans.

That he originally contemplated the conquest of the whole of Gaul is not at all what I wish to advance; for with him, as well as with every other man, it is probable that his views extended with the extension of his power, and that those things which at first were too vast for even ambition to grasp, soon appeared to court his endeavours, as victory took one great step after the other on the road to general dominion. Nevertheless, that the spirit and intention of conquest was in his heart, there can be no doubt; and even if he proposed to bound his acquisition of territory to the banks of the Meuse, the Seine, and the shores of the ocean, the remnant of the Roman power was the first obstacle that in policy he was bound to overcome.

Aided, then, by the principal tribes of Franks, he marched directly upon Soissons. Syagrius was prepared to meet him; but, after a severe conflict, the Romans were routed, and their unhappy leader, flying from the field of battle, took refuge with Alaric, king of the Visigoths. Daring in his own nature, and elated with his victory, Clovis instantly sent messengers to the Gothic king, demanding that Syagrius should be given up to him, and boldly threatening war in case of refusal.

Alaric had lately succeeded Euric or Evaric in the kingdom of the Goths; and, on what motive it is hard to say, he stained the first years of his reign by violating all the duties of hospitality in regard to the unhappy

Roman, and by yielding him to the demand of his barbarous enemy.

His after-life showed that Alaric neither wanted courage, nor firmness, nor activity; and yet, by one of those strange contradictions which are sometimes found in the human character, he began his career with an action which can be accounted for on no other principle than the basest timidity.

With Syagrius in his hands, Clovis soon made himself master of all that remained of the Roman possessions in Gaul; and then, with the same barbarous spirit which he evinced in many an after-circumstance, he caused his captive to be butchered in prison. Such an action, however, was quite in harmony with the feelings of the age; and the often-repeated anecdote of the silver vase, the circumstances of which occurred at this period, is chiefly valuable as a proof of the uncivilized state of the Franks even then; showing how little, except in number, their armies still differed from a horde of plundering savages. The facts, as related by Flodoard and Gregory of Tours, are as follows: The cities of the Romans which fell into the hands of the Franks after the death of Syagrius were all more or less subjected to pillage; and even if Clovis, from political motives, extended a share of protection to the great body of his new subjects, he does not seem in any degree to have respected the Christian churches, which were stripped of all the rich plate and ornaments that had decorated them under the imperial government. The sacred buildings of Rheims, one of the first cities that had embraced Christianity in Gaul, were not exempt; and, among other articles of value carried off was a silver vase, of immense size and exceedingly curious workmanship.

At that time, the fame of St. Remi, the most eloquent and talented churchman of the day, was spreading far and near through Gaul; and even the idolatrous monarch of the Franks either felt or affected no small veneration for the virtues of the Christian prelate. As bishop of Rheims, St. Remi, either from some particular idea of sanctity attached to that vase, or from its great value, sent messengers to Clovis to complain of the violence which had been committed, and to beg the restitution of that particular urn at least, which he described. "Follow me to Soissons", replied the king to the messengers; "there the booty is to be divided, and, if it be in my power, the prelate's desire shall be gratified".

On their arrival at Soissons, the troops were assembled; and the whole mass of plunder being displayed before the army, the king, pointing to the urn, which lay conspicuous on the glittering heap, turned to the soldiers whom he had led so often to battle and to victory, and, before proceeding to determine by lot, as was customary, the part which each man was to have in the spoil, he begged that the vase might be assigned to him.

Many of the soldiers instantly expressed their consent; but one, either jealous of the invasion of established customs, or coveting the splendid prize himself, raised his axe, and, dashing it down upon the vase, exclaimed, in answer to the king's demand, "Thou shalt have nothing here but that which fortune shall give to thee by lot".

For a moment all were dumb with astonishment; but at length, the general voice having assigned the vase to Clovis, he returned it to the messengers of the bishop, in the state that the axe had left it.

The passions that swelled in the heart of a barbarous monarch at such an outrage as had been offered to him on this occasion may be easily conceived. He smothered them, however, for a time, although both his power and his popularity might have supported him had he given way to his resentment and possibly in this very instance of the strong command he possessed over himself is to be traced the source of that great influence he acquired over others.

It must not be thought that his anger was forgotten, though it slept; and, after lying dormant for a whole year, it suddenly awoke, the instant that a pretence of justice was afforded to his wrath, by the misconduct of him who had been so severely exact in his allowance to the king. At the general assembly of the people, called the Champ de Mars, when, by old custom, all the warriors of the nation presented themselves before the monarch, to show that their arms and equipments were kept bright and in good condition, the young soldier who had struck the vase appeared, with evident signs of negligence in the state of his weapons. The king paused before him with a frowning brow, remarked the slothful carelessness evinced in his rusted arms; and catching his battle-axe from his hand, cast it down upon the ground disdainfully, exclaiming, "None show themselves here with such ill-ordered arms as thine. Thy lance, thy sword, thy battle-axe, are all disgraceful to a soldier".

The young man stooped in silence to pick up his axe, but, as he did so, Clovis, with a blow of his weapon (called a francisque), smote him to the ground never to rise again, crying, "So didst thou strike the vase at Soissons!". The true motive of the blow spoke out in the words that accompanied it; but, as he had refrained when the offence was given, and retaliated not till justice was joined with vengeance, his followers admired rather than murmured, and saw nothing in their barbarous leader but a chief who knew equally well when to bear and when to punish. A modern people would have looked deeper; but the separation of motives from actions is the art of a much more refined nation than that of which I write.

Pursuing steadily his ambitious purposes, Clovis went on from conquest to conquest. At first, the dominions which he had won from the Romans seemed to have bounded his designs towards the south; and we find the scene of all his wars, for the first fifteen years of his reign, in the northern and western parts of Gaul, on the banks of the Wahl and the Rhine. Even passing those rivers, he subdued part of the country beyond; and, in the midst of such continual struggles for increase of territory, his marriage took place with Clotilda, niece of Gondibert King of Burgundy, a circumstance which affected his fortunes more than any of his victories. Not that Clotilda brought him any fresh possessions for she seems to have had no dower but her beauty and her virtue. She was a Christian, however; and with the zeal of love and conviction, she endeavoured incessantly to inspire her own faith into the bosom of her husband. For long the monarch resisted al her entreaties, and there were indeed many obstacle to his conversion. The people he commanded were fervent idolaters, and it might be dangerous and difficult to stand among them alone in a new religion. Under his nation's gods, he had fought and conquered; and we must not, in our own imaginations, endow Clovis with a spirit so much superior to his age, as not to be affected by superstitions then common to all men of all creeds.

The very manner of his conversion was superstitious, and, if I may make use of the term, heathen. After resisting for years the solicitations of Clotilda, the monarch, on seeing his army giving way in every direction before the Germans at the battle of Tolbaic,—now Zulpich, near Cologne—, suddenly addressed a prayer to his wife's God, vowing to abandon all other gods, if he would yield him the victory.

As he spoke the Franks rallied, the Germans were defeated; and Clovis, beholding a miracle in his rapid change of fortune, determined to adhere to the vow he had made in the time of danger. On considering this event, I was inclined at first to suppose, that Clovis, perceiving the great influence of the Catholic clergy, and how much they might aid him in the schemes of conquest that he meditated, had embraced their faith upon political motives; and that the superstitious historians of the day had decorated his conversion with a miracle. This hypothesis, though specious, and yielded, I own, with reluctance, will not bear closer observation; for if we take care to avoid the common error of looking at events characterized by the spirit of a different age through the medium of modern feelings and manners, we shall find that, unless we attribute to Clovis extended views and schemes of policy far beyond any recorded of those times, the motives for his conversion to the Christian faith must remain as they are stated by the historians,—the solicitations of his wife, acting upon superstitious feelings common to the age, and enforced by an extraordinary coincidence, at a moment of danger and excitement.

Nevertheless, the act of embracing the Christian religion at a time when his whole people were heathens, when all the independent tribes of his own nation, and the kings that governed them, were in the daily habit of destroying the temples and persecuting the ministers of that doctrine which he was about to receive, was a bold and a great measure; and, joined with the success that accompanied it, showed a mind, however uncivilized, powerful in itself, and confident in its own powers.

It was not without some examination that Clovis professed the faith, nor without precaution in regard to his people. After having listened attentively to the eloquent predication of St. Remi, he declared himself satisfied, and ready to receive baptism; but, at the same time, he assembled his army, and communicated to them his design.

It is more than probable that the troops were already aware of the intentions of the king, and that means had been used to induce them to follow his example, for three thousand of the most illustrious persons of his army instantly avowed their willingness to abandon the idols of their forefathers, and to embrace the doctrine of salvation.

This number was sufficient, though the greater part of the army still remained obstinately heathens. The first stone was laid—the conversion of his people begun—and Clovis trusted for the rest to time, and his own powers of mind.

Easter being near when this occurrence took place, that festival was appointed for the ceremony of baptizing the newly converted monarch and his followers; and a strange and interesting sight it must have been, to see the splendid barbarians, who conquered, not only the Romans, but the conquerors of Rome, present themselves at the altar of God, to solicit pardon in the name of the divine teacher of peace and good-will.

The account of the baptism of Clovis, as given by Flodoard, and confirmed by the still earlier account of Gregory of Tours, is curious in various points of view. In the first place, it shows the high pitch of power, of boldness, and of wealth to which the Church of Rome had, even then, arrived; and it puts in strong contrast therewith the barbarous simplicity of the Frankish king.

On the morning appointed for the ceremony, we read, that "The streets, from the dwelling of the monarch to the cathedral, were decorated, and hung with fine linen and rich carpets; tapestry and white veils were suspended from the portals of the church; a thousand perfumed tapers filled the temple with both odour and light; and the people, in an atmosphere of balm, imagined that they breathed already the air of Paradise". At the hour determined, the procession set out from the palace, commenced by the clergy, bearing in pomp the holy evangelists, with banners and crosses, and singing the hymns and canticles of the church. Next appeared St. Remi, leading the royal convert by the hand, accompanied by the queen and the monarch's sister, with an immense multitude of the most distinguished Franks, eager to follow the example of their chief.

As they proceeded onwards towards the cathedral, Clovis, struck with the splendid ceremonial of the Roman church, which had been displayed in all its full magnificence to honour his baptism, turned to the prelate, and betrayed the state of his religious knowledge by asking, if what he saw were the kingdom of God which had been promised to him. "No", replied St. Remi; "it is but the beginning of the road which conducts thither". The king then entered the church, and approached the baptismal font, when the bishop, with a burst of that impassioned eloquence for which he was celebrated, exclaimed, with a loud voice: "Bend thy head humbly, Sicamber, before thy God! Destroy that which thou hast adored! Adore that which thou hast destroyed!". After this bold address, he took the monarch's profession of faith, gave him baptism, and received him into the Christian church, baptizing at the same time the warriors who followed the king to the font, as well as an immense number of women and children.

His conversion to the Christian religion had, as I have already said, an immense influence upon the fate of Clovis. The clergy of the Roman church, thickly spread over every part of Gaul, without excepting the dominions of Aquitaine and Burgundy, had already courted the Franks, even when governed by a heathen monarch; but now that he professed the same faith with themselves, they spared neither exertions nor intrigues to facilitate the progress of his conquests.

It does not enter into the plan of this Introduction, which necessarily must be as brief as is consistent with perspicuity, to follow the reign even of the founder of the French monarchy through all its circumstances; suffice it, that in a short time the event of several wars left the Franks masters of the whole of that part of Gaul situated within the Rhone, the Rhine, the ocean, and the Loire.

In Burgundy their warfare had been successful, but not advantageous. They had gained battles, but acquired no territory; and though their policy had been conducted with much barbarous art, it had proved as fruitless as their victories. Clovis then turned his designs against Aquitaine, and, after several years of preparation befitting so great an enterprise as the conquest of that vast tract of country lying between the Loire and Pyrenees, he put himself at the head of his army, and marched directly towards Poitiers. In the neighbourhood of that city, Alaric, King of the Visigoths, who had collected an immense army in Spain, and crossed the Pyrenees with as hostile intentions towards Clovis as those which Clovis entertained towards him, had paused in his advance, to wait the arrival of Theodoric the Great, and the Goths of Italy.

With such a powerful ally, joined to his own overwhelming forces, it is probable that Alaric doubted as little of success as the monarch of the Franks. The stake for which they played was great,—no less than the empire of the whole of Gaul. Each had much to lose, and each had much to win; and each cast his whole power upon the chance.

But though the troops of the Franks are said to have been inferior in number, they possessed, in other respects, great advantages over the Goths. A long series of wars, with scarcely an interval of peace, had rendered them firm, hardy, and skilful and a long series of victories, without a check, had given them confidence in themselves, and in their leader.

If we are to believe the Catholic historians, no miracles were wanting that might encourage Clovis on his march. But having purposely abstained hitherto from citing any of the puerile superstitions with which the clergy of that day either deceived themselves or others, I shall not pause to do so on the present occasion. It is nevertheless difficult to abstain from saying something on the subject, when these pretended miracles, however distinct in object and in nature from the great and glorious manifestations of power that accompanied the divine Author of our religion, or even from those which vouched the inspiration of the prophets of old, have been too often confounded therewith by the weak, the malicious, and the vain of latter days, for the purpose of sneering at the one while they ridiculed the other.

Alaric remained inactive, while Clovis advanced with rapidity; and thus the Goths lost and the Franks gained the great advantage of being the attacking party. The two armies met on the plains of Vouglé, within a few miles of Poitiers, and in a very short space of time the empire of Gaul was decided. The Goths gave way on every side; and, though Alaric made the most immense exertions to conquer fortune, and win the great stake for which he strove, the route of his troops was soon complete. Both monarchs fought in person, like common soldiers; and it is said that they met hand to hand in the battle, when Alaric fell beneath the sword of his rival.

The death of their king rendered the confusion of the Goths irremediable. They fled from the field in every direction. The fallen monarch's son, with what forces he could collect, retired into Spain, where he succeeded to the throne of that country; while Clovis, with his victorious army, marched on through the territories which the Goths had possessed in Gaul, and subjected the whole land to the sway of the Franks. The Pyrenees became now the southern boundary of Clovis's dominion, and the kingdom of France may be said to have begun.

The Frankish king had yet rivals to subdue in the heart of his kingdom. I have already mentioned the various tribes of the nation which inhabited the north of France, and pointed out, that though they seemed, by prescription, to consider the chief of the Sicambri as the head of the confederate nation, yet each was governed by its own monarch, and probably by its own laws, of which we have instances in the Salique law, and the *Loi ripuaire*.

It was not, however, to be supposed that an ambitious warrior like Clovis, who had conquered all that opposed him, and extended his dominions in such an immense proportion, would leave the petty chieftains of his race—over whom he had risen so high by victory and genius—in tranquil possession of the territories which they held parcelled out through his kingdom. To seize upon their lands was an injustice; but it was an injustice so common in the age, that it followed as a matter of course; and the only choice seemed to be in the manner of performing it. Clovis, following the bent of his natural disposition, selected, in all instances, the most sure means of obtaining his object, without at all considering whether it was cruel, or whether it was base.

Sometimes he advanced to his purpose of overthrowing his kindred kings, with the boldest, sometimes with the most artful steps; but the termination was ever bloody and barbarous. In one instance he incited the son to murder the father, and then himself caused the assassination of the son. In another, he stirred up the Leudes, or Companions of the King of Cambray against their sovereign; and when, after an ineffectual struggle, the unhappy monarch was seized by his army and given up with his brother to their barbarous relation, Clovis slew them both with his own hand, saying they were a disgrace to his family for suffering themselves to be chained; adding, that it was better to die than endure ignominy. Thus, having found means, by the slaughter of all his kindred, to annex their dominions to his own, the monarch of the French, who had begun life but the chieftain of a barbarous tribe, found himself, in the prime of his manhood, the sovereign of one of the richest and most extensive kingdoms of the world. What plans he would have formed to secure and improve his conquests, and to what uses he would have applied his power, had his life been extended to the usual period allotted to man, it is impossible to say. From the means he employed to acquire, however, it is probable that his measures of security would have been bloody and remorseless. But, at the same time, we may fairly presume that he would have used the immense authority he had so cruelly obtained, for the general good of his subjects and the benefit of his successors, both from the instances of wisdom he evinced in the collection and publication of the Salique law,—certainly one of the best and most comprehensive of the barbarous codes—, and from the influence he exercised over the council of Orleans, which founded the liberties of the Gallic church.

That he was famous among even the people of his age, when rumour and fame had not, as in the present day, wings as rapid as the wind, may easily be judged from the fact of the Emperor Anastasius having bestowed on him consular honours, and sent him the purple. That he was great, his conquests and his acquisitions announce sufficiently. But that he was happy in his fame, or secure in his greatness, is more than doubtful. To the last day of his life, his mind seems to have been tormented with fears of rivalry; and he is reported to have complained to his assembled people, after having destroyed all his kindred, that he remained, like a traveller among strangers, having no relation to succour him if adversity should arise. "Not that he was sorry for their death", says the Bishop of Tours, with emphatic simplicity; "he spoke thus only from cunning, that he might discover if he had any relations still living, to the end that he might kill them". I translate the words almost literally; and they are those of one of his eulogists.

Could such a man be happy? No. It was time for him to die ; and he expired at Paris in the forty- fifth year of his age, five years after the overthrow of Alaric.

It unfortunately remains a fact, notwithstanding all that has been said on the subject, that a monarch who is by no means a good man may be a very good king. To be really great, he must be both. Clovis had many of the requisites for greatness; but not the whole. His higher qualities and his brighter talents were those least to be expected from his situation. His vices were those of a barbarian. Cruel, cunning, remorseless; he was the northern savage endowed with power. Clear-sighted, temperate, firm, with grand purposes, extensive views, and steadiness of execution, he was worthy of a better age.

All laws are apparently susceptible of a division into two great classes. The first embraces those laws which—instituted to provide against cases that may or may not happen, or may be qualified by various accessory circumstances—must ever be more or less vague, undefined, and varying, according to the varying circumstances of society. The second is that class of laws by which certain events are regulated that must necessarily occur in the course of nature; and which, consequently, may be provided against by clear and established rules, in every nation, according to its wants and situation.

Of this last class are the laws respecting the succession to kingdoms and inheritances; but, of course, it is not in the infancy of a nation that great precision can be given to rules, even concerning inevitable events; and accordingly, we find, during the reign of the first race of French monarchs, very little regularity obtaining in respect to the transmission of the sceptre. Indeed, the only absolute law upon this point, acting invariably during their dynasty, seems to have been that article of the Salique code by which women are excluded from inheritance.

At the death of Clovis, his four sons succeeded him, and parted among them that kingdom which it had been the business of his life to unite. It is not, however, my purpose to trace here the tedious series of the Merovingian kings. It is sufficient for my present object to mark three circumstances of interest in their history; namely, the first application of the Salique law in the succession to the throne, —the first shadowy outline of a Court of Peers—, and the rise and progress of that immense power, which converted the maires of the palace into kings.

It may not be unnecessary, however, to pause for one brief moment on the general state of the country. The population, which covered the face of Gaul, was now more mixed and confused than ever; consisting, however, of two distinct bodies. One of these, the Franks, was indeed pure and separate from the allay of any foreign blood; and, already possessing all civil and military power, was gradually advancing to the appropriation of all lands and territorial privileges. The other consisted of a thousand different races,—the original Gauls forming a great proportion. With these were the descendants of the Romans, their conquerors; the Leti, and other nations to whom the Romans had apportioned various parts of the Gallic province; several tribes of Goths, such as the Taifali, who had submitted after the defeat of Alaric; Saxons, Huns, Germans; and, in short, portions of all the swarms of barbarians that had aided to dismember the falling empire of

Rome. These, however, exclusive of the Armoricans, constituted but one class,—the conquered; and for them the choice of but two sorts of fate was open,—the church or slavery. There were exceptions, but exceptions prove nothing against a general rule.

Even before their emigration from Germany, in common with the rest of the German tribes, each nation of Franks was distinguished by two grades, or classes, in their society. The common bulk of the nation formed the first; but from these were selected a number of persons, called by the name of *leudes*, or *fideles*. Probably, in the first instance, they were but the voluntary warriors who accompanied the chief of their tribe upon any of his warlike expeditions. They grew into more importance, however, as the nation acquired territorial possessions; tracts of land were assigned them, as the recompense for their services ; and an oath was exacted from them, on their admission to the order, which, accompanied as it was by various solemn ceremonies, would seem the origin of feudal investiture.

Although persons were no longer elevated to the station of *leudes* by talents and courage alone, under the successors of Clovis the order still continued. It is very difficult to say, though we find them often mentioned in history, what were the duties, and what the privileges, of these *leudes*. Certain it is, that their prerogatives were not hereditary before the year 695; and whatever services they, by their oath, promised to the monarch, it appears that he, in return, gave them especial protection. The Salique law calls them *Homines qui sunt in truste regis*; and the formula of Marculfus mentions, that six hundred sous, then an immense sum, was the penalty for killing one of the anstrustions—a title I believe to have had the same signification with *leudes*.

At all events, it is clear that we have here an order of nobility; and it is little less clear that this order has proceeded gradually, with various changes, but without intermission, to the present day. I have said this much from a belief, that to trace institutions and to mark each step in the progress of society can never be uninteresting to the reader or the writer. On the same principle I shall also pause to remark, that during the reign of Clovis the arts and manufactures of the Romans became more familiar to the Franks. Their works in gold and silver we find carried to a very high pitch of perfection prior to the days of Charlemagne; and from the progress of the superfluous and ornamental arts we may always deduce a considerable advance in the more useful ones. In the luxuries and elegances of the table also they had made no small advance. Wine had been known in Gaul for ages, as well as beer. Hydromel, it is probable, was introduced by the Franks themselves. Cider was made, and was judged worthy of forming part of a banquet offered by a king. Table-cloths were used where the table was neither of such splendid materials as to be shown for the purposes of ostentation, nor covered with flowers. Napkins also were employed; but it is probable that they were used merely for washing before and after the repast. Spoons of silver, cups of the precious metals, wrought richly and ornamented with jewels, are mentioned within a few years of the reign of Clovis, as well as vinaigrettes, and several utensils with the use of which we are not now acquainted.

It might be supposed that all these objects of luxury, the manufacture of which implies great progress in art, had formed part of the plunder which the barbarous nations had taken from the Romans; but by the will of St. Remi we find various articles of silver stated to have been wrought at Laon : and directions are also given therein for converting some large pieces of plate into lesser ones, with precise orders for the manner in which they were to be chased and engraved. From this we discover that such arts were still pursued under the government of the Franks; and from the same document we have reason to infer that the weaving of many sorts of cloth, fringes, and tapestry, was also still carried to great perfection, though linens and silks were imported through Marseilles. Notwithstanding these facts, much, infinitely much, had been lost by the fall of the Roman empire, and more was still to be lost; for hitherto, of course, the tide of barbarism had not so completely effaced the traces of Italian civilization as it did after having flowed on for many years.

In the mean while language also naturally began to undergo a great change. The influx of so many northern nations, each bringing a dialect of its own, as may be well supposed, soon supplanted the Latin tongue, which the Romans—according to their wise policy of making their language and their institutions the chains wherewith they bound the nations they conquered—had rendered general in Gaul by the constant habit of more than four centuries. The lower class of people could not be expected to speak the tongue of the Romans in its purity; and the Latin generally used in Gaul at the fall of the empire, was necessarily adulterated with a great intermixture of Celtic terms. The Gothic, the Saxon, and the Vandal jargons added each something to corrupt it as they passed. Then came the Franks, who, retaining the country they had conquered, gave more expressions than any other tribe to the dialect of the people, though the great men, and the court of their own nation, still affected to speak the tongue of their German fathers. Thus, the *langue rustique*, or *Romane*, became, after several centuries, the general medium of communication among the people; while the Latin, in any degree of purity, was only found among the ecclesiastics; and the *Franc teutch*, or *Theotisque*, still remained the language of the monarch and his court, which distinction continued long after the reign of Charlemagne himself.

To return, however, to the successors of Clovis After the death of that monarch all the disorders and miseries of a divided empire succeeded. Brother warred with brother; and whatever alliances they formed for the purpose of turning their arms against some external enemy, generally ended in producing treachery or disunion among themselves, on account of the plunder taken, or the dominion acquired. At length two out of four of the Frankish monarchs died, and their male descendants being extinct, the kingdom remained divided between Childebert and Clotaire, the third and fourth sons of Clovis. No greater union, however, reigned between them now than while the kingdom had been separated into a greater number of parts; and eternal quarrels and intrigues continued till the death of Childebert, who, leaving but two daughters, Clotaire, his brother, in exercise of the Salique law, took possession of his whole dominions.

Whether that the law itself was new, and yet unsanctioned by that long custom and common application which renders law indisputable, or whether it was that in seizing the treasures of Childebert, as well as his dominions, Clotaire committed an action unwarranted by the code which assigned him the land, it is difficult to say : but, evidently from the apprehension of his right being in some way contested, the new monarch of France banished the widow and daughters of his brother immediately after that prince's death. It is probable, however, that the law was decisive as to the succession, or, instead of banishing his nieces, he would, in all likelihood, have followed the common practice of the day, and ended the dispute by murdering them.

After the death of Clotaire ensued a new division of the kingdom, new wars, new intrigues, new assassinations, offering a picture of anarchy, blood, and horror, more dreadful, perhaps than any in the range of time. If it be possible to add a deeper shade to a scene of crime where unbridled passions of every kind carried human nature to the extreme of blood-guiltiness, it will be found in the fact, that the principal instigator and actors in all the massacres of this period, belonged to that sex which by frame weak, and by nature gentle, seems formed as much to calm man's violence as to sooth his sorrow. But neither Fredigonde nor Brunehault,—the one stained with the blood of her husband and her husband's children, and the other, who died with the murder of five successive kings upon her head—, neither surely deserved the name of woman. I will not pause, however, on such scenes of horror, but, passing over the reigns of the sons of Clotaire, only stay for a moment to point out a trait of generosity which shines brightly among the awful darkness of all around it. Assassinated by his wife Fredigonde and her paramour Landri, Chilperic, one of the monarchs of France, left but one son, an infant of four months old, surrounded by jealousies and dangers on every side. In such a state of things it seemed a natural consequence that the late king's brother Gontran, and his nephew Childebert, either should divide the kingdom, or that Gontran, who had many causes of provocation against Chilperic, should seize upon the whole inheritance, and ensure his possessions by putting the infant heir to death. Gontran, however, seems to have been formed of different clay from the kings of that age; and marching upon Paris, he took his young nephew under his protection, caused the cities and the nobles to swear fealty to their new monarch, and weeping bitterly for the murder of his brother, defended his child against all danger, while at the same time he rendered justice to all those whom Chilperic himself had plundered, redressed the wrongs of the people, and brought back justice and security, which had been long turned from their course during the former reign.

This child of four months old, possessing the smallest portion of the French empire, and menaced from his cradle with every danger that could beset life and property, became afterward sole possessor of Gaul, under the name of Clotaire the Second, and governed well and wisely for many years. In his reign we find several of the Roman titles which were attached to particular offices under the empire, now adopted by the Franks, and forming a class of official nobility, if I may use the term, which soon after became hereditary. Thus the names of duke and count, derived from the Roman dux and comes, are common in all the writings of the seventh century. At first they seem to have been employed by the Franks merely as military distinctions, but they soon became attached to local governments, and in the end, though several centuries after, they were rendered hereditary, a quality which, it is curious to remark, was at this time only attached to the station of king.

At what time the person invested with the dignity of count by the Merovingian kings first began to exercise in the provinces the functions of judge is difficult to be determined with precision, but that he did so long before the time of Charlemagne, is beyond all doubt. Possessing authority to administer what was termed high and low justice, or to decide in all but ecclesiastical cases, it is probable that the provincial counts, when their titles became hereditary, retained the same privileges; and that thus arose that part of the feudal system which attributed the dispensation of justice to the high nobility.

In addition, however, to the counts I have just mentioned, I find, in the very reign of which I am now treating, another officer called the Count of the Palace, or Count Palatine, whose functions are much better defined, and whose office existed till the dynasty was changed a second time, at the accession of Hugh Capet. There are instances mentioned even afterward, but few.

The duties of the counts of the palace were very distinct from those of the maires of the palace, and comprised the general administration of justice, not only, as has been supposed, in cases where the mere household of the king was concerned, but in all those instances where, from any circumstances, the highest authority was sought.

It is true that one of their chief avocations was to hear and judge in all cases where the king's interest, either personal or royal, was affected; but at the same time, all appeals from the courts of the provincial counts fell under their cognizance, and all causes of sufficient importance to call for the royal decision itself were referred to them, as the officers on whom the king reposed a duty which would have been too operose to be joined with the other occupations of government.

Under the successors of Clovis, the functions of count of the palace were performed by one person : though afterward we find several joined in this trust at one time. His decisions were without appeal, and affected all cases; but this attribute, which might have proved dangerous, received some check from the sort of counsellors by whom he was assisted, called *Scabini Palatii*. The power indeed remained with him; but the exercise of power is always controlled, even by the presence of persons who, though they cannot prevent, may oppose its abuse. Nor was it by the presence of those counsellors of the palace only that the immense authority of the count was restrained. Many individuals of the higher and more esteemed of the nobility, as it then existed, were often called by the king to assist at the decisions of this count palatine; and, perhaps, in this may be traced the faint shadow of the king's Court of Peers. At all events, there is a strong similitude between the two institutions. The king was effectually, in the one as well as in the other, the head of the judicial court, and was often present at its judgments. The persons called to sit in each were the same; and the only material difference that existed in the constitution of the two assemblies was, that in the latter a fixed rule had been adopted with respect to the members who composed it, and that the right of appearing there was a privilege, not a concession. Institutions of any very great importance are rarely founded at once, but generally proceed for years, gaining slowly form and stability. Nor are they, generally, the effect of any one cause, but rather of the combination of many precedents, which by accumulation, not only form laws, but also institute tribunals.

Another fact occurs in the reign of Clotaire the Second, which gave rise to circumstances extremely like the meeting and judgment of the Court of Peers, such as we find described many centuries afterward. Having associated his son Dagobert to the throne, Clotaire ceded to him that part of France which had been called, while separated, the kingdom of Austrasia. On what terms this cession was made we cannot at present ascertain; but it appears that a part of the territory was retained by the king, which Dagobert imagined justly belonged to the domain assigned him. A violent contest succeeded between the father and the son, in consequence of which twelve of the nobles, among whom were several bishops, were called upon to terminate the difference by a judgment. Their decision was unfavourable to Clotaire; but he yielded without resistance, and placed his son in possession of the whole of the territory in dispute.

That the assembly called on the present occasion was totally distinct and different from the national assembly, from the *Plaid*, or from any other ordinary court, is perfectly susceptible of proof; yet I do not mean in the least to say that the tribunal by which this judgment was given was the usual meeting of an organized court, which went on continuously into after-years. We know historically that it was not; but it is the reiterated occurrence of such events that, in the end, very often produces regular institutions.

Another officer of the crown at this time, and one of the highest, was the maire of the palace, though hitherto he had made no step towards that immense influence which his situation commanded in after-days. The maire of the palace was, in fact, merely master of the king's household; and took the name of *major domus regiae*, or *gubernator palatii*; and we have no reason to believe that, previous to the reign of Clotaire the Second, any power was intrusted to him further than that which the title implied.

In the reign of that prince, however, a degree of separate authority seems to have been confided to the maires of the palace; and we find that on the whole of France being once more united into one monarchy, Clotaire appointed maires for each of the kingdoms into which it had been formerly divided. The very separation of the office from the existing royal household seems to imply that its functions had by this time become different; and Fredigaire, or Idatius, as he has been wrongly called by some, marks particularly that Herpon, sent as *maire du palais* beyond the Jura, was killed in a rebellion, while acting the part of a wise judge and governor.

In the reign that followed, the authority of the maires of the palace, though greatly increased, was kept within due bounds by the powerful mind of Dagobert; and even after that mind had been injured by debauchery and indolence, his prompt and warlike character supplied the place of greater virtues, and held in check the ambition of his followers. Nevertheless, that ambition had full scope to extend itself during the infancy of the two sons of Dagobert, between whom the kingdom was divided after his early death.

The men, however, whom he had appointed to superintend the affairs of the realm during the minority of his children, seem to have justified his choice. Pepin the elder, to whom the government of Austrasia was confided, with the young king Sigebert, and Ega, who directed the education of Clovis the Second, both seem to have done justice to their charge to the end of their lives; but the space allotted to either was brief. Neither of them lived more than three years after their lord; and they died, leaving the kingdom to anarchy, bloodshed, and devastation.

The power of the maires of the palace had now begun to extend itself to every department of the government; and, after a very short lapse of time, that power was so strongly confirmed, that Ebroin, who had been long disgraced and confined in a monastery, issued forth on the accession of Theodoric, or Thieri, to the throne of France, and compelled his sovereign, by force of arms, to receive him as maire. He had previously murdered the noble who had been elevated to that post during his absence; and, after having perpetrated such an act, it may be well supposed he reigned supreme.

His whole soul seems to have been given up now to the accumulation of his wealth and the extension of his authority, however base and bloody were the means to be employed for that purpose. A clever but somewhat fanciful writer has seen, or imagined in the character of Ebroin, the defender of the people against the aggressions and encroachments of the nobility; but I confess that I can find no trace of any two parties such as those to which he refers, and certainly no earthly cause for supposing Ebroin to have been a martyr to anything but cupidity, cruelty, and ambition. There was no popular party—all was a chaos formed of the rude, irregular, and contending passions of individuals. The dukes, the counts, the bishops, the patricians,—all struggled for their own aggrandizement—all sought to wring new privileges from the crown, or to rob new territories from their neighbours. Someone, more strong or more talented than the rest, inflicted himself on the monarch as his *maire du palais*, attached such of the nobles and *leudes* to his own party as he could win by presents, promises, and favours, and stood in open warfare against all the rest; who each, on their part, waited but the opportunity to snatch the dignity from him that possessed it. The monarchs, if by chance they were endowed with any energy of disposition, struggled, but struggled in vain, to cast off the yoke of their more than royal ministers; and if they were, as usually happened, weak and slothful, they continued to exist, governed instead of governing, and committing the meanest fault of which kings can be guilty— lending their name to the tyranny of others. Thus, immersed in effeminacy, debauchery, and sloth, ran on a long race of kings, called in history the Sluggard Kings, or les *rois fainéants*; till at length Chilperic the Second endeavoured to shake off the chains with which his race had been so long shackled.

The effort was made, however, at an unhappy moment, and against a man whose energy as a politician, and skill as a warrior, rendered him the most tremendous adversary that a king could encounter. I speak of the famous Charles Martel. Chilperic was defeated; Charles was acknowledged maire du palais; and, as if but to give him opportunity for the display of his extraordinary powers, enemies sprang up on all sides, and were conquered as they arose. The Saxons, the Prisons, the Gascons, and the Saracens were one by one overthrown; the whole of France was reduced to obedience; and Charles Martel was king in all but the name. But he was king of a land which had lost all that makes a throne desirable,—arts, sciences, peace, and stability. The seas of blood which had been poured out in the intestine struggles of the French nobles had washed away every tincture of literature which had been left by the Romans. The arts and the commerce which, even as late as the reign of Dagobert, had been seen flourishing in luxuriance, were now all crushed under the iron steps of civil war. Long arrears of hatred and vengeance had been accumulated between each family and each province of the land. No principle of law or justice remained to restrain the strong, to protect the weak; and no acknowledged power of legislation existed, except in the sword. Such was the state of the kingdom over which Charles Martel fixed his sway. It is not my purpose here to trace his victories, or recapitulate the enemies by which he was attacked. It is sufficient to say, that under his administration order was in some degree restored by the sole vigour of the hand which held the reins of government; but the sciences which had fled, and the arts which had been lost, remained unrecovered till a brighter era opened, and a more comprehensive mind awoke, to recall the treasures of the former days.

Having so far given a sketch of the progress of France, however short and imperfect, I must pause for a moment to notice some of the changes which had taken place in Italy, since Odoacer had wrested the sceptre of the Caesars from the weak hands of Orestes and his son.

On this subject I shall be still briefer. Odoacer was not long suffered lo enjoy the undisputed possession of his usurped dominions. Theodoric, the Ostrogoth, a man of extraordinary talents and many high moral qualities, blended with many of the vices of his age and his nation, invaded the territories which Odoacer had usurped, and after both conquest and perfidy obtained the sovereignty of Italy. His virtues and abilities once more promised peace and prosperity to Rome; but his faults delayed the progress of improvement, and his death transferred the power to a line of weaker and less fortunate princes than himself.

The victories of Belisarius, and the majestic successes of the eunuch Narses, are too well known to call for recapitulation. Suffice it, that the talents, virtues, and firmness of that last great man snatched I he whole of Italy from the dominion of the barbarians, and, as Exarch of Ravenna, he governed the ancient territories of Rome from the Alps to the Ionian Sea, in the name of the Emperor of the East. The exarchs became the sovereigns of Italy; but Justinian, by mile, and equitable laws, endeavoured to ensure, from oppression the people whom he yielded to the certain evils of delegated sway. The bishops of Rome, or popes, were the mediators who procured from the Eastern emperor this benefit for the varied inhabitants of Italy; and to those bishops themselves Justinian intrusted some part of the civil government of the state; which perhaps may be looked upon as the first small nucleus round which they afterward collected the immense mass of their temporal power.

For but a short period Italy, as a whole, remained attached to the empire, and free from barbarian invasion. The ingratitude of a court he had served, and a people he had delivered, drove Narses into resistance if it drove him not to treachery; and Italy, laid open to the Lombards, was soon divided between the monarch of that people and the Exarch of Ravenna.

Thus it continued for many years in continual struggles between the Romans and the barbarians, during the dangers and uncertainties of which perilous times the great fabric of the Roman church was first placed upon a solid foundation, by the genius and virtues of Gregory the First; and was raised up, stone by stone, by his more interested and ambitious successors.

At length, about a century and a half after the Lombard invasion of Italy, the Emperor Leo, the Iconoclast, by attempting, with fanatic violence, to reform the superstitious worship of images, once more separated the Roman territories in Italy from the Eastern empire; and the separation was forever. After having succeeded in the East in pulling down the sacred images which for many years had been revered through the whole Christian world, and having, with vulgar intemperance, insulted the obnoxious clay, the emperor issued his commands to his western subjects, enjoining the same destruction of the statues, and the same abandonment of all material representations of spiritual objects. But the people of Italy were less disposed than even the Greeks to yield a system of devotion which gave tangible forms as a link between faith and imagination; and they also had greater facilities of resistance.

The decrees of Leo were rejected with contempt and abhorrence; the bishops of Rome proclaimed his doctrine heretical; warned, admonished, and finally excommunicated the emperor himself; and all Italy rose at once to throw off the yoke of the East. Many and ineffectual attempts were made both by arms and negotiations to reduce Rome once more to obedience; but the bonds were broken, and though no new emperor was elected for many years, the two countries were absolutely and in fact separated from each other. For a time some of the forms of a republic were resumed; but the pope, who had been the guide and the support of the people in their resistance, now became their chief and their ruler. It is not improbable that his government would have gone on with a regular increase of domination, and that the same results which were afterward obtained would have been equally produced, had no danger and necessity forced the pope to call in the aid of a great foreign ally, when the reciprocation of benefit and support extended and strengthened the power of each.

The danger which thus compelled the bishops of Rome to apply for assistance to the rulers of the Franks arose from the growing demands and ambitious policy of the Lombards.

That nation had strenuously supported the Church of Rome in her separation from the Eastern Empire; but soon took advantage of the dissensions which followed, and the weakness of all parties, to seek extension of territory and aggrandizement by conquest. For a time remonstrance, negotiation, and threats withheld the Lombards from attempting the actual conquest of Rome; but at length the prize appeared too tempting for longer forbearance, and Astolphus, King of the Lombards, prepared to reduce the whole of Italy to his dominion. The Roman pontiff had no resource but to call the ruler of the French nation to his deliverance.

That ruler was the maire of the palace. Astolphus, as I shall notice more fully hereafter, was twice defeated; Rome and the power of the church were secured; and the family of Heristal laid up for future years a title to support from the apostolic see.

This digression has necessarily conducted me farther than the reign of Charles Martel, who, during the first encroachments of the Lombards, could only afford the Roman pontiff the aid of intercession and remonstrance with his enemy. The danger of his own situation at that time, the host of domestic and foreign adversaries by which he was threatened, and the painful anarchy which prevailed through the kingdom he was called to rule, chained him to the soil of Gaul till he had successively triumphed in almost every part of the Frankish territories. But he did triumph over every attack, silenced enmity, crushed faction, and overcame revolt. A more general government was instituted, foreign enemies were driven from the land, and many provinces which the feebleness of former ministers had suffered to be detached, were now regained and consolidated.

The kingdom being once more united, the people accustomed to the domination of maires of the palace, the king's existence forgotten, and the usurped authority strengthened by a thousand victories, Charles probably thought it useless, if not contemptible, to decorate the power which he held by his own right hand with a title which many a reign of weakness had rendered degrading. He made war or peace in his own name, he granted dignities and domains without mention of the king,— he raised up, he cast down, he commanded, he reigned. Such sway sufficed him; and he was content. Not so his son Pepin, who succeeded, and for some years reigned with his brother Carloman. As long as the latter was joined with him in authority Pepin contented himself with the name of maire du palais; and thus designated, the two brothers, in perfect union, governed, and fought, and triumphed together. But to make use of the eloquent words of the Bishop of Meaux, Carloman, disgusted with the age, in the midst of his greatness and his victories, yielded his power into the hands of his brother, and voluntarily turned to monastic seclusion.

From that moment the crown became Pepin's object. To take it was not difficult, for it had been long within reach: but to secure it to himself and to his successors was not so easy a task. The dangerous precedent of dethroning his king he knew might be fatally made use of by others; more especially against himself and his family, whose illegitimate possession might ever strengthen the pretences of rebellion. It is true that rights are inherent, and never can be created where they do not exist; but in that barbarous age rights were undefined; and though Pepin might easily have founded his title on the will of the people, he well knew that there too was an expedient that might ever be commanded by the great and the successful. As some prop to the uncertain basis of popular election, he resolved to strengthen the foundation of his dynasty by the most solemn sanction of the church. That sanction was easily obtained; for the church was in hourly need of military support; the people shouted their consent; Childeric was dethroned and confined in a monastery; and Pepin, having been solemnly crowned by the papal legate at Soissons, assumed the style of king, after having long possessed the power.

THE AGE OF CHARLEMAGNE

FROM THE BIRTH OF CHARLEMAGNE

TO HIS ACCESSION.

AD 742 TO AD 768.

The precise birth-place of the greatest man of the middle ages is unknown; neither have any records come down to us of his education, nor any particulars of those early years which are generally ornamented by the imagination of after biographers, even when the subject of their writing has left his infancy in obscurity. Eginhard, who possessed the best means of knowledge, frankly avows that he was himself ignorant; and the manuscript of a contemporary author, whose propensity to anecdote gives a value to his details, which neither the style of his composition, nor the accuracy of his statements, could bestow, is defective in that part which might have afforded some information, however vague, regarding the youth of Charlemagne. The year of his birth, however, as ascertained by computation from other data, seems undoubtedly to have been AD 742, about seven years before his father, Pepin the Brief, assumed the name of King.

His mother was Bertha, daughter of Charibert, Count of Laon; and concerning her early union with Pepin, a thousand pleasant fables have supplied the place of all accurate information. Although one of the papal epistles to Charlemagne insinuates that Pepin at one time contemplated a separation from Bertha, for the purpose of marrying another woman, it is evident that she was loved and honored by her husband, from the fact of her having shared in the new and solemn spectacle by which Pepin attempted to consecrate, in the eyes of the people, his usurpation of the supreme authority.

To the forms usually observed on the accession of a new monarch of the Francs, Pepin added various ceremonies which had never before been used in Gaul. Amongst these, the most striking, from its novelty, was the unction which had been instituted for the kings of Israel, and which was readily performed for the Frankish usurper by the famous Boniface, Archbishop of Metz. In all the solemnities which dignified the elevation of her husband, Bertha was a partaker; and many have been the laborious struggles of historians to discover, or invent, various complex and political motives for so very natural an occurrence; but it would seem, that the simple desire of distinctly marking that his personal elevation to the royal station implied the elevation of his whole family, and the permanence of the kingly office in his race, was the sole view of the new sovereign of the Francs. The influence which she exercised over her husband, and the reverence which her children always displayed towards her, render it probable that to Bertha herself was entrusted the early education of Charlemagne. Still it is greatly to be regretted, that we do not possess any details of the tuition under which the mind of that prince put forth, between infancy and manhood, those grand and splendid qualities which, hidden in the darkness that overhangs his youth, shine out immediately on his accession to the throne, like the rising of a tropical day, which, we are told, bursts forth at once in its splendor, unannounced by the slow progress of the dawning twilight.

Nevertheless, although nothing is known of the minute particulars either of his domestic instruction or his early habits, there was a grander species of education to which he was subject, and of which we have better means of judging: I mean the education of circumstances. It is a common influence of troublous times, not alone to bring forward, but to form great intellect. The familiarity with scenes of danger and excitement—the early exercise of thought upon great and difficult subjects—the habit of supporting, encountering, and vanquishing, the very proximity of mighty schemes and mighty changes,—must necessarily give expansion, vigor, and activity, to every faculty of the mind, as much as robust exercises and habitual hardships strengthen and improve the body. In the midst of such uncertain and eventful times, and surrounded by such grand and animating circumstances, was passed the youth of Charlemagne, and though we cannot discover whether paternal or maternal care afforded the means of cultivating his intellect or directing his pursuits, to a mind naturally great and comprehensive, like his own, the world was a sufficient school—the events by which he was surrounded sufficient instructors.

The first act performed before his eyes was the consummation of all his ancestor's ambitious glory, by the mighty daring of his own father: and this instance of the ease with which great deeds are achieved by great minds, was a practical lesson and a powerful incitement. The first act of his own life—a task which combined both dignity and beneficence—was to meet, as deputy for his father, the suppliant chief of the Roman church, and to conduct him with honor to the monarch's presence. The event in which he thus took part, and which afterwards affected the current of his whole existence, originated in the unhappy state of Rome, which I have before slightly noticed, and in the continual and increasing pressure of the Lombards upon that unstable republic which had arisen in Italy, after its separation from the empire of the East. The second and third Gregory had in vain implored the personal succor of Charles Martel to defend the Roman territory from the hostile designs of their encroaching neighbors; and Zacharias, who had succeeded to the authority and difficulties of those two pontiffs, had equally petitioned Pepin for some more effectual aid than remonstrances addressed to the dull ear of ambition, and menaces which began to be despised.

Under Stephen, who followed Zacharias, and ascended the papal chair soon after the elevation of Pepin to the sovereign power, the danger of Rome became still more imminent; for Astolphus, the Lombard King, contemning alike the threats of an avenger who did not appear, and the exhortations of a priest who had no means of resistance, imposed an immense tribute on the citizens of Rome, and prepared to enforce the payment by arms. But by this time the popes or bishops of Rome had established a stronger claim upon the rulers of France than that which they had formerly possessed. The instability of Pepin's title to the crown, had made him eager to add a fictitious authority to the mutable right of popular election; and, having, as we have before seen, joined to the voice of the people the sanction of the Pope, he divided between two, a debt which might have been dangerous or burdensome while in the hands of one. By this means, however, he gave to the Roman pontiffs a claim and a power; and Stephen now resolved to exert it in the exigency of his country.

In the moment of immediate danger, when Rome was threatened by hostile armies, and her fields swept by invading barbarians, the prelate, with a worthy boldness, set out from the ancient queen of empires, as a suppliant, determined to apply, first for justice and immunity at the court of Astolphus, the King of the Lombards, and, in case of rejection, then for protection and vengeance, at the hands of the new monarch of the Francs. Astolphus was deaf to all petitions, and despised all threats. Ravenna had fallen, and Rome he had determined to subdue. But the Pope pursued his way in haste; and, traversing the Alps, set his foot with joy on the territories of a friend and an ally. The French monarch was then returning from one of his victorious expeditions against the Saxons; and the messengers from Stephen met him on the banks of the Moselle.

The most common of all accusations against the human heart, and, I might add, against the human mind, is ingratitude. But in an uncivilized state of society, where rights are less protected, and mankind depend more on the voluntary reciprocation of individual benefits and assistance, than on fixed rules and a uniform government, the possession of such emotions as gratitude and generosity, would seem to be more necessarily considered as a virtue, and the want of them more decidedly as a crime, than in periods or in countries, where the exertions of each man is sufficient for his own support, and the law is competent to the protection of all.

Besides a feeling of obligation towards the Roman pontiffs, which the new sovereign did not hesitate a moment to acknowledge and obey, the call of the Pope was perfectly consonant to Pepin's views and disposition, as a man, a king, and a warrior. To welcome the Bishop of Rome, therefore, the monarch instantly dispatched his eldest son Charles, then scarcely twelve years of age, and every honor was paid to the head of the Catholic Church that reverence or gratitude could inspire.

This is the first occasion on which we find Charlemagne mentioned in history; but the children of the Francs were trained in their very early years to robust and warlike exercises; and there is every reason to believe that great precocity, both of bodily and mental powers, fitted the prince for the office which was entrusted to him by his father.

From the distinction with which Pepin received the prelate, and from the bold and candid character of that monarch, little doubt can exist that he at once determined to protect the Roman state from the exacting monarch of the Lombards, by the effectual and conclusive interposition of arms. The King of the Francs, however, had still something to demand at the hands of the Pope; and the remonstrance of Astolphus, who pleaded hard by his envoys against the proposed interference, raised Pepin to the character of umpire and judge, enhanced the value of his mediation, and gave him a claim, not likely to be rejected, for some return on the part of Stephen. In regard to many of the particular circumstances of this time, contemporary historians are silent; and Anastasius, who lived at a later period, when the papal power had obtained, in a great measure, the ascendancy which it so long possessed, is so evidently incorrect in regard to several of the numerous details he gives, that great caution is necessary in receiving his account.

With those anxious fears for the stability of his authority which must always attend usurpation, Pepin eagerly sought every means of strengthening his title to the throne of France; and, not content with the pontifical sanction already given, determined on obtaining from the Pope, during his visit of supplication, some new act of recognition and consecration. On a positive promise of aid from the monarch of the Francs, Stephen formally absolved him for the breach of his oath of allegiance to Childeric; and repeated the ceremony of his coronation in the church of St Denis. Nor were precautions wanting to guard against any future exercise of the same popular power, which had snatched the crown from one monarch, and bestowed it on another. The Pope launched his anathema at all those who should attempt to deprive the Carolingian line of the throne they had assumed; and Charles and Carloman, the two sons of Pepin, were crowned together with their parents, by the hands of the Roman pontiff.

As he had chosen by the papal sanction to prop his authority, originally raised upon the sandy foundation of popular election, the French monarch was of course moved by every principle of prudence, as well as by the remembrance of his promise, to strengthen and support the Roman Church. Almost immediately on the arrival of the Pope, Pepin dispatched messengers to Astolphus, requiring him to abandon his demands upon the city of Rome, and to cease his aggressions on the Roman territory. Astolphus refused to comply; but, as he well knew the power of the Frankish nation, he sought to avert the storm which threatened him before he prepared to encounter it. Carloman, the brother of Pepin, who had resigned his inheritance in France, abandoned the world, and sought the best desire of human nature, peace, in the shade of the cloister, was at that time dwelling in a monastery, within the limits of the Lombard dominions. The eye of Astolphus immediately fell upon him, as a fit messenger to his brother; and he was compelled by the orders of his abbot to journey into France, and to oppose, at the court of the French monarch, the wishes and designs of the pontiff.

A custom, which must be more particularly noticed hereafter, existed at this time amongst the Francs, of determining upon war or peace, at the great assembly of the nation, in what was called a *Champ de Mars*; and though the Maires of the Palace had frequently violated this ancient institution, Pepin, who courted popularity, called upon his people, in almost all instances, to sanction any warfare he was about to undertake.

In the present case, where greater and more important interests were involved, he did not fail to add the consent of the nation to his own determination; and, at the Champ de Mars, held after his coronation, he announced to the nobles of the land his resolution of defending Rome from her enemies by force of arms. In the same assembly, his brother Carloman is said to have remonstrated publicly against this purpose; but the assertion is founded on the faith of after historians, whose evidence is doubtful, if not inadmissible. In the dim obscurity which hangs over these far ages, the more important facts only appear distinct; and those which are clearly known, in regard to the transactions of which we speak, are simply, that the nobles of France, concurred completely in the views of the king, and that Pepin marched with an immense army towards the frontiers of Italy; leaving Bertha, his wife, and Carloman, his brother, at Vienne, in Dauphiny, where Carloman died before the monarch's return from his Italian expedition.

The Lombards, warned of the approaching invasion, immediately occupied the passes of that mountain barrier, which nature has placed for the defence of the Italian peninsula. A battle was fought amongst the hills; the Lombards were defeated; and the Francs poured down into the ancient territories of the Romans. Pepin marched forward with that bold celerity which distinguished all his race; and at once laid siege to Pavia, within the walls of which Astolphus had taken refuge. The war was carried on by the Francs with all the unsparing activity of a barbarous nation: and, while the

Lombard capital was invested on all sides, bands of plunderers were spread over the country to ravage, pillage, and destroy.

Astolphus at length submitted to the power he was in no condition to resist; and, opening a negotiation with Pepin, he agreed to yield the exarchate, and the Pentapolis, which the monarch of the Francs had pledged himself to re-annex to the territories of Rome. Forty distinguished hostages were given to ensure the performance of the treaty; and Pepin retired from Italy, satisfied that he had compelled the restitution of possessions which had been unjustly withheld.

Perhaps the most important point of discussion in the history of the middle ages is now before us, and one, in regard to which, a greater variety of different opinions has been offered and maintained, than any other question has elicited. The formal and distinct connection of the exarchate of Ravenna, and the territories of the Pentapolis, with the Roman domains, forms the basis of the temporal throne of the Popes, and, consequently, has been a subject of warm contestation in all its parts, between the friends and the enemies of the Romish Church.

It is neither necessary nor fitting here, to state even the most prominent of the many conclusions to which authors have come upon this question; nor to endeavor to refute errors or correct mistakes, farther than by a simple statement of the ascertained facts, and a few deductions from them.

When Italy threw off the dominion of the Emperors of the East, its language was more submissive than its actions; and the authority of the empire was acknowledged long after its arms were resisted, and its power was at an end. As some sort of government, however, was absolutely necessary, the Romans, as I have already stated, recalled many of the forms of the old republic, and though tacitly submitting to their Popes, or Bishops, who led, counseled, and protected them, they still, as a senate and people, named their own governors, and entrusted that portion of their freedom which they were obliged to sacrifice for defence, to whomsoever their own wisdom or necessities might dictate. The office of exarch, which had been instituted by the Emperors for the government of their Italian provinces, was still continued by the Roman people as a means of obtaining protection; and the persons who filled it were by them elected, under the names, which had become synonymous, of Exarch or Patrician.

By fraud or violence, and probably by both, the Lombards, who had first armed in defence of the Romans against the Emperors, took possession of Ravenna and its dependencies; but the Popes never ceased to claim that territory, originally in behalf of the Roman people, and ultimately in the name of the Roman Church.

The rulers of the Francs, beginning with Charles Martel, had been successively elected by the senate and people of Rome to the post of Patrician, or Exarch; and, consequently, were bound, by the fact of accepting that office, to maintain the integrity of the Roman territory. Pepin, therefore, in his expedition against Astolphus, was only fulfilling one of the duties of the exarchonate, and re-annexed the recovered tract to the rest of the appendages of Rome, rather as an act of restitution, than of donation. As the separation of Italy from the empire of the East had originated in an ecclesiastical dispute, the interests of the state became identified with that of the Church. Gradually, in after ages, the Popes acquired the supreme power over the whole territory; and, anxious to find a title of more weight than mere possession, they assumed that the act of Pepin was the gift of a province, conquered by the Frankish king, directly bestowed upon the see of Rome, rather than a successful campaign of the exarch for the recovery of a province belonging to the republic. They afterwards attempted to support this pretence by a supposititious donation of a part at least of the same district by Constantine; and the Pontiff, in their letters, alluded more and more strongly, as the progress of years obscure the memory of realities, to fictitious rights which fictitious gifts had created.

Whatever was the nature of Pepin's restoration of the Exarchate and Pentapolis, the terms in which it was expressed were verbal; and even in the famous letter of Pope Adrian to Charlemagne, wherein he boldly declares the donation of Constantine, which was supposed to have taken place in remote and indistinct times, he touches most tenderly upon those after gifts of the same territory which were subject to immediate examination and refutation.

Individual ambition continually defeats its purpose by hurrying too rapidly towards its object; but a number of men, in long succession, conducting a permanent establishment, in which their own personal interests are entirely merged, often acquire a fearful superiority to those around them, by the calm regularity of their progress in advance, and the passionless caution by which they secure each advantage as it is obtained. The march of the papal power was slow and gradual. The Exarchate was re-annexed to Rome; the Pontiffs subsequently chose to believe it bestowed upon the Church, and on that hypothesis founded their temporal dominion, while, by similar means, they extended the limits of their spiritual authority. Nevertheless events, which will soon come under review, will show that the monarchs of the Francs looked upon the whole transaction in a different light, and considered all the temporal, and part even of the ecclesiastical power in the provinces which they had restored to Rome, as still vested in themselves in their quality of Patrician, or Exarch.

Although the youth of the Frankish nation were often permitted to bear arms at a very early period of life, it does not appear whether Charlemagne did, or did not, accompany his father in the first expedition against the Lombards. Several years follow, in the records of that period, without mention of the future monarch. During that lapse of time, Pepin again invaded Lombardy, in order to enforce the execution of the treaty which Astolphus had entered into the year before, and which he had unscrupulously broken, as soon as the sword of the Franc was withdrawn from his throat. The Lombard king was again driven to submission, and forced to begin the restitution which was demanded; but he did not live to complete it; and, after his death, which took place in consequence of a fall from his horse, Desiderius, who had commanded a part of his troops, was elected King of the Lombards, by the influence and support both of Pepin and the Pope,—a subject of which I must necessarily speak more hereafter.

In the meantime, Charlemagne continued to advance towards manhood. Successive wars, the fruits of a barbarous and unsettled state of society, where rights were undetermined, and law was in its infancy, afforded a continual school for the acquisition of that military knowledge and that corporeal strength, which, in those times, supplied the place of science in government, and talent in command. Early taught by his father all that was then known of warfare as an art, Charlemagne had but too frequent opportunities of gaining practical experience. It is more than probable, from the known habits of his nation, that he accompanied his father in most of his campaigns; but the first occasion on which he is decidedly stated by the chronicles to have followed the King to any of the many military expeditions which consumed the reign and the talents of Pepin, was on the renewal of the war with Waifar, Duke of Aquitaine, whose ambitious turbulence neither clemency could calm, nor punishment repress.

This struggle with the Dukes of Aquitaine, which continued with greater or less activity during two hundred years, is worthy of some attention. At that time, as already remarked, the right of succession was, in most cases, vague and undefined, and in none more so than in the transmission of the crown. Indeed, there are many reasons for believing that the chiefs of the Francs were originally elective, as was the case also with the Lombards, and that the royal office became hereditary by the progress of gradual innovation and customary submission. However this might be, it seems clear, that the Dukes of Aquitaine had some immediate connection with the Merovingian Kings of France, and some collateral claim upon the throne itself—the existence of which claim and connection, has caused much greater disputes amongst the antiquaries of modern times, than it did amongst the princes of their own day.

It does not appear, in any degree, that this title was put forth, or considered of consequence, in the times to which this book refers. Pepin was seated safely on the throne; the Dukes of Aquitaine are never found to have disputed his right; and their consanguinity with the Merovingian Kings would be unworthy attention, were it not necessary to show, that they stood in a different relationship to the French monarchs from the other dukes or governors of provinces, and claimed the territory they possessed, not indeed as independent sovereigns, but as hereditary, though subordinate princes, holding their feof,—or *beneficium*, as it was called under some circumstances,—not by the will of the reigning monarch, but in right of clear descent.

On various occasions, the Merovingian Kings themselves endeavored to restrict the power of the Dukes of Aquitaine to the same limits as that enjoyed by the simple governors of a province; and the charter of Charles the Bald expressly states, many years afterwards, that they only possessed the duchy of Aquitaine in the name of the Kings of France. Nevertheless, it is beyond doubt, that Dagobert, to end the continual claims of the children of his brother Charibert, granted to his nephews the whole of Aquitaine as a *perpetual lordship*, on condition of tribute and homage; which is the first clear instance of a direct hereditary *feof*. Standing thus in a position totally different from that of any other of the French noble of the time, the Dukes of Aquitaine were continually trying the new and unascertained power which they held, against the monarchs by whom it had been conceded, and still more frequently against the maires of the palace, who afterwards governed in their name.

In the time of Charles Martel, Eudes, Duke of Aquitaine, was constantly in revolt, whatever phantom king shadowed the Merovingian throne; and all the moderation of the hero of that age, could never bind the turbulent prince to his alliance, nor all the exercise of his tremendous power, awe him to obedience and to peace. Continually defeated, Eudes still rose from his temporary submission, and, the moment that the presence of his conqueror was removed, allied himself to anyone who would aid him in the breach of those promises and treaties which fear and necessity had alone extorted. Charles, on the contrary, still triumphed and forgave; and, although the Duke of Aquitaine had even leagued with the Saracens, at once the enemies of his faith and his country, their defeat was followed by his pardon.

After the death of Eudes, the same turbulent spirit descended with the inheritance; and, though the territories he left were divided between his three sons, the rulers of the French found that the enmity of the Dukes of Aquitaine was transmitted entire. Hunald, who, as eldest of the three, had received Aquitaine for his portion, was soon forced to submit, by Charles Martel, and did homage, not to the Kings of France, but to the Maire of the Palace. Yet the spirit of revolt subsisted still; and no sooner had death unnerved the hand of the victor, than Hunald was once more in arms, plundering the provinces of Pepin and Carloman. Again subdued, the courage of the Duke sank. Remorse for having blinded his brother Hatton, operated, together with superstition and disappointment, to give him a temporary disgust to the world; and, resigning his territories to his son Waifar, he retired into the cloister.

No greater degree of tranquility accrued to France from this change in the government of Aquitaine; for Waifar proved still more rebellious and turbulent than his predecessor; and Pepin had soon to take arms, in order to put an end to his incursions. Several of these expeditions against Aquitaine are mentioned in the chronicles of the time; but that in which Charlemagne first appears in a military character, is marked as having been preceded by two years of peace,—an extraordinary duration of tranquility, in times when the scepter ever implied the sword.

The nominal cause of warfare on the present occasion was the plunder of Church property by Waifar; and, on the approach of Pepin, the Duke promised immediate restitution, at the same time giving hostages for his future conduct. In those days, falsehood seems to have been sufficiently frequent to teach caution to the most unsuspecting; yet credulity—always a quality of an infant state of society—was carried to a very extraordinary height. Pepin, after having been repeatedly deceived, again trusted his rebellious subject; and Waifar, who, by his apparent submission, had alone sought to gain time for preparation, forgot his promises as soon as he could collect an army; threw off his allegiance; and, adding outrage to revolt, advanced into the territories of France, ravaging the country with fire and sword.

But the vengeance of the monarch was prompt and powerful. Accompanied by his eldest son, Pepin took the field, entered Aquitaine at the head of immense forces, and, with rapidity almost incredible, subdued the whole province, from Auvergne to Limoges. Here Charlemagne had one of those examples of grand and extraordinary celerity in the movement of immense armies, which he afterwards so often practiced himself with magnificent success. In the course of a very few weeks, many hundred miles of an enemy's territory were conquered. Speed set preparation at defiance, and surprise changed resistance into terror. In this, as in almost all other wars, the people were made the expiatory sacrifice, to atone for the faults of their rulers. Blood and flame wrapped one of the finest districts in France, and ruin and destruction marked the consequences of the vassals' revolt, and the vengeance of the sovereign.

During four years Pepin pursued the war against Aquitaine, displaying many instances of extreme clemency and extreme rigor, the causes of which dissimilarity of conduct, at different times, must remain in darkness; as the chronicles of that age do not explain the motives, and the historians of after years have only substituted hypotheses for facts. The greater part of the revolted country at length submitted, and Remistan, the uncle of Waifar, himself joined the party of the king, and bound himself, by the most solemn oaths, to aid the monarch as a vassal and a friend. His engagements, though voluntary, were as frail as those of the rest of his family and but a short time elapsed before he was again in arms against the sovereign who had trusted him, pursuing his designs with all the acrimonious virulence of conscious treachery.

The territory of Limoges and Bourges, where Pepin had built himself a palace, and established his residence, was ravaged by the orders of this faithless ally; and, not content with simple aggression, Remistan had the criminal boldness to appear, with hostile purposes, within sight of the monarch he had insulted, and the friend he had betrayed.

The fate he courted soon overtook him. Not long after he had presented himself before Bourges, he was taken in an ambush laid by some of the officers of the king, and was brought bound into the royal presence.

The character of Pepin might doubtless have derived a fictitious air of magnanimity in the eyes of after ages, from a display of clemency on this occasion; but it can hardly be denied, that mercy to Remistan, after the gross treachery he had committed, and the blood he had caused to flow, would have been anything but mercy to the rest of France.

The justice of his execution, which has been denied, depended upon whether he maintained rights as an independent monarch, and was a conquered king, rather than an arrested subject. The fact, however, is clear, that, whatever were his original claims to royalty, his ancestors had renounced them in a thousand instances; and also that, whatever force had been used to compel that renunciation on their part, he himself had acknowledged voluntarily the sovereignty of Pepin, and had actually served him as his liegeman. Unless, therefore, rights are to be looked upon as mere matters of caprice, and obedience to an established government is to be granted and withdrawn, at the pleasure of each individual, Remistan was in reality the treacherous and revolted vassal of the French king; and, while his pardon would have been an act of folly, his punishment was but a deed of justice.

No clemency was shown: Remistan was instantly condemned and hung; and the war of Aquitaine was soon after terminated for the time, by the death of Waifar, who appears to have been slain by the hands of his attendants, probably instigated by Pepin himself. On this point, it is true, we have no certain information, the only passage in the ancient chronicles which hints at the agency of the French monarch in the death of his rebellious vassal, leaving the matter still as a doubtful report.

Such means of destroying an enemy were but too common at that period; and, though the frequency of the fact can in no degree be brought forward to justify or even palliate a great moral offence, it at all events gives more probability to the rumor of its having been committed.

Pepin had many motives for seeking to bring the war in Aquitaine to as speedy a conclusion as possible, amongst which was the defection of Tassilo, Duke of Bavaria, who, but a short time before, had sworn allegiance to him, and acknowledged himself in the most solemn manner a vassal of the crown of France. The precise duties which he took upon himself by this oath and acknowledgment, we do not discover; nor is it easy to distinguish what was the distinction at that time between this higher class of vassals, and the inferior nobles more immediately within the jurisdiction of the monarch. The feudal system, the seeds of which had been long sown, was beginning to rise in different directions; but was far from possessing that great and extraordinary form which it afterwards assumed. Each particular age in the world's history brings forth the peculiar institution suited to the character of society at the time; but it does so slowly and by degrees, as necessity prompts the desire of alteration, and experience presents the mode. No sudden and general changes have ever been attended with permanent success, for although, by reiterated experiment, and the accumulated experience of many, it is impossible to say what degree of perfection may be ultimately reached, it would seem that the mind of man is incapable of conceiving at once any great and universal system. Each age may improve upon the last; and each individual epoch may produce and perfect the scheme of society necessary for itself,—at once the consequence of its existence, and the type of its character. But still the creation of great institutions is like the sculpture of a statue, and a thousand slight blows from Time's chisel are required, to change the marble ruggedness of the mass into the perfect and harmonious form.

At the time of which I now speak, the feudal system, the chief institution of the middle ages, was yet in its first rudeness, and a number of accidental circumstances were still required to give it consistency, solidity, and extent. It is impossible, and would be of little use, to trace all the events which contributed to that effect. The revolt and subjection of vassals—the power of some monarchs and the weakness of others—the rights of different orders, mutually wrung from each other—and the imperative necessity of some fixed barrier, however frail, between the claims of various classes,—gradually produced a state of society fitted to those times, and those times alone.

Amongst these causes were such insurrections as those of Waifar and of Tassilo. But though Pepin succeeded in subduing the former, and in annexing almost the whole of Aquitaine to the crown, the complete subjection of the dukedom of Bavaria was reserved for his successor.

On his return from his last and most successful expedition against Waifar, the monarch of the Francs was seized with a low fever at Saintes, which preyed severely upon a constitution shaken by mighty cares and never ceasing activity. His first resource under the depression of sickness was a humble petition for aid at the shrine of St Martin of Tours, which had been rendered famous as a place of marvelous cure, by the folly and ignorance of the age, and the impudence and talent of its prelates. But the malady of the King was not one of those in which mental medicine can prove efficacious; and, however great might be his faith or superstition, Pepin returned, weaker and nearer to death than he went. He then proceeded to Paris; and took up his abode in the monastery of St Denis, where his sickness each day advanced more and more rapidly. At length, the period came when the approach of death forced itself upon his conviction; and after having, with the consent of the principal men of the kingdom, divided his whole dominions between his two sons, Charles, (afterwards called Charlemagne,) and Carloman the younger, he died at the age of fifty-three.

Between Pepin and his father, Charles Martel, there existed a strong point of resemblance in their excessive promptitude of resolution, and their wonderful rapidity of execution, which qualities combined, formed the great secret of their power and their success. In other respects they differed from each other essentially. Charles Martel, despising the superstition of the day, oppressed the church; and, contented with his own power, contemned and circumscribed that of the nobility. Pepin, on the contrary, with greater ambition and greater piety, courted both the clergy and the nobles; and easily did away the phantom king, under the shadow of whose name Charles Martel had been satisfied to rule severely the other orders of the state.

Charles Martel left to his sons the regal power. Pepin transmitted to his children both the power and the name,—which is in all ages a great addition. As in war, an earthen mound, which an infant could crawl over with ease while unopposed, becomes, when defended, an important post; so in policy a mere title, which, abstractedly considered, is but air, very often becomes, in the struggle of contending parties, a mighty barrier and a strong defence.

In assuming the hereditary title of his Merovingian predecessors, however, Pepin unfortunately adopted also their system of dividing the succession—a system which had distracted the dominion of their race, and proved the destruction of his own.

FROM THE ACCESSION OF CHARLEMAGNE AND HIS BROTHER, TO THE DEATH OF CARLOMAN AND THE REUNION OF THE KINGDOM.

FROM 768 TO 771

The two sons of Pepin,—Charles, known in modern history by the name of Charlemagne, by which title I shall in future designate him, and Carloman, his younger brother,—succeeded, at the death of their father, to one of the most fertile, the most extensive, and the most powerful kingdoms, which Europe has beheld since the fall of the Roman empire.

The Pyrenees, the Alps, the Mediterranean, and the ocean, were boundaries supplied by nature to defend it from aggression, and to limit its extent; and the Rhine seemed intended for the same purpose by the same beneficent disposer. But rivers, however large, are ever very feeble and inefficient barriers between nations; and continual struggles had taken place upon the German frontier of France, from the period of the first establishment of the Frankish dominion in ancient Gaul, to the accession of the Carolingian race, the consequences of which struggles affected the whole reign of Charlemagne.

Without attempting to trace the progress of aggression on either side, and without joining in the censure often cast upon the barbarian tribes, for pursuing that system of migration which nature herself dictated, and for giving way to that thirst of conquest which was the first motive in their advance towards civilization, I must touch briefly on the causes which, during so long a period of the middle ages, rendered the northeastern limit of France the scene and object of incessant contention.

The spirit of predatory migration affected the whole people of the north of Europe from the moment that the population became so general and so dense, in relation to the means of support, as to require a relief and force an outlet. The first impulse might be given by some accidental circumstance, unconnected with any regular design of seeking more abundant fields, or more extensive hunting grounds. It might be afforded by the vagabond habits of the Scythian herdsmen, who peopled a great part of the north, and by their pressure upon the more settled nations, whom they either infected with their own desire of wandering, or drove forth by their superior power.

However that may be, it is not necessary to examine the remote and difficult question of national origins, in order to discover, amongst the various tribes who quitted the north to conquer and plunder the more civilized and enfeebled parts of Europe, two very distinct modifications in their principles of action, which led to great and important results. Some of these nations, whether they derived such a peculiar character from their native stock, or from some fortuitous circumstance, passed rapidly from country to country, contenting themselves with pillage, rapine, and destruction; sometimes returning to their own country after a successful expedition; sometimes proceeding to ravage some other land; but never dreaming of settling themselves anywhere, till centuries of roaming had obliterated the first character of their savage state, and gradually blended with them different races of a milder blood.

Other tribes again, whether driven from their native habitation by strife with a superior power, or actuated by the general spirit of migration, seemed still to covet some fixed abode; and though often forced by circumstances to change from place to place, showed at each step the same inclination to settle, like a swarm of bees which congregate upon a thousand various points, before they find a spot where they can hive at last.

The first mentioned class of invaders appears to have been animated in their expeditions by the desire of moveable plunder alone; the second class seemed to have acquired the more refined idea of territorial acquisition; though both were at the same time inspired by the spirit of conquest, the first great passion of a savage people.

Of those who seem more or less to have felt the wish for permanent establishment, the Goths, the Burgundians, the Lombards, and the Francs were the principal. The Francs fixed their dominion in the last portion of that civilized and fertile territory, towards which the stream of barbarian invasion was continually tending. The same desires which had led them forth, still animated the nations they had left behind; and, on taking possession of the Roman dominions in Gaul, they had to turn upon those who followed, in the very same path by which they had entered; and to defend what they themselves bad wrung from the Romans against the tribes of kindred plunderers, which trod upon their steps.

Thus the German frontier became a scene of incessant strife; but the Francs were a young and warlike people, mighty in adolescent energies, and tremendous in indefatigable activity. Far from contenting themselves with the barrier of the Rhine, the desire of conquest, which had made them masters of Gaul, led them to strive for dominions beyond the natural limits of the land they had obtained and in their struggles against the nations which followed—with forces concentrated for one great object, and with regularity of government ensuring stability of purpose—though sometimes defeated, and often repelled, they restrained the barbarians with whom they had to contend, and retained, as well as acquired, extensive territories on the farther bank of the Rhine. The boundaries of these territories were, from the very manner in which they were held, vague, uncertain, and varying from day to day, so that it is now impossible to draw with any precision the line of frontier which in this direction separated France from the uncultivated tribes of the North, at the epoch of the death of Pepin, and the accession of his sons.

The provinces beyond the Rhine, however, were considerable and, together with the rest of the Frankish possessions, formed the most extensive, as well as most powerful of the European monarchies. This descended without dispute to Charles and Carloman; but several circumstances accompanied the transmission of the supreme power to their hands, which are worthy of notice. I have before had occasion to point out the uncertain character of the succession to the crown of France, during the domination of the first race; nor is it very easy to discover any universal principle by which this important point was regulated. The will of the dying monarch seems to have been of some effect in the allotment of his dominions amongst his children; but the general assembly of the nation was always called upon to confirm or explain the dispositions of the former king.

It is difficult also to conceive the permanent unity of the people as a nation, while the territory was divided between two or more monarchs; and the only means we have of accounting for the long existence of such a state of things, is to look back to the original constitution of the Francs, as a German tribe, and to remember that, in that day, nations, not countries, formed the true divisions of mankind. This was a natural consequence of the migratory habits of the northern hordes, who, having no fixed habitation during many years, were long before they suffered the spirit of national union to deviate, in any degree, into local attachment.

The French, therefore, remained one people, however the state might be divided, or the country allotted; and the inheritance which Pepin transmitted to his sons, was not an united rule over the whole, but the government of a certain portion of the nation, and the possession of a certain portion of territory, severally assigned to each, while the general coherence of the Francs, as a people, remained unbroken.

The exact division of the country which took place upon the death of the great over-thrower of the Merovingian race, is involved in much obscurity; for the two best authorities of the time are in direct opposition to each other. Eginhard, the friend and servant of Charlemagne, assigns to him that portion of France called Neustria, with its usual dependencies;

while the continuators of Fredigarius, give him Austrasia, declaring Neustria to have been the portion of Carloman. The latter prince, however, according to both accounts, was crowned at Soissons, which was sometimes included in the kingdom of Austrasia; and Charles was, on the same day, inaugurated at Noyou, which always formed a part of Neustria.

The question, in regard to these two provinces, is indeed of little moment; as the difficulty is only an historical doubt of the present day, concerning a point which, notwithstanding the discrepancy of contemporary statements, seems to have been perfectly clear in those times, and gave rise to no consequences of any import. Charlemagne and his brother appear to have been perfectly satisfied with the division of the northern part of France, and each took possession of his own; but the sovereignty of Aquitaine, reunited to the crown by the arms of Pepin, proved a cause of doubt and disagreement between the two princes, which might have ended in open warfare, had not the early death of the younger intervened. On this subject also the Fredigarian Chronicle and the account of Eginhard are totally at variance. The first declares that Pepin, in dying, divided Aquitaine between his sons; but Eginhard positively states, that that province was attached to the portion of Charlemagne. In all probability, the matter was left in doubt, both by Pepin and the national assembly; but even a doubt where equal partition was regarded as a right, very naturally created coolness and jealousy towards his brother in the mind of Carloman, and loosened the bonds of kindred affection.

The quarrels of those persons in high stations, between whom Heaven, for their mutual defence and support, has established the close ties of blood, afford to the interested and ambitious so many means of gain or aggrandizement, that there would be ever found many to foment them, even were vanity, weakness, and malice, not continually ready in a court to promote hostility and render disunion irreparable. Carloman, apparently a feeble and easily governed prince, found plenty, both of knaves and sycophants, in his palace, to prompt his anger against his brother, and drive him on to acts of unkindness, if not aggression. Thus, their reign began in coldness and suspicion; but peace was still maintained, by the influence of their mother, Bertha; and the insurrection of a part of their dominions, seemed to furnish a motive for union and for mutual support.

It unfortunately happened, however, that the war, to which they were thus called as allies by every principle of good policy, had for its site and its motives, the very territory of Aquitaine, which had been the cause of their own dissension. Hunald, the father of that turbulent and unfortunate prince, from whom Pepin had wrested, after a nine years' contest, both his *feof* and his life, no sooner beheld the throne of France once more occupied by two young and inexperienced monarchs, than, encouraged by the too evident disunion which existed between them, he issued forth from the cloister to which he had devoted himself; called Aquitaine to arms; and, working upon the mind of a warlike but inconstant people, easily raised an army, and declared his sovereignty and independence.

Charlemagne instantly prepared to repress his rebellious subjects, and called upon Carloman to aid him in his design. Carloman promised his support; and even advanced into Poitou to confer with his brother on the conduct of the war; but their meeting terminated in a manner unsatisfactory to either; and Carloman returned to his own dominions, refusing to take any share in the expedition. In regard to his reasons for thus withdrawing the assistance he had promised to his brother, we have no information; and though it has been supposed that he wished to make the partition of Aquitaine the price of his support, and retired in resentment on refusal, it is better not to venture a conjecture in the utter absence of recorded fact.

His defection in the hour of need drew forth at once the great and overpowering energies of his brother's mind. The revolted Duke was at the head of a large and increasing army, and was carried on by the power of a fresh and hitherto successful enthusiasm in a bold, adventurous, and excited people. The forces of the young monarch, on the contrary, were but scanty in number; and, suddenly deprived of the aid on which he had confidently relied, he was left alone, unknowing alike the extent of his own powers, and of the attachment of his people, to lead the Francs to the field for the first time, against a warlike race and a desperate enemy. He paused not, however, for a moment; but pursued his expedition undaunted; and combining in his own person all the military talents of his ancestors, with high qualities entirely his own, he subdued the revolted provinces with a celerity of movement, and a decision of action, hardly equaled in ancient or in modern times. Notwithstanding the small army which he brought into the field, it would appear that the energetic activity of the young monarch surprised and terrified his opponent. Hunald fled without fighting; and, hard pressed by Charlemagne, only escaped into Gascony by his superior knowledge of the country, the complicated mazes of whose mountains were unknown to those by whom he was pursued. The place of refuge which he chose was the court of his nephew, Lupo, Duke of Gascony, who had joined in the revolt of Aquitaine, although his rebellion had never proceeded to actual warfare with the young monarchs of France. This asylum proved anything but a secure one. The ties of blood, indeed, connected the fugitive chief strongly with him, whose protection he claimed; but it must be remembered, that Hunald, in the day of his power, had, in a fit of ambitious jealousy, deprived his own brother Hatton, the father of Lupo, of his sight.

In almost all barbarous nations, where law is not sufficient for the chastisement of crime and for the reparation of wrong, revenge is considered as a virtue, and principle gives permanence to what is originally but a transitory passion. Lupo at first received his uncle with an appearance of hospitality; but Charlemagne advancing to the banks of the Dordogne, sent on messengers to summon his vassal the Duke of Gascony, to yield the rebellious subject who had taken refuge at his court, and to make atonement for his own revolt by instant submission and compliance. Obedience waited the command of the King; and Lupo, notwithstanding the ties of kindred and the rights of hospitality, made no scruple to deliver up the man who had robbed his father of his sight; thus at once avenging the ancient injury of his house, and securing both pardon and favor from the young monarch, to whom he at the same time acknowledged his homage and dependence.

Clemency was a natural quality in the mind of Charlemagne. It seldom if ever deserted him, even when age had taken from the first softness of the heart; and, in the whole course of a long life, we find few or no instances of cruelty recorded against him, while every historian rings with the praises of his moderation and gentleness. The single example of great severity which I shall have to notice hereafter, was the effect of that stern, though perhaps necessary policy, from which the mind of youth impetuously revolts. But in the present instance, young and happy himself—in the possession of those physical powers, and that ease of corporeal sensations which give natural amenity to the disposition and also blessed with that inexperience of abused lenity and of unrequited kindness, which leaves the heart free to act—cruelty could scarcely form a part in the character of Charlemagne.

No bloodshed stained his triumph over Hunald, gratified the revenge of Lupo, or blackened the Gascon's treachery by its consequences; and the young monarch spared his rebellious subject, though prudence, and even humanity, taught him to guard against future insurrection.

While waiting the return of his envoys from the court of Lupo, Charlemagne dedicated his time to the construction of a fortress on the banks of the Dordogne, in order both to employ his own troops, and to overawe the turbulent people of Aquitaine; and, after Hunald had been delivered bound into his hands, he contented himself with confining him to a seclusion scarcely more strict than that of the monastery which he had abandoned for the purposes of rebellion. The submission and obedience of Lupo, who had been an accessary, if not a participator, in the insurrection, was received as sufficient atonement; and thus the war, which had been boldly undertaken, and vigorously carried on, was terminated both with prudence and humanity.

This display of energy and power was anything but pleasing to Carloman; and the jealousy which he entertained towards his elder brother, was greatly increased by the triumphant expedition, in which he might have gloriously shared, but which he had ignominiously abandoned. Men were not wanting in his court to urge him on to open hostility, and it required every effort of calmer and wiser counselors to obviate the approach of internal warfare. Nor was the disagreement between the two French princes nourished in secret or brooded over in silence. Their disputes were heard throughout Europe, and became matter of rejoicing to the enemies, and of terror to the allies, of France.

A mediatrix, however, still existed of sufficient influence to avert actual war. Bertha, the mother of Charles and Carloman, was equally beloved and honored by each of her children; and her good offices between them, succeeded, though with difficulty, in maintaining peace, and producing an apparent reconciliation between the brothers. Having accomplished so far her excellent intention, she turned her whole thoughts towards the restoration of that general tranquility which had been so long a stranger to Europe. Her zeal in the cause of peace now led her to form the scheme of an alliance, which, however thwarted by the violent passions of others, and however unfortunate in its event, was wisely and nobly designed by her in whom it originated. This was a union with the court of Lombardy, and an extension of the relations between the various states of Italy and France. For the purpose of conducting the negotiations in person, the Queen set out for the Roman territory; but took occasion to pass through Bavaria, in order to avert a rupture between Tassilo, Duke of that country, and his sovereigns, the Kings of France. Having opened a communication between the Duke and Charlemagne, which afterwards produced the effects she desired. Bertha proceeded to Italy, on her journey of peace and reconciliation.

In the meantime, several changes deserving of notice had taken place in the relative position of the Lombards and the Romans, since the last expedition of Pepin, which rendered the interposition of Bertha not unnecessary. The death of Astolphus, against whom the arms of the Frankish monarch had been turned, had occurred immediately after his submission, and a struggle ensued for his vacant throne. Desiderius, who had commanded for Astolphus a considerable body of troops, and who to some military talent added great hypocrisy and much barbarian cunning, instantly determined to seize the crown of his dead master, and made every preparation for that object. But a strong party was soon formed against him, at the head of which appeared Rachis, once King of Lombardy, but who, in former years, had abandoned the robe of royalty for the monastic gown. Desiderius soon found that his influence amongst the Lombards was quite insignificant, compared with that which Rachis could oppose to him;

and the wily aspirant, rather than yield the prize at which he aimed, resolved to strengthen his power, by alliance with two persons who had proved the most formidable enemies of his nation, namely, the Roman pontiff and the monarch of the Francs.

Pepin, who was then still alive, was entirely guided in this instance by the Pope; and Stephen the Second willingly promised his aid to the ambitious soldier, on condition that Desiderius would undertake to fulfill to the utmost all those engagements which Astolphus had left unaccomplished at his death. The Lombard, who scrupled to break no promises, had little hesitation in pledging himself to whatever was demanded as the price of assistance and support. He acceded to every particular which the papal envoys were instructed to require, and bound himself by the most solemn vows, to the completion of the treaty of Pavia. Stephen, forgetting, what experience should have taught him long before, that oaths to hold ambition are but as the green withes wherewith the Philistines bound the limbs of the Hebrew giant, believed the sincerity of the Lombard, armed, threatened, and solicited, in his favor; and, finally, seated him on the throne for which he struggled.

The moment his object was attained, the promises of Desiderius were forgotten, and their fulfillment skillfully evaded. Pepin was at this time fully occupied with the wars of Aquitaine; and the Lombard, seeing that the Roman pontiff was not likely to receive any speedy assistance, proceeded by degrees from refusing restitution to renewed aggression, and finally struggled, both by art and arms, to recover the territory which the French monarch had formerly wrested from the usurping grasp of his predecessor.

Though the dominion of the Eastern Empire had been cast off by the people of Italy, no declared and precise separation had yet taken place. The two countries were disunited, in fact; but the Greeks held some small territory on the peninsula; the words of absolute disjunction had not been spoken; and the Emperors still kept up their claim upon Italy, and their hope of recovering it. Aware, that in all the struggles between the enfeebled power of Constantinople and the Roman states, a thousand opportunities would be afforded to the Lombards for aggrandizement and rapine, Desiderius called the Greeks back, to the Italian shores, and endeavored to allure them to the attempt, by promising the aid of all his forces. In the dangers and difficulties with which these intrigues enveloped them, the Popes had again and again recourse to Pepin; and Paul I, who succeeded to his brother, Stephen II, seems to imply, by the many expressions of gratitude and obligations which fill his letters, that the monarch of the Francs, though still prevented, by the wars of Aquitaine, from personally chastising the treachery of the Lombard king, had exercised some effectual influence, from time to time, in behalf of the Roman, church.

To Paul—after the mad attempt to establish the lay Pope Constantine, who became the victim of his own ambition, was deposed, and blinded— had succeeded Stephen III, one of the weakest men who ever filled the apostolic chair. His election had hardly taken place, ere he sent messengers to Pepin, praying for the continuance of that assistance which had been afforded to his predecessor. But Pepin was, by this time, no more; and Sergius, the faithful friend and envoy of the Pope, found Charles and Carloman sovereigns of France. The ready activity of the two young Kings was easily worked upon by the eloquence of the papal legate; and a mission with some troops, was dispatched by each, to give protection and assistance to Stephen, then the inveterate enemy of Desiderius, and of the whole Lombard race.

Itherius, charged with this mission to Italy by Charlemagne, executed it with care and circumspection, and contrived to give much satisfaction to the pontiff, without embroiling his master in a distant contention, at a moment when the monarch was engaged in suppressing the revolt of Aquitaine. He remained no longer in Rome than the duty he had to perform required; but Dodo, the commissioner of Carloman, either by desire of the monarch, or for his own purposes, protracted his stay in Italy, and warmly advocated the cause of the Roman church against the King of the Lombards. Combining with Sergius, the *nomenclator* of the Holy See, and his father Christopher, he attempted to enforce the restitution of the Roman lands and cities, and urged in his purpose with imprudent haste, so that all ended towards open warfare between the Francs and the Lombards.

It was at this time that Bertha, the mother of the French princes, undertook the work of pacification, and conceived, that, by uniting her eldest son Charlemagne to the daughter of Desiderius, the King of Lombardy might be induced to restore the contested territory to Rome, and that tranquility might be recalled to Europe. Her journey into Italy, and its object, soon reached the ears of Stephen; and all the influence of the Roman church was exerted to prevent an alliance between the hereditary friend and protector of the Popes, and a daughter of the inimical Lombards.

A letter of the weak pontiff, upon this subject, still remains, showing a lamentable want of dignity and temper, with common decency lost in vehemence of expostulation. Innumerable base and degrading epithets are applied to the Lombard race; and few languages could have supplied the prelate with more vulgar and dirty abuse than he has found in the elegant tongue of the Romans. Every obstacle, also, that the most politic ingenuity could devise, was thrown in the way of the proposed marriage; but the motive for abstaining, which surely should have been the most conclusive in the eyes of the young monarch, had it really existed, was his own union with another woman.

That Charlemagne had already had a son, called Pepin, by a person named Himiltruda, is known; but that the character of the connection between him and the mother of his son was but temporary, is evident. It is certain that the nation of the Francs did not consider it as a legitimate marriage; nor, even if they had, would it have proved an insuperable obstacle, for the bonds of that engagement, on which so much of the safety and welfare of society depends, were of no very strong and tenacious quality in the barbarous age to which our eyes are now turned. Divorces were easily and frequently obtained; and there were even cases where no formal interposition of the law was necessary to legalize a second marriage, while the husband or wife of the first was still living. The Pope, however, selfishly fearful of the new alliance, insisted strongly upon the indissolubility of the existing union, whatever it was. He not only remonstrated, but threatened, and even proceeded to anathematize all who should neglect his warning.

Notwithstanding his menaces and his wrath, the marriage took place, and before long, a change in his own feelings, induced Stephen himself to look upon it with a more lenient eye. Neither excommunications nor interdicts were then such formidable engines as they afterwards became; and, ignorant of the powers of the thunder they possessed, the Popes, in the infancy of their dominion, contented themselves with launching the bolts at molehills, with which they afterwards learned to bend the mountains. Though a weak man, Stephen III was too wise to assail his benefactors; and the storm of malediction with which he had threatened the proposed espousals hung suspended on his lips the moment they were completed. At the same time, Desiderius made some concessions to the Roman see, and succeeded in once more persuading the pontiff that he was willing to become his ally, and restore to Rome all that his predecessors had snatched from her sway. Nor did his dissimulation stop there; but, as Sergius and Christopher had been the constant and talented opponents of the Lombard power, and had not only counseled the Pope in his resistance, but had counseled him well, he contrived, by the artful agency of Paul Affiarta, who possessed the spirit, and acted the part, of tribune of the people, to blacken the character of those two faithful servants in the eyes of the feeble prelate. Stephen was easily deceived: the unhappy Sergius became the object of his dread and apprehension; the Lombard king was called to Rome by the blinded pontiff to defend him against his best friends; and, in a weak and ill concerted effort, made by Sergius, Christopher, and Dodo, to take possession of the Lateran, and exclude the foreign monarch from the city, the people abandoned them at the command of the Pope, and those three leaders fell into the hands of their enemies.

The two Romans were given up to the wrath of Desiderius and Affiarta; and though the sanguinary history of the Roman prisons is ever obscure, it is believed, that Christopher, after having submitted to the horrible operation which doomed him to endless darkness, died of the consequences; and that Sergius, his son, was strangled in his dungeon. Dodo, the Franc, was only allowed to escape out of respect or fear for Carloman, his master, whom it was wise to conciliate, and dangerous to outrage. With that prince, Desiderius, it is evident from many circumstances, kept up a constant and intimate correspondence towards the close of the year 770, and, as one of the learned Benedictines has observed, we have reason to regard it as more than probable, that the coldness of Carloman towards his brother Charlemagne, is to be greatly attributed to the machinations of the Lombard. Though it is unwise in general to imagine, in a remote age, those extended views of policy which seem the produce of a more enlightened state of society, yet the profound art of Desiderius is established beyond a doubt by all his actions; and the project of weakening a mighty and dangerous power, by fomenting disputes between the two monarchs who swayed it, was certainly within the scope of even barbarian cunning.

His efforts to create divisions, and increase dissentions, were greatly weakened by the influence of Bertha over both her sons, an influence which she ever employed to promote union; and the magnanimous character of Charlemagne himself, was a still greater obstacle in the way of such attempts. Neither coldness, suspicion, nor even anger, on the part of his brother, could provoke him to one hasty word, or one rash act; and it would appear that this moderation was not wholly without effect, even on Carloman himself, who, after many long, and, on his part, violent discussions, was at length reconciled to the kindred monarch in so public a manner, that congratulations on their restored affection forms the subject of one of the papal letters.

After the death of Sergius and Christopher, the confidence placed by the Pope in the King of the Lombards, was strong, in proportion to the weakness of his own understanding. All his opinions of Desiderius and his nation were changed; and, without remembering that he had very lately indulged in the most violent and unchristian abuse of both the sovereign and people of Lombardy, he now poured forth, with the same facility, a torrent of ill-judged and unseemly praise.

This change of sentiment may have tended greatly to allay his wrath at the marriage of Charlemagne with the daughter of Desiderius. But, at all events, the humane policy of Bertha seemed, for some time, quite successful. She visited the court of Desiderius, paid her vows at the shrines of the most esteemed saints in Italy, brought back her proposed daughter-in-law to France, witnessed her union with Charlemagne, and saw the papal opposition cease. Italy was tranquillized; the Roman pontiff was reconciled to his dangerous neighbor; and, in Bavaria, the Queen's intercession had been anything but in vain. Charlemagne had readily consented to peace, on the first overture of Tassilo, and dispatched Sturmius, abbot of St Fulda, to negotiate with his disaffected vassal. Terms were easily concluded with a clement king; and the aspect of all things promised tranquility to the world.

Such auguries, however, soon proved false. But, though the germs of future warfare lay hid in all the circumstances of the peace—though the ambition of Desiderius looked upon it merely as a temporary means —and the turbulence of Tassilo only regarded it as a short repose, — yet the first blow given to its stability was by Charlemagne himself; and a personal repugnance to the alliance he had formed, produced the same evil consequences as ambition, revenge, or any of those passions which we are accustomed to regard as the grander impellents of human nature. Some strong disgust seized on the monarch of the Francs towards his Lombard wife; and he determined on seeking, through the lax laws of divorce which then existed, the only means of deliverance in his power. His purpose was not effected, without considerable opposition from his nobles, his relations, and his mother Bertha. The latter, who had cemented the union of her son with the Lombard Princess, could not, of course, behold its speedy dissolution, without great pain; nor could she contemplate the consequences without apprehension. She argued, she remonstrated; she threatened to withdraw from the young monarch her society, which she knew he loved, and her counsels, which she knew he esteemed; and his immoveable resolution produced the only serious disagreement which ever troubled the intercourse of Bertha and her son.

Charlemagne persisted in his determination, and pursued his object without pause. The cause of divorce on which he insisted, incurable sterility, tom natural defect, has been more than once admitted as valid in the case of monarchs; and the King found no difficulty in inducing his bishops to dissolve the marriage. Desideria was repudiated; and Charlemagne, whose temperament and desire of offspring did not permit of his remaining unmarried, immediately raised to his bed Hildegarde, the laughter of a noble family in Swabia, who proved a more happy and more prolific wife.

It was not to be expected, that Desiderius should forget the insult offered to his race; and the means which had been employed to unite the Lombards to the Francs by the bonds of peace, thus became the cause of new disunion, and added personal hatred to political opposition. The enmity of the Lombard King towards Charlemagne was at once taken for granted throughout Europe, and was acted upon by all who were themselves inimical to the monarch of the Francs; so that the court of Pavia became a general refuge for the fugitives from Gaul. Hunald, Duke of Aquitaine, appears to have been the first who made it his asylum. How he effected his escape from the confinement to which Charlemagne had subjected him, is not now to be discovered; but, after a very short imprisonment, we find him seeking protection at Rome. Whether the Pope, Stephen III, by this time cured of his mistaken friendship for the Lombards, and fearful of offending his best supporter, Charlemagne, refused to receive Hunald in his flight; or whether he himself, doubting the inviolability of a sanctuary, whose chief guardian was his successful enemy, abandoned it voluntarily, does not appear; but it would seem that his stay in Rome was very brief. In all probability, as soon as he heard that the daughter of Desiderius had been put away by Charlemagne, calculating on human nature, he sought refuge at the Lombard court. No evil, however, thence accrued to the French monarch. The long, unhappy, and turbulent existence of Hunald was now drawing near a terrible close; and, having either embraced some heresy obnoxious to the Lombards, or abandoned Christianity altogether, he was stoned to death, within a short period after his arrival at Pavia.

Another fugitive soon appeared at the court of Desiderius with claims and rights which gave that monarch new hope of dividing and neutralizing the power of the Francs, and of avenging the insult he had received in the person of his daughter.

Late in the year 771, Carloman, the sharer of the French monarchy, expired; and, though no mention is made by any of the annalists of the precise cause of his death, except that it proceeded from some disease in the ordinary course of nature, there is reason to believe that his decease was sudden, as we find no attempt, on his part, to secure the succession of his territory to his children, nor any dispositions in regard to its partition between them. Scarcely had the funeral ceremony been performed, and the body of Carloman laid in the earth at the church of St Remigius of Rheims, when the evident disaffection of her husband's vassals and the fear of a brother, towards whom that husband had ever shown both jealousy and suspicion, induced Giberga, the widow of the dead king, to fly to Italy. This step Eginhard pronounces to have been unnecessary in itself; but it was certainly in no degree surprising, at a time when the immediate succession to the throne depended upon the choice of the people; and when the death of a competitor was often considered necessary to the security of a successful candidate. Her flight, therefore, was not extraordinary; but when, instead of trusting to the protection of the church, she chose, as the place of her refuge, the court of her brother-in-law's profound enemy, Desiderius; and solicited him to establish her children on the throne of their father, without the consent, and contrary to the customs of the nation; she seems to have acted with hasty passion rather than with prudent care. She chose to trust to the arms of strangers, which could never prevail where national affection was wanting. Very few of her husband's nobles accompanied her into exile; and the rest, forming the great body of the nation, unanimously declared Charlemagne their king.

Were it necessary here to reiterate all that has been before said concerning the uncertain nature of the regal succession in France, it might be clearly shown, that, in all instances, hereditary right was only acknowledged by the people in a limited sense, requiring to be accompanied by the specific consent of the nation; nor can it be doubted, that no repartition of the kingdom was held valid without the confirmation of the General Assembly of the Francs. This popular power had been preserved by frequent exercise under the whole of the Merovingian race, and had been confirmed most strikingly by the deposition of Chilperic and the elevation of Pepin. The right, therefore, of the nobles of Carloman's dominions, to choose his brother for his successor, was undeniable; and many circumstances induced them to do so without hesitation.

A reign of two years over a considerable portion of the French people, had already sufficiently displayed the character of the young monarch, to show that he possessed all those talents requisite to lead a barbarous nation, in difficult and momentous times. The nobler, the finer, the grander qualities of his mind and his heart, it is probable the rough chiefs of his warlike people neither saw nor estimated; but it was the peculiar attribute of that great prince, to add to feelings and powers which would have ornamented the brightest times, those animal abilities and ruder perfections, calculated to dazzle; captivate, and control the age in which he lived. His courage, his skill, and his activity, as a commander, were well known throughout the land; and, after the death of his father, his liberality and protection had been extended to all the faithful friends and adherents of the great king to whom he succeeded. He was thus esteemed, admired, and loved, by the clergy, the soldiers, and the people; and it is anything but wonderful, that such a leader should have been the universal choice of the Francs, in preference to an infant monarch and a female regent.

In accepting a crown which the nation had every right to bestow, Charlemagne was justified. He committed no crime—he violated no law— he was no usurper. But whether it would not have been nobler to have preserved the throne of their father for his brother's children, is a question not so easy of solution. The appearance of such an action would certainly have been more magnanimous, whether the reality were so or not; and where a doubtful procedure redounds to the advantage of the person who adopts it, the world is ever ready, and often just, in attributing it to a selfish cause. Nevertheless, a number of truly patriotic motives, to a mind so extensive in its views as that of Charlemagne, might act in opposition to kindred affection and native generosity. The good of the people that he was called to govern certainly required some other rule than that of women and children. Too many instances were before his eyes of the fatal effects springing from such an administration, for a doubt upon that point to enter his imagination; and, on the other hand, even if the nation would have consented to his governing in the name of his nephew, till the child grew up into the man, it is evident that his sister-in-law, Giberga, anxious for the supreme power herself, would never have yielded her assent. At the same time, it must be remembered, that the very proposal would have been an attack upon the rights of the French people to a voice in the succession of their monarchs, which Charlemagne was then in no condition either to make or to support.

Other motives undoubtedly concurred to determine the young King in his acceptance of the crown. If we may judge from the immensity which he afterwards accomplished, and from the steadiness and unity of design with which he pursued the general civilization of Europe, we shall find cause to believe, that great scheme to have been the offspring of his mind at a very early period, and to suppose, that all the power he acquired was regarded by him only as the means of accomplishing a vaster purpose. To reason thus of any vulgar conqueror would be idle, but the life of Charlemagne, taken as a whole, justifies the argument; and if such were his general views, he could not doubt that, in his hands, the union of the whole French empire would be more beneficial to itself in every part, to Europe, and to the world, than any portion of that power could be, entrusted to a woman and a child. Let it be granted that, even under this view, Charlemagne was ambitious; and, had he violated any right—had he usurped the power which he accepted, the end could not have justified the means, and his ambition would have been criminal. But the Francs had a just title to offer him the crown; he had an equal title to accept it; and if he did so for the benefit of his country, or for the benefit of mankind, his design was great, and his ambition was noble and glorious.

Whatever were his motives, Charlemagne received without hesitation the homage of those subjects who, since the death of his father, had been placed under the dominion of Carloman; and the whole of France was again united beneath one scepter.

The empire which was thus given at once to his command was, beyond doubt, the most powerful in Europe in every point of view. Italy was divided and exhausted; Greece was weak and debased; the north was portioned amongst various tribes, and, under the government of each and all, was still barbarous and distracted. England, separated into many kingdoms, was inefficient as a whole; and Spain was still agitated and employed by the bloody struggles of her different conquerors. But France, blessed with a hardy and a vigorous race, innervated by luxury, and unweakened by divisions, comprised the whole extent of country from the Mediterranean to the Ocean, from the Pyrenees to the Alps. A regularly organized state of society existed, though that state was far from perfect. Her laws, though scanty, were well known, were mild, and were more generally enforced than those of any other country. Her population was numerous, and her produce sufficient for her population. Her resources of all kinds were immense, and those resources were now entrusted to one, who, with extensive and extraordinary powers, combined love for his country and feeling for mankind.

FROM THE DEATH OF CARLOMAN TO THE CAPTURE OF PAVIA.

771 TO 774.

The intrigues of Desiderius were strengthened and directed by the presence of the widow and children of Carloman; but whether Charlemagne, strong in the love and support of his people, despised the weak machinations of his enemies in Italy, or whether a more pressing danger in the north called first for his attention, certain it is, that the immediate effort of his arms, after reuniting the two great parts of the French monarchy, was turned against those barbarian tribes who still ravaged the German frontier of France. With a pertinacity which nothing could overcome, and with a ruthless disregard of oaths, engagements, and ties, which no chastisement could correct, they, year after year, pillaged and desolated the transrhenane dominions of the Francs, slaughtered the inhabitants, and carried off the wealth of the country.

The chief of these nations was that people, or confederation of tribes, called the Saxons, of whom the Frisons were either a mere branch, or else perpetual allies. With the origin of the Saxons, I am not called upon to meddle. Suffice it, that the first mention of such a people in history, is to be found in Ptolemy, who flourished in the second century of the Christian era. They were then an insignificant tribe, inhabiting, with several others, the small peninsula of Jutland, and possessing three islands at the mouth of the Elbe. Their territories, however, were soon augmented, partly by aggression on the neighboring states, and partly by coalition with other nations, who—feeling that, as numbers formed the truest strength, union was the surest policy,—combined with the Saxons, to participate in the plunder which that race continually acquired, and gradually lost their distinctive appellations in the general name of the people with whom they associated themselves.

In the time of Charlemagne, the possessions of this great league were very extensive, stretching, at one point, from the banks of the Rhine, nearly to the Oder, and on the other hand, from the North Sea, to the confines of Hesse and Thuringia. Warlike in their habits, vigorous in body, active and impatient in mind, their geographical situation, operating together with their state of barbarism, rendered them pirates, extending the predatory excursions, common to all the northern tribes, to the sea, as well as to the land.

A thousand circumstances had combined, in the course of several hundred years, to lead the Saxons to carry on their warfare upon the waves. The fleets which the Romans had built before their eyes, as well as the maritime alliance which two Roman rebels, Carausius and Magnentius, had entered into with Germany, for the purpose of obtaining support in their usurpation of the purple, taught the barbarian confederates both naval architecture and naval skill. Thus, while the art was gradually forgotten by the declining Romans, the Saxons went on in progressive improvement, and at length became, properly speaking, the only maritime people at that time in Europe.

In an age, and amongst a people, where plunder and conquest were the only substitutes known for general commerce, the Saxons felt the great advantage of possessing all the insulated positions, which could afford shelter to their frail and ill-constructed vessels. They held, from an early period, greater part of the islands scattered round the mouths of the German rivers; and soon beginning to extend their dominion, they captured, at different times, all those on the coast of France and in the British sea. Not contented, however, with this peculiar and more appropriate mode of warfare, the Saxons who remained on land, while their fellow-countrymen were sweeping the ocean, constantly turned their arms against the adjacent continental countries, especially after the conquest of Britain had, in a manner, separated their people, and satisfied to the utmost their maritime cupidity in that direction.

Surpassing all nations, except the early Huns, in fierceness, idolaters of the most bloody rites, insatiable of plunder, and persevering in the purpose of rapine to a degree which no other nation ever knew, they were the pest and scourge of the north. Happily for Europe, their government consisted of a multitude of chiefs, and their society of a multitude of independent tribes, linked together by some bond that we do not at present know, but which was not strong enough to produce unity and continuity of design. Thus they had proceeded from age to age, accomplishing great things by desultory and individual efforts; but up to the time of Charlemagne, no vast and comprehensive mind, like that of Attila, had arisen amongst them, to combine all the tribes under the sway of one monarch, and to direct all their energies to one great object.

It was for neighboring kings, however, to remember that such a chief might every day appear; and, once more leading on the barbarians of the north, might extinguish in blood the little light that still remained in Europe, if some means were not taken either to break their power, or to mitigate their ferocity. Such was the state of the Saxons at the reunion of the French monarchy under Charlemagne; and it would seem, that the first step he proposed to himself, as an opening to all his great designs, was completely to subdue a people, which every day ravaged his frontier provinces, and continually threatened the very existence of the nations around.

Against them, consequently, were turned the first efforts of his arms, as soon as he became the sole sovereign of France; but to overthrow and to subjugate was not alone his object. Doubtless, to defend his own infringed territory, and to punish the aggressors formed a part of his design; but beyond that, he aimed at civilizing a people whose barbarism had been for centuries the curse of the neighboring countries, and, at the same time, communicating to the cruel savages, who shed the blood of their enemies less in the battle than in the sacrifice, the bland and mitigating spirit of the Christian religion.

That in the pursuit of this object he should have ever committed, either on a principle of policy, or of fanaticism, or of necessity, a great and startling act of severity, is to be much lamented. But no inference can be drawn from a single fact in opposition to the whole tenor of a man's conduct; and Charlemagne proved incontestably, by every campaign against the Saxons, that his design was as much to civilize as to subdue. These wars have been made the subject of bitter accusation against him, and it has been said, that his true policy should have been to defend his frontier by a strong line of fortresses; but we have only to turn our eyes for one moment to the invasion of the Eastern empire by the Huns, in order to find an example of the utter inefficacy of fortresses in staying the progress of barbarian armies. The hundred castles of the Illyrian border impeded not one hour the march of Attila; nor did the greater cities, though fortified by all that the united experience of Greece and Rome could suggest to strengthen them, offer any more effectual obstacle to the barbarian. The fate of the East was tried and decided in the field; and thus, with France, no fortresses could have defended her frontier from an enemy, whose inroad was ever as rapid and as destructive as the lightning. The Saxons were not less fierce, active, or vigorous than the Huns; and Charlemagne had but one choice—either boldly to seek and subject them by force of arms, to soften their manners and change their habits by the combined effect of law and religion—or, to wage constant, bloody, and disadvantageous war with them on his own frontier while they continued in separate tribes, and, if ever they united under one great chief, to risk his crown, his country, and the world, wherever and however they chose to call him to the field.

His resolution was immediately taken and, the year after the death of his brother and the choice of the people had placed him on the throne of the reunited kingdom, he held a great diet of the nation at Worms, and announced his intention of leading his warriors to the chastisement of the Saxons. Many of those who heard him had suffered, either in their property or through their relations, from incursions of the barbarians; and all willingly assented to an expedition which proposed to vindicate the insulted honor of France, and punish the spoilers of her territory. The military preparations of the young monarch were soon completed; and, entering the enemy's territory, he laid waste the whole land with fire and sword, according to the cruel mode of warfare in that day. No force appeared to oppose him, and he penetrated, without difficulty, to the castle of Eresburg, where a garrison had been left. The fortifications were speedily forced by the Frankish soldiers, and a much more important conquest followed than that of the castle itself, namely, that of the famous temple of the Irminsula, or great idol of the Saxon nation. The temple consisted of an open space of ground, surrounded by various buildings, ornamented by everything rapine could collect and offer at the altar of superstition. In the centre rose a high column, on which was placed the figure of an armed warrior; and gold and silver, lavished on all the objects around, decorated the shrine, and rewarded the struggle of the conquerors.

Nearly at the same spot, it would appear, the famous battle took place between Arminius and Varus, in which the Roman was signally defeated, and Germany freed from the yoke of the empire. The grateful Germans, we are told, in memory of their emancipation, and in honor of their liberator, raised a rude pillar on the spot, calling it *Hermansaule*, or the pillar of Arminius. But, as years passed by, and many a barbarian tribe swept over the country, the occasion of its erection was forgotten—the name was corrupted to Irminsul—the reverence of the people for the monument of their victorious struggle deviated into adoration—and the statue of their triumphant general became an idol, to which many a human sacrifice was offered. It is more than probable, indeed, that Mars, the god of battles, had supplied the place of the conquering German in the minds of his succeeding countrymen; and it seems certain, that this idol was not alone the object of veneration to one particular tribe, but was considered as the great tutelary deity of the whole people.

Its capture, therefore, was naturally an ominous event in the eyes of the Saxons; and, following rigorously his purpose of extinguishing their

Pagan rites, Charlemagne at once overthrew the vain object of their worship—an old and convincing mode of proving the impotence of false gods. The fane was at the same time demolished, the pillar was cast down, and buried deep below the surface of the earth, and three days were consumed in the work of destruction. This long delay, in the heat of summer, and in a dry and barren country, saw the waters of the rivers round about exhausted, and exposed the army of the Francs to all the horrors and difficulties of a general drought, in the midst of an unknown and inimical country. To advance was impossible; to retreat was perilous in the extreme; and Charlemagne was placed in a situation both painful and dangerous. One of those happy accidents, however, which, forgotten in the fate of meaner men, are marked and remembered when they second the efforts of those whose genius and whose perseverance raise them to great eminence—intervened to save the monarch and his army. While the troops were reposing, during the heat of the day, a sudden torrent filled the bed of a river, which had lain, for many days, dry before their eyes. The soldiers devoutly believed that a miracle had blessed and rewarded the destruction of the idol; and, elevated in mind as well as refreshed in body, they marched boldly on to the banks of the Weser, ready to fight with all the burning zeal of fanaticism, or to die with the iron constancy of martyrs.

Neither battle nor bloodshed proved necessary. Disunion amongst themselves, a wasted country, and a powerful enemy, were quite sufficient motives to induce the Saxons to offer once more that nominal submission, which they had so often rendered, and so often thrown off.

Charlemagne had not yet experienced their utter faithlessness himself, though the history of his predecessors furnished him with many an instance of pledges given and forgotten, and treaties entered into and violated, by the same barbarian enemy. His clemency, however, taught him to overlook the past; and, seeking rather to reclaim than punish, he accepted the twelve hostages which the Saxons offered as sureties for their future tranquility, withdrew his troops, and left the missionaries to effect by persuasion, what the sword is impotent to enforce.

It is worthy of remark, that in the course of this campaign, which may be taken as an example of the system of hostilities pursued by the Saxons against the Francs through the whole war, no general battle was fought. Scattered in various bands, a sort of federative republic without any general government, the Saxons seldom, if ever, could collect a sufficient force to oppose the great and formidable armies of the Francs. A country but slightly cultivated, and property entirely moveable, afforded them the means of abandoning the land with little risk or loss; and they vanished before the footsteps of an invading enemy, or only appeared to harass his march, and out of his supplies. Whenever he showed any inclination to advance far into the country, they obtained his absence by pretended submission, and by oaths never intended to be observed; and the moment they were freed from his presence, they endeavored to repay themselves for any damage he had occasioned, by ravaging and spoiling his frontier provinces.

In the present instance, either Charlemagne was deceived by their submission, or trusted to the capture of their fortress, and the destruction of their great idol, to intimidate and repress them. At the same time, many circumstances combined to call the young monarch back to France, and after receiving the Saxon hostages, he returned to his own country with all speed. New wars and new conquests lay before him. The storm which had been gathering in Italy, though it broke not immediately on his own head, by falling on a friendly power, whose regard for his interest had drawn it down, required him in honor and justice to interpose.

Various changes had taken place in the Italian peninsula during the expedition into Saxony, which ultimately brought about some of the greatest events in the whole of the French monarch's magnificent career. The intrigues which Desiderius had not for a moment ceased to carry on, in order to deceive and plunder the weak pontiff of the Roman church, had been principally conducted by the well-known Paul Afiarta, one of the most wily and subtle negotiators of the day. Endowed with a persuasive and popular eloquence, devoid of all moral feeling, and without any fixed principle but ambition, he had allied himself with Desiderius, in order that, supported by the Lombards, he might govern Rome, by a double influence over the prelate, and the populace. With the people he was ever a favorite, and for some time he was successful with the Pope; but, before the close of his pontificate, Stephen, notwithstanding the weakness of his understanding, began to discover how completely he had been deceived by the Lombard, and to perceive that the restoration of the contested cities was more distant than ever.

His mind was not sufficiently firm to make any equal and vigorous efforts in defence of the Roman state and he lived not long enough, after having opened his eyes to the treachery of the Lombard King, to display many of those passionate and indecent struggles, which were more in accordance with his temper and understanding. During the last few months of his life, he did little to free himself, although he saw the bonds with which he had suffered his hands to be enthralled; and dying, he left the Roman mitre nearly in the gift of Afiarta.

Adrian, who succeeded to the vacant chair, well understood the dark and ambitious character of the popular leader; but as the Roman citizens had then a principal voice in the election of their bishops, he dissembled his feelings towards Affiarta, till he himself was placed securely in the pontifical seat, by the unanimous consent of the clergy and people.

Nor even then did he venture at once to traverse the designs of the demagogue by open opposition. Affiarta was still honored and employed; and his approaching disgrace was concealed under the appearance of an honorable embassy to the court of Desiderius. Had a distant mission to an inimical monarch been proposed to the wily Roman, he would probably have suspected his danger, and refused to absent himself from a city where his safety was ensured by his influence over the multitude; but when the road laid before him was short, and the monarch to whom he went was his own immediate confederate, he saw no risk, and undertook the task. The opportunity, also, for conferring with Desiderius, seemed the most favorable that could be chosen; and Afiarta set out for Pavia, in the full belief that he was carrying on his own purposes to their consummation.

Still Adrian wisely refrained from any hasty attempt to execute his designs against the traitor, who had betrayed his predecessor, and was preparing to betray him also. He suffered Afiarta to reach the Lombard court, and to transact both the public business with which he was charged, and the private intrigues on which he was intent. But, in the meantime, the influence of the demagogue fell gradually lower and lower amongst the people of Rome, while that of Adrian, who was not himself deficient in popular talents, increased in a great degree. The Pope then found that, supported by his own favor with the citizens, and their fickle forgetfulness of their former leader, he could venture to do justice; and as the false minister was returning from his embassy, he was arrested at Ravenna by the bishop of that city, tried, condemned, and executed for the murder of Christopher and Sergius.

The exact chronology of the other events of this period is somewhat obscure; and I have separated the fate of Afiarta from the circumstances affecting Charlemagne, as I could not discover what was the part which the Roman took in any of them. It is certain, however, that Adrian was scarcely seated in the chair of St Peter, when the Lombard King, seconded probably by Afiarta, repeatedly and anxiously pressed the pontiff to acknowledge the children of Carloman, who were then in exile at his court; and to consecrate them as the rightful sovereigns of that part of France which their father had possessed during his life.

The enmity of Desiderius towards Charlemagne was both personal and political; and his object in the present instance was easy to divine. Perfectly impotent himself to invade with effect the territory of France, or to injure the monarch of an united people, he hoped, by establishing a new claim upon the Francs, supported by the sanctifying authority of the church, to raise up a powerful party for the children of Carloman in that monarch's former dominions, and thus to create the means of attacking Charlemagne, both by drawing a large body of Francs to his own cause, and weakening his enemy through their defection.

For the purpose of gaining the pontiff, it would seem that he once more renewed his often violated oaths of making full restoration of every part of the Exarchate and Pentapolis. But Adrian was too wise, either to trust to vows whose fragile nature had been so often proved, or to abandon the alliance of a firm and powerful friend, for the promises of a feeble and treacherous enemy. His decided refusal to anoint the children of Carloman, together with the death of Afiarta, drew down upon him the utmost wrath of Desiderius. The Lombard King had not only accompanied his solicitations with promises in case they were granted, but also with threats in case they were rejected; and these threats he proceeded immediately to execute.

Taking advantage of the absence of Charlemagne in the north, and the difficulties of the Saxon warfare in which he was engaged, Desiderius prepared to follow the universal policy of his predecessors, and to aim at the possession of the whole Roman territory. His first act was the farther dismemberment of the Exarchate, from which he seized the cities of Faienza and Commacchio; an act of violence considerable in itself, but which was only the prelude to greater aggression.

The Pope remonstrated both by letters and ambassadors; but in vain. The cities remained in the hands of the Lombards; and Desiderius, at the head of a large army, entered the papal territory, and marched upon Rome itself. Adrian had no forces whatever with which he could keep the open country against the power of the Lombards; but, though straitened in every way, attacked much more rapidly than he had expected, and blockaded in the very heart of the Roman states, he remained firm and inflexible. A spark, caught from the flame of that ancient courage, which had so often shone forth in other days amongst the palaces and temples wherein he stood, seemed to blaze up in the pontiff's heart; and Adrian resolved once more to defend the walls of Rome. The old gates, which had seen many a barbarian torrent ebb and flow, but which were now too much shattered by the siege of time to promise long defence, were taken down by his order, and new ones erected in their place; an action which at once gave additional courage to the citizens, and expressed to his enemies his unconquerable determination. Rome, however, could sustain no protracted blockade, and the aid of the Francs was absolutely necessary to save from fresh capture and spoliation the city which had herself extended conquest so far.

Even to implore such aid was a task of difficulty. By this time the whole of the surrounding country was in the hands of the Lombards, and the only means of communication still open between Rome and France, was by the Tiber and the Mediterranean. No European nation except the Saxons could be considered at that time as a maritime people. The Greeks, indeed, amongst the remains of all the mighty things which had come down to them from the golden age of the empire, possessed the ruins of a navy; and the Venetians were just beginning to aspire to dominion at sea; but the citizens of Rome were little accustomed to trust themselves to the waves; and the attempt to pass into France by the Mediterranean was, confessedly, one only to be thought of, because every other passage was obstructed. Nevertheless, an ecclesiastic of the name of Peter was found to undertake the task; and having accomplished the marine portion of his journey in safety, he arrived at Marseilles, from which place he was obliged to traverse almost the whole of France to Thionville, where, during the winter, Charlemagne was reposing after his expedition against the Saxons, and rejoicing in the birth of a son.

Admitted to the presence of the young monarch of France, the papal envoy urged, in strong language, the propriety and the duty of succoring Rome and her pontiff. Nor are the precise terms in which this demand was couched unimportant, as affecting, particularly, the only question by which the position and government of any country in the present day, is immediately connected with the age of which I speak. The messenger appeared before the King, "demanding", says the Chronicle of Moissiac, "that he should free the Romans from the oppression of King Desiderius", adding, that "he, Charlemagne, was the legitimate guardian and defender of that people, because Stephen the Pope, of blessed memory, had consecrated him to the Roman Patriciate, anointing him with the holy unction".

Charlemagne immediately saw that both policy and honor required him to interfere in behalf of Rome, and to support a prelate, whose resolute adherence to his cause, had brought upon him the danger against which protection was implored. Still, though thus moved by every inducement which could influence a person in his situation, though beyond all doubt warlike as a man and ambitious as a monarch, Charlemagne did not hurry on to an invasion of the Lombard territory without consideration and reluctance, nor mix in the strife of the neighboring powers—though one was his avowed enemy, the other his attached friend—without endeavoring to bring about peace by intercession, and to obtain justice by negotiation.

With a spirit of moderation, such as perhaps no monarch ever displayed but himself—notwithstanding certainty of success, confidence in his own tried powers, the enthusiastic support of his people, the urgent solicitations of a friend, a just cause for warfare, and the prospect both of glory and advantage—Charlemagne employed every milder means ere he unsheathed the sword; and paused long, in the hope of still avoiding war ere he broke the happy bonds of peace.

Desiderius, however, confiding in the advances he had already made against Rome, in the army he had raised, and in the possession of the Alpine passes, rejected every pacific offer. Twice in the course of the spring, did envoys from the sovereign of the Francs visit the court and camp of that monarch, proposing terms of peace, and offering even to buy the justice with gold which was refused to solicitation; and twice they were sent back by the Lombard, with insulting messages of arrogant refusal.

The situation of Rome had, by this time, become eminently hazardous; and Charlemagne felt that farther delay would be an act of injustice to his ally. The very consciousness of power had rendered the monarch scrupulous in its exertion, but, once driven to action, not a moment was lost, not an energy was unemployed. The Lombard had provoked him long, and, beyond doubt, began to imagine that his tardiness of resentment proceeded weakness; for the crafty and the base con-tinually deceive themselves, by attributing the actions of others to motives which would have influenced themselves. But Desiderius soon found, that, like the snow gathered on the mountains which overhung the Lombard kingdom, the spirit of Charlemagne, though long tranquil, was moved at length only to overwhelm everything by which it was opposed.

The general assembly of the Francs, or the field of May, was held at Geneva; and some time was spent in deliberating on the measures necessary to render the first efforts of the war successful. While these consultations were proceeding, the French monarch, still anxious for peace, once more sent messengers to the King of Lombardy, giving him notice and information of the vast preparations he had made to support Home by force of arms; but offering, even then, on hostages being given for the restitution of the captured cities, to withdraw his troops, and leave his expedition unaccomplished.

Desiderius rejected the last hope of peace; and Charlemagne proceeded to force his way into Lombardy, the first, but the most difficult and most important stop in the war. The strongest barrier which the hand of nature can pile up to separate rival nations, and mark the true limits of distinct countries, lay before him, in the gigantic masses of the Alps. But war was now decided on; and, undeterred by frowning precipices and everlasting snows, multiplied obstacles, difficulties, and dangers, Charlemagne advanced upon his way; and, separating his army into two divisions, he directed one, under the command of his uncle, the Duke Bernard, to cross the mountains by the Mons Jovis or Mont Joux, while he himself led the other into Italy by the passage over Mont Cenis.

To conduct a great force, consisting principally of cavalry, through two of the most difficult and precipitous mountain passes in Europe, was an undertaking which even the mind of Charlemagne, all bold and confident as it was, would not have conceived, had it not been absolutely necessary to conquer such difficulties in the outset, to ensure ultimate success.

His many attempts to obviate the approaching warfare, and the continual rumor of his military preparations, had put the enemy on his guard, and had given time for every measure of defence. All the easier passes of the mountains were already occupied, and even fortified, by the Lombards; and no way remained of forcing an entrance into Italy, but by unequal and most hazardous battle, or by the long and painful march which he determined to accomplish. It would seem that on this passage of the Alps great and extraordinary conquerors have taken a pleasure in trying the extent of their powers.

Hannibal, Charlemagne, and Napoleon, have each undertaken, and each succeeded in the enterprise; but of all these, perhaps, the monarch of the Francs had to contend with the greatest difficulties, with the least means of success. The Carthaginian, it is true, was harassed by enemies, and the Corsican was burdened with artillery; but the one could call to his aid all the resources of ancient art, whose miracles of power shame our inferior efforts and the other could command all the expedients of modern science, to support his own energies, and to smooth the obstacles of his way. Charlemagne stood alone in the midst of a barbarous age, when the knowledge of ancient Europe was extinguished, and the improvements of modern Europe were unknown, upheld solely by his own mighty mind in the accomplishment of an undertaking which he himself had conceived.

The design, however, was eminently successful. Notwithstanding the difficulty of procuring provisions, and all the dangers attendant upon the march of a large force of cavalry over steeps and glaciers, snows and precipices, the army passed in safety, and began to pour down upon Italy. Few troops had been stationed by the Lombards to guard a passage considered almost impracticable; and those few were instantly put to flight, by the first body of Francs who traversed the mountains. The rest of the invading army followed, after a difficult and wearisome march; and the reunion of the two divisions took place at the foot of the descent. From the successful expedition of the Duke Bernard, with one great body of his nephew's troops, the tremendous mountain over which he forced his way received the name, which it retains to the present day, of the Great St Bernard. It had before borne the appellation of Mons Jovis, from a temple to Jupiter, which ornamented the side of the acclivity; but the name of the Heathen deity was soon forgotten in the exploit of the Christian warrior; nor has the same passage, effected in an after age by another mighty conqueror, been able to snatch from the uncle of Charlemagne the glory of the great enterprise which he achieved, or to efface his name from the majestic object with which it is inseparably connected.

The news of this sudden appearance of the Frankish army, in a quarter where they had been so little expected, passed like lightning to Desiderius, who hastened instantly with the main body of his forces to oppose the enemy, before they could quit the narrow defiles in which they were entangled. Collecting all his troops, he took possession of the pass of La Cluse, and made a demonstration of defending it with vigor. But Charlemagne, having fortified his camp in front, detached a considerable force through the mountains, to turn the flank of the Lombards. This movement was instantly perceived by Desiderius; and, struck with sudden terror lest his retreat should be cut off, he abandoned at once his projects of resistance, and, flying to Pavia, left the country open to the Franks.

Strong fortifications and abundant provisions secured to Pavia the means of long defence; while the Franks, naturally impatient, and unaccustomed to the protracted operations of a regular siege, were likely to be foiled by one which promised every difficulty that skill, resolution, and despair, could oppose to their efforts. But the mind of Charlemagne possessed those extraordinary qualities which are only recorded of the very greatest men, and which bend to the will of the individual so gifted, even the natural character of those brought in contact with him. Determined that his conquest of the Lombards should be more effectual than that of his father, Charlemagne resolved not to abandon his design for vows which might be broken, and submission which would certainly be feigned. The siege of Pavia, therefore, was undertaken with the determination of carrying it on without pause or compromise; and the Francs themselves, yielding their national haste and eagerness to the purpose of their King, evinced a degree of patience new to all their habits.

The defence of Pavia had been undertaken by Desiderius himself; but Verona also, one of the strongest towns of his dominions, he determined to maintain against the enemy, while he left the rest of the Lombard cities very nearly to their fate. The government of Verona he entrusted to his son Adalgisus; and thither also the wife and children of Carloman were sent, for their greater security, as to a place not exposed, like Pavia, to the first attack of the invaders. At the same time, Autcarius, a Frankish noble, who had accompanied Giberga to Lombardy, was invested with a share of that command for which the youth and inexperience of Adalgisus rendered him not fully competent.

The supposition that the resistance of Pavia would long retard the progress of Charlemagne against Verona proved to be fallacious. From the first, the Frankish monarch seems to have determined to reduce the Lombard capital rather by absolute blockade, than by more active measures and, as a large portion of his troops were thus unemployed, no sooner had he seen the trenches completed round that city, than he led a division of his army against Verona. Astonished at the rapidity of his progress, and cut off from all communication with Desiderius, Adalgisus lost heart, and, instead of attempting to occupy and divide the invading force by a spirited resistance, he abandoned the army committed to his care, and, leaving Verona, fled, first to Pisa, and thence to Constantinople. He was destined never to revisit Lombardy; but his existence at the court of Constantine, the enemy both of the Popes and of Charlemagne, was long a subject of disquietude to the conqueror of Italy.

Verona, abandoned by the prince, surrendered almost immediately, and the widow and children of Carloman fell into the hands of the victor. What was the conduct of Charlemagne to the beings thus cast upon his mercy, has not yet been discovered. The eldest son of the dead Carloman is never again mentioned in history, and a vague and improbable tale is all that has reached us concerning the second. That tale, however, if it be true, shows that the monarch treated his nephew with kindness; and the general character of Charlemagne may well justify our belief so far, whether the whole be true or not. The same darkness is spread over the history of Giberga, which involves that of her children; and the only farther account we have of Autcarius, is a laudatory composition in praise of a person of a somewhat similar name, which, however, is by no means clearly proved to be applicable to the follower of Carloman.

No sooner had Verona fallen, than the victorious monarch hastened back to press the siege of Pavia; and his designs on Italy gradually extending themselves with time, opportunity, and experience, he began to contemplate a longer absence from his native country than he had at first proposed, in order to effect completely what he had so boldly undertaken. His wife and children, therefore, received directions to join him in the camp before Pavia; and their coming gave a new proof to the Lombards of his unchangeable resolution, and afforded to his soldiers a demonstration of the persevering patience with which he intended to carry on the siege.

Although the capital still held out, the other cities of the Lombard kingdom one by one surrendered to detached bodies of the Francs. Few of them offered any resistance, and in general the people seemed not unwilling to amalgamate themselves with a great and conquering nation. Pavia, nevertheless, was defended long with all the energy of valor, and the pertinacity of despair. The abundant stores with which it had been supplied, managed with care and frugality, kept up the spirits of the inhabitants, and preserved the obedience of the garrison. Days, weeks, and months passed by; summer, autumn, and winter fled; and yet the city maintained its resistance, though the whole of the rest of Lombardy had submitted.

At length, as the high solemnity of Easter ap-proached, Charlemagne prepared to visit Rome, leaving to his officers the task of carrying on the siege during his absence. Various motives induced him to undertake the journey; and those extensive views of general policy, that on all occasions showed him the utmost extent of advantage which could be reaped from any measure, taught him to look upon a visit to the ancient capital of the world as a means of extending his power, and deriving the greatest benefit that could accrue from his expedition to Italy.

Lombardy, except the capital, whose resistance could not be effectual, was already conquered; and the Frankish monarch regarded that country as his own, by the right which, with very few exceptions, had hitherto alone bestowed dominion, and trans-ferred the scepter from one race to another. He was King of Lombardy by force of arms; but at Rome he was to be received as Patrician, and Ravenna looked upon him as Exarch,— titles which had previously been mere names, but of which he now intended to exercise the rights. The people of Rome, by their voluntary act, had named him Patrician, or military governor; and both his father and himself had been called upon to perform the most arduous duties of that station, without exercising any of the power which the office implied. But Italy was now at the monarch's feet; and Charlemagne, without the least desire to trample on it, prepared to take upon himself the full character of Patrician, and to govern, though his government was of the mildest quality.

The news of his approach flew rapidly to Rome; and the supreme pontiff, at once animated by original feelings of regard and esteem, grateful for services rendered, and mindful of benefits to come, prepared to receive the conqueror of his enemies, in the ancient queen of empires, with all the solemn splendor which suited the man, the occasion, and the scene.

In the meantime, Charlemagne set out from Pavia, accompanied by a considerable army, and an immense train of bishops, priests, and nobles; and, passing through Tuscany, he advanced by rapid journeys upon Rome. Shouts and songs of triumph greeted him on the way; towns, castles, and villages, poured forth to see him pass; the serf, the citizen, and the noble, joined in acclamations which welcomed the conqueror of the Lombards; and dead Italy seemed to revive at the glorious aspect of the victor. Thirty miles from the city, he was met by all those who could still boast of generous blood in Rome, with ensigns and banners; and at a mile's distance from the walls, the whole schools came forth to receive him, bearing in their hands branches of the palm and the olive, and singing, in the sweet

Roman tongue, the praises and gratulations of their mighty deliverer. Thither, too, came the standard of the cross, with which it had been customary to meet the Exarchs on their visits to the city; and truly, since the days of her ancient splendor, never had Rome beheld such a sight as entered her gates with the monarch of the Francs.

It was now no savage army come to ravage and to spoil, with hunger and hatred in their looks, and foulness and barbarism in their garments. On the contrary, a long train of the princes and nobles of a warlike and beautiful nation, mingling, in the brilliant robes of peace, with all the great of a people they had delivered, entered the gates of Rome, and, amidst songs of victory and shouts of joy, were led forward, through all the splendid remains of ancient art, the accumulated magnificence of centuries of power and conquest, by a monarch such as the world has seen but once.

Above the ordinary height of man, Charlemagne was a giant in his stature as in his mind; but the graceful and easy proportion of all his limbs spoke the combination of wonderful activity with immense strength, and pleased while it astonished. His countenance was as striking as his figure; and his broad high forehead, his keen and flashing eye, and bland unwrinkled brow, offered a bright picture, wherein the spirit of physiognomy, natural to all men, might trace the expression of a powerful intellect and a benevolent heart.

On so solemn an occasion as his entry into Rome, the general simplicity of his attire was laid aside; and he now appeared blazing in all the splendor of royalty, his robes wrought of purple and gold, his brow encircled with jewels, and his very sandals glittering with precious stones.

As he approached the church of St Peter, and was met by the Exarch's cross, the monarch alighted from his horse, and, with his principal followers, proceeded on foot to the steps of the cathedral. The marks of his reverence for the shrine of the apostle were such as a sovereign might well pay, whose actions and whose power left no fear of respect being construed into submission. In the porch, near the door, he was met by Pope Adrian, attended by all his clergy, clothed in the magnificent vestments of the Roman church; and while loud shouts rent the air of "Blessed be he who cometh in the name of the Lord!" the pontiff held his deliverer to his heart, poured forth his gratitude, and loaded him with blessings.

The meeting was one of great interest, both to the priest and the monarch. I know no reason why, in examining the characters of princes, we should endeavor to set them apart, in their sentiments, from the rest of human beings, and not believe them to be actuated by the same affections as their fellow men. Though Charlemagne was a great conqueror and a clear-sighted politician, an ambitious king and a dauntless warrior, we know that he had a heart full of the kindest and the gentlest feelings; and there is every reason to believe, that all the finer emotions of his bosom were affected by his meeting with the Roman pontiff. That he revered Pope Adrian as a prelate, and loved him as a man, his afterlife sufficiently evinced; and when he met him, for the first time, in the midst of Rome, he must have remembered that, sooner than bring discord and strife into his dominions, the old man before him had dared the enmity of a powerful and vindictive monarch, had seen his country wasted and destroyed, and had exposed himself to be besieged in a vast, but ruined and depopulated city. We may well believe, then, that the feelings of reverence and affection he expressed were the genuine emotions of the young sovereign's heart. Such feelings on his part, while the Pope, on the other hand, acknowledged in him the saviour of Rome, and the deliverer of the church, could not fail to create between them a bond of sympathy and regard such as circumstances seldom suffer to exist amongst the great of the earth. The friendship, thus begun, continued through their mutual lives; and, with the invariable fortune of union between the good and wise, tended immensely to the safety and prosperity of both.

After the arrival of the monarch, several days were spent in celebrating the solemnities of Easter; but neither the Pope nor the King neglected those matters of temporal jurisdiction, which were now tending towards a more clear and decided establishment than Italy had known for many years. Charlemagne was evidently received as sovereign by the Pope himself, and by the whole people of Rome. He was crowned with the diadem of the Patricians, or Exarchs, and exercised, for the first time, the extensive sway with which that office invested him. In whatever manner Pepin had re-annexed the Exarchate and Pentapolis to Rome, that act, it is clear, was in no degree such as to exempt those territories, or even Rome itself, from the dominion of the Patrician. On the entrance of Charlemagne into the city, there was no struggle, dispute, or misunderstanding about authority. It was assumed by him at once, and granted by the clergy and the people as the undoubted right of the Patriciate; nor did he ever cease to use the supreme power, first as Patrician, and afterwards as Emperor, from his arrival in Italy to the close of his life and reign. To him all great causes were referred; the Pope himself appeared before him as before his judge; and we find repeated instances of his having extended his jurisdiction to ecclesiastical, as well as civil affairs, throughout the whole of the Roman territory.

Nevertheless, there is every reason to believe that Adrian solicited, and that the monarch granted, considerable territories, to be held by the Church of Rome, though solely conceded as by lord to vassal, and by no means independent of the Patrician. A great variety of forms had by this time been introduced amongst feofs and benefices; and what were the feudal privileges granted on the present occasion, what those reserved, is very difficult to ascertain; for, though the Popes have since asserted that the donation of Charlemagne was written, the original deed has never been seen by any one; and through the whole correspondence of the pontiffs with that monarch, we find no mention made of such an instrument. So far from it, indeed, that, within a few months of the gift, a contest took place between Adrian himself, and Leo, Archbishop of Ravenna, concerning the limits of the district granted by Charlemagne to the Church of Rome, which would have been at once determined by the production of the monarch's charter. This, however, was never done, and the Pope was obliged to apply to the King of the Francs, in order to establish the facts. Such an event seems to determine the question; for it must not be forgotten, that the dispute was not about a small portion of frontier land, which the ambiguity of language might render difficult to define; but about cities and provinces, in regard to which no doubt could have been entertained, if any written deed had existed to establish the papal claims.

The limits of the territory granted remain equally uncertain to the present day. The papal historians declare, that the gift of Charlemagne included, besides the Exarchate and Pentapolis, the whole of Corsica, Parma, Mantua, Reghio, and Bardi, with the Venetian provinces, and a considerable part of the Tyrol, as well as Spoleto and Beneventum. But the Popes themselves, with more moderate wisdom, never, in their letters to the donor, speak of anything beyond the Exarchate and Pentapolis, except the territory of Spoleto; and though it is not improbable that Charlemagne might, as Gibbon asserts, give that to which he had no right—for rights were then but badly defined—it is not at all likely that he should give what he did not possess, which is implied by the more than doubtful account of Anastasius.

Some slight mention appears to have been made about this time, of a prior donation from Pepin to the Holy See; but not in such terms as to call for opposition or confutation, even had Charlemagne been inclined to resist the transfer of the property from the people to the church. That he was not so, is sufficiently evident from his own gift to the Popes, of those provinces which his father had re-annexed to the Roman state, with the addition of Spoleto. But, at the same time, it is to be remarked in regard to this famous donation, that even then existed the custom of granting considerable territories to the principal churches and monasteries under the dominion of the sovereign, as a feudal property to be held of the crown; nor can I look upon the gift of Charlemagne in any other light, though various after circumstances seem to prove, that the people of the city of Rome still continued to regard themselves as an independent republic till the hour that the Patrician was saluted Emperor. To hold these territories even as a vassal of the Frankish monarch, was still, in the opinion of the Pope, a great step gained; and we never find that he made any opposition, or offered any remonstrance, to the many acts of sovereignty exercised by Charlemagne within the very provinces bestowed, although those acts were, in several instances, such as were seldom justified by the feudal tenure of any lands in that day.

Satisfied with the assertion of his authority by a temporary exhibition of the Patrician power, Charlemagne seems to have required little immediate return from the pontiff for the services he had rendered to Rome and the church. After regulating some clerical affairs of little interest, he hastened back to Pavia, where his presence at the head of the army had become necessary, for the purpose of supporting and encouraging his soldiers under the wearisome labors of the longest and most difficult siege which the Francs had ever undertaken. At the same time, many circumstances imperatively required that he should press the Lombard capital to its immediate fall, and turn his steps towards his own paternal dominions.

One of the most urgent of these circumstances was the state of his northeastern frontier, from which continual accounts of the most alarming character reached him in the heart of Italy. It appears, that no sooner had the news of his absence from France spread abroad, than the Saxons hastened to take advantage of so favorable a moment, and to avenge their recent subjection, by ravaging the borders of their conqueror's territory. Flame and the sword desolated the land; and though, on one occasion, a panic, which the monks willingly mistook for a miracle, caused the barbarians suddenly to fly, at the very moment they were advancing to burn the church of St Boniface, at Fridislar, their terror was soon forgotten, and their devastation recommenced.

With these motives for activity stimulating his mind, Charlemagne took vigorous measures to render the blockade of Pavia more severe than ever. No living thing was suffered to enter or to quit the city but the birds of the air; and though Desiderius still resisted with desperate resolution, famine soon began to undermine the courage of the Lombards. The hopelessness of rescue, the subjugation of the whole country round, the weariness of restraint, the known clemency of the victor, and the miseries of a protracted siege, all acted on the hearts of the Pavians, and at length, about the middle of the year, they threw open their gates to the Francs.

To compensate for the obstinate resistance, which they feared the conqueror might construe into crime, the Lombards in the city delivered up Desiderius, his wife, and daughter, to Charlemagne, without any stipulation in their favor; and, indeed, seem themselves to have relied entirely on the mercy of their conqueror. Their reliance was not in vain: no cruelty stained the glory of the triumph. Pavia did not even suffer from plunder; and the treasures found in the palace of the vanquished Desiderius repaid the Frankish soldiers for their long fatigues, though no part went to swell the stores of their own liberal monarch. A medal was struck upon the occasion of the fall of Pavia, but Charle-magne did not permit any painful act of triumph to crush the iron into the flesh of the Lombards. Their institutions were still left to them inviolate; and the monarch of the Francs appeared amongst them less as a conqueror, than as a father.

He instantly, however, took the title of King of Lombardy, and was crowned with the iron circle which the monarchs of that country had assumed after their settlement in Italy; but the choice was still left to the people of the land, in all cases, whether they would be judged by their own, the Roman, or the Frankish law. A few additions, indeed, were made to the Lombard code; but even this was done with a sparing and judicious hand, and was softened with the pretence of supplying the laws which had been lost or forgotten.

The disposition, also, which the Lombards had shown to amalgamate themselves with the Francs, met with every encouragement from the great French monarch, whose desire was ever to win, rather than to compel. He received the oath of homage from the Lombard nobles; and, as if that oath could not be broken, trusted them, in general, with the entire government of their towns and provinces, confided in their faith alone, and strove in everything to smooth the way for the complete union of the two nations, taking care that the humiliation of overthrow should not impede the progress of pacification and concord

These regulations required some time to perfect; but, at length,

Charlemagne once more set out for France, and reached it in the middle of August, leaving but few troops in the Lombard kingdom. Pavia, the capital, and a small number of frontier towns, received garrisons, but the people in general had evinced willingness in their submission; and Charlemagne, too strong to be fearful, was too noble to be suspicious.

Adalgisus, however, was now at the court of Constantinople, whose emperor still looked towards Italy with envy and regret; and it was not at all unlikely, that the peace of Charlemagne's new kingdom might soon be troubled by the intrigues of the Emperor of the East. Desiderius, with his wife and daughter, were carried or sent into France by the conqueror, and, apparently, were obliged to embrace the monastic life; for we find that the dethroned monarch was first committed to the charge of Agilfred, Bishop of Liege, and was afterwards conveyed to the monastery of Corbie, where he lived for some time in the practice of mild virtues and superstitious observances, and died at an unknown period.

Whether the peace that he now enjoyed, compensated for the splendor that he had lost, and the calm contemplations of the cloister were sufficient occupation, after the troublous ambitions of the palace, history does not mention, though it insinuates that he was happy. But still, there can be little doubt, that the consciousness of having cast away empire for revenge, must have mingled remorse with memory, and forced many a regret upon his mind,—especially when he reflected that his own intrigues had worked his downfall, and learned, from the moral voice of the irretrievable past, that had he been virtuous, he might have continued great.

GEORGE JAMES

FROM THE CONQUEST OF LOMBARDY TO THE BEGINNING OF THE SPANISH WAR.

774 - 777

The life of a monarch, at all times one of difficulty and rare, is ever, in barbarous ages, an existence of continual labor and incessant strife. Nor can even a decree of civilization greatly superior to the age in which he lives, raise a king above a constant war with the barbarism around him, nor grand views for the weal of human nature effect anything for his own peace and tranquility. On the contrary, every general effort to benefit the race of our fellow creatures, must always have to struggle against narrow prejudices and petty interests; and there is unhappily too much reason to believe that very extended views, in royal bosoms, only afford new cause for strife, added to the many which unceasingly assail a throne.

Neither, in an uncultivated state of society, before reason had learned to curb desire, or long experience had shown the fruitlessness of contention, could even predominant military power and the gift of victory ever secure the duration of peace without, indeed, some one man could, by a godlike mind, render conquest universal, and obedience permanent. And yet, peace being, as the great Spaniard beautifully says, the true object of war, so warfare must still, in a barbarous age, be the only means of peace, however vain the treaties obtained may prove, however transitory be the tranquility that follows.

The most pacific disposition, joined to the most benevolent mind, would never have won for Charlemagne the repose of his German frontier; but, in fact, the disposition of that monarch, by the habits of his nation—by the circumstances of his country—by the character of his age—by the education of his youth—by the constitution of his body—by the very qualities of his mind—was warlike. His benevolence showed itself continually in his government, in his laws, in his efforts to soften and to civilize, in his treatment of enemies, in his affection for his friends, in his placability after personal offence, and in his active intercession for the unhappy and the unfortunate. In all these points, the beneficence of his heart rose above the rudeness of his age, trampled on its prejudices, and cast away its passions, but still by nature he was a warrior, and he could not have remained a king unless he had been a conqueror.

The nations around never suffered him to withdraw his hand from the sword; and, as fast as by victory he had crushed one of the hydra heads of war, another was raised to attack him at a different point. Scarcely had he entered Italy, to the succor of Pope Adrian, ere, as already mentioned, the

Saxons, whom he had so lately subdued, were again in arms; and, secure in the absence of their conqueror, and the difficult warfare before him, were ravaging at their leisure the transrhenane provinces of France, and burning all that they could not carry away. No sooner, however, had Pavia surrendered, and Italy received his law, than Charlemagne hastened to the scene of danger. Pausing, himself, at Ingelheim; on finding that the enemy had disappeared, he dispatched four armies into the heart of Saxony, to punish the aggression of the people, while he made preparations to attempt their complete subjugation in the ensuing year.

For fifteen months his kingdom had been without his presence, and a great accumulation of internal business had, of course, taken place during his absence. The immense activity of the young monarch, however, left nothing long unconcluded, although all the affairs of his extensive dominions, which were in any degree important, were transacted by himself alone.

To conceive the possibility of such an undertaking, the habits of that great monarch must be considered, and also the extraordinary constitution both of his body and his mind. Gifted with a frame, the corporeal energies of which required little or no relaxation, and which, consequently, never clogged and hampered his intellect by fatigue, Charlemagne could devote an immense portion of his time to business, and, without taking more than a very small portion of sleep, could dedicate the clear thoughts of an untired mind to the regulation of his kingdom, even while other men were buried in repose. He was accustomed, we are told, to wake spontaneously, and rise from his bed four or five times in the course of each night; and so great was his economy of moments, that the brief space he employed in putting on the simple garments with which he was usually clothed, was also occupied in hearing the reports of his Count of the Palace, or the pleadings of various causes, which he decided at those times with as much clear wisdom as if listening to them on the judgment seat.

Some lighter exercise of the mind was nevertheless necessary even to him; but this was principally taken during his repasts, when he caused various works to be read to him, which did not require the severe attention that he was obliged to bestow on judicial investigations. The subject of these readings was, in general, the history of past times, and works upon theology, amongst which the writings of St Augustin are said to have afforded him the greatest pleasure.

By the constant employment of moments which would otherwise have been wasted to the intellect, an extraordinary mass of business was easily swept away; and, at the end of the very year in which he returned from Italy, a number of acts, diplomas, charters, letters, judgments, and affairs of all kinds, can be traced to Charlemagne himself, the dispatch of which, together with all those that must have escaped research, would be utterly inconceivable, were we ignorant of what were the habits of that great and singular man.

While Charlemagne was thus employed in France, the armies sent against the Saxons penetrated into their territory in four different directions. Three of these hosts met with considerable opposition; but, after contending for some time successfully with the enemy, they returned, to pass the winter in their own country, loaded with spoil and crowned with victory. The fourth army found the land abandoned by the Saxon troops; but a great part of the wealth of the nation had been left behind, and the Frankish soldiers amply, repaid themselves for the ravages which had been committed on their own frontiers, during their absence in Italy.

The Saxons, however, were still unsubdued; and a fortress which

Charlemagne had repaired at Eresburg, had been attacked, the garrison defeated, and the walls razed to the ground. The frontiers of Hesse, which had suffered the most from the Saxon inroads during the preceding year, were still open to the enemy; and everything in the state of Germany, called for immediate attention and exertion on the part of the French king. As soon, therefore, as the general assembly of the people could be held, he collected his forces, and entering Saxony at the head of a considerable army, he captured the castle of Sigisburg, restored the fortress of Eresburg, and, marching on to the Weser, forced the passage of that river, which a multitude of the enemy attempted for a time to defend. He thence pursued the Ostphalians, or Eastern Saxons, to whom he was for the time opposed, across the country towards the Oder, on the banks of which river he arrived without impediment.

The extraordinary rapidity of his movements seems to have daunted and surprised the Saxons, even more than his power or skill; and, on his sudden appearance at the Oder, Hasson, chief of the Ostphalians, with the other leaders of his tribe, met him, in order to tender hostages for their submission. The clemency of the conqueror was not yet exhausted. The hostages were once more received; and, turning towards the sea, Charlemagne, in like manner, accepted the promises of the Angrarians, another tribe, which had likewise been in arms against him.

Notwithstanding the bold and daring character of all his military movements, the Frankish monarch had not thus left behind him an immense tract of hostile country, without taking measures to keep open the communication with his own resources; for while he advanced into the very heart of Saxony, he stationed a considerable body of Francs upon the banks of the Weser, to guard the passages of that river, and to secure the means of retreat.

None of the dangers which surrounded him, however, escaped the Saxons; and that part of the nation who, inhabiting the western side of the Weser, were called Westphalians, soon perceived all the advantages which their position in the rear of the monarch's army afforded them. It was evident, that, in the midst of an inimical country, covered with woods, and intersected with rivers, a thousand perils and difficulties would attend his retreat, if the force left to maintain the communication with France were once cut off. To this purpose, then, the first efforts of the Saxons were directed; and, as the Francs on the Weser were in possession of an entrenched camp, stratagem was employed to render that advantage of no avail. In the absence of the monarch, the discipline of the troops who had remained behind was a good deal relaxed; and, with that national want of caution, which may be still traced in their descendants, the Francs of the reserve suffered a considerable body of the enemy to mingle with some of their foraging parties, which were returning towards nightfall. The Saxons thus penetrated into the heart of the camp; and, in the darkness, easily opened a way for the entrance of their companions.

The Francs, suddenly attacked in their sleep, before they were aware of the proximity of an enemy found myriads of hostile swords at their throats; and before they could recover from their first surprise, a great number were sacrificed to their own imprudence. But discipline in that day was of less consequence than in the present times; and in a hand-to-hand fight, such as then raged in the encampment of the Francs, the individual exertions of each man were of almost as much consequence as the union of the whole. Gradually, the Francs forgot their first panic, roused themselves, rallied, resisted, overcame; and before morning, the Saxons were defeated, and in full flight.

Nevertheless, flight did not bring them security; for Charlemagne himself, who never yielded one unnecessary instant to repose, was by this time returning towards his rear guard. Rumors of the attack upon his camp reached him on his march, and gave such speed to his movements, that he arrived on the spot as the Saxons were in the act of flying from the scene of their overthrow. A hundred thousand fresh swords were added to those which already smote the fugitives; and a fearful number of the enemy paid with their lives the penalty of their bold attempt. This defeat entirely dispersed the Westphalians for the time; the rest of the hostile tribes had already given hostages for their future tranquility; the whole land was bowed in apparent submission; and Charlemagne, leaving garrisons at Sigisburg and Eresburg, now led his victorious army back to their native country.

The repose of Germany was only temporary; but, in the meanwhile, the joy which the capture of Pavia and the fall of the Lombard kingdom had occasioned in Rome, began to be obscured by storms in Italy itself, and gathering clouds in other quarters of the political horizon. Scarcely had Adrian, after Charlemagne's return to France, written to his great protector, a letter full of blessings and thanks, than he had cause once more to solicit his presence in Italy, and to address him as a suppliant, rather than congratulate him as a friend. The first disquietude which the Pope was destined to suffer, proceeded from that contest which I have already noticed, with Leo, archbishop of Ravenna, who persisted in detaining the whole of the Pentapolis, and various cities of Aemilia. These he declared he had received as a donation from the monarch of the Francs; and a long and tedious dispute ensued, which could never have taken place, had a written deed existed to authenticate the right of the Holy See. But more serious and general dangers soon began to menace Italy; and two after epistles of Adrian are found full of matter affecting the immediate interest of

Charlemagne.

The state, in which Lombardy had been left, must here be considered, at the risk of repeating some facts which have been before mentioned. On the fall of that kingdom, Charlemagne, instead of pursuing the course of policy common both in the days which preceded, and those which followed his reign, by dividing great part of the territory he had just acquired, amongst such of his followers as he desired to reward or promote, left the Lombard nobles in full possession of their land, and merely claimed their homage as their new sovereign. This was instantly yielded, with every sign of joy and willingness; for to escape with life, liberty, and fortune, was an event which seldom, at that period, befell a conquered people.

At first, the Lombard lord, feeling no compassion for their former King, who, for his own ambition and revenue, had exposed them all to spoliation and abasement, gladly saw the scepter transferred to a clement and generous prince, and joyfully welcomed the unexpected termination of the war. But conquest had loosened, if not broken, the bonds of society. Charlemagne left them to their own counsels. The steel-clad myriads of the Francs, which had spread terror and dismay amongst them, were withdrawn; fear was forgotten; a distant monarch was despised; ambition sprung up in the heart of every one; and each of the Lombard nobles entertained some project of breaking his vows of homage, and making himself independent.

It was some time before unity of purpose rendered general disaffection formidable. The first attempt was conceived with no extended views, and was the simple effort of a turbulent vassal to free himself from his engagements, and establish a separate state. This took place in the case of Hildebrand, Duke of Spoleto, the homage of whose duchy had been resigned by the King in favor of the Holy See. Possibly, encouraged by the resistance of the Archbishop of Ravenna, that noble learned to despise the rule of the Roman prelate, and hoped to emancipate himself from the oaths which bound him to Charlemagne, now that the monarch had transferred his allegiance to a weaker power. He seems, at first, to have laid no more comprehensive plan, than that of resisting an authority whose temporal force was small, and whose spiritual thunders were then feeble and almost untried.

Greater schemes, however, soon followed. Rodgaud, Duke of Friuli, one of those in whom Charlemagne had placed the greatest confidence, and to whom he had entrusted the greatest power, began to conclude that he also might free himself from the authority of him to whom he had pledged his faith. Although his duchy was powerful and important, including a considerable portion of the Tyrol, and stretching far round the Venetian Gulf, he very well knew that a force which had crushed the Lombard kingdom, while entire, could not be successfully opposed by any detached part. But yet he hoped, that—by leaguing together once more, all the disjointed members of the state, and by giving to all, the energy of a common cause, and of individual danger—he might be able to recover the independence of those territories which had been lost by the general apathy, under the reign of Desiderius. Gradually, these views extended and changed. He found that his personal influence was not sufficient to form that bond of union which he desired; he doubted that the activity of his confederates would be equal to his own; and he naturally turned his eyes elsewhere to seek for farther support and assistance. At length, trusting to chance and his own skill to reap the greatest benefit from the enterprise, the Lombard chief conceived the design of calling back Adalgisus from his exile at Constantinople; and proposed to him the total subjugation of Italy, by the aid of the Eastern empire.

Such negotiations passed rapidly between Lombardy and the Grecian capital. Adalgisus, who had been received with favor, and invested with patrician honors, by the Emperor, welcomed with gladness the hope of recovering the territory of his father; and the Emperor Leo, who had succeeded Constantine Copronymus, joyfully perceived a chance of reuniting under his stray the long divided empire of Rome.

But Leo was neither by mind nor by body fitted for great undertakings. Had his father Constantine been still alive, it is probable that the enterprise would have been accomplished, or at least commenced, before the monarch of the Francs was aware of the conspiracy. The preparations of Leo, on the contrary, were weak and dilatory. The sloth with which he proceeded, gave full time for rumor to use her wings. Pope Adrian, watchful on all occasions, obtained information of the impending danger, and instantly dispatched messengers to France, beseeching aid for himself, and pointing out the perilous situation of the Frankish monarch's new dominions.

The envoys of the pontiff reached France while Charlemagne was still absent, pursuing his successful expedition against the Saxons; and the news of the conspiracy of Rodgaud, and the danger which menaced his Italian territories, met him as he returned towards his own country. Perils, with him, were always encountered as soon as known; and, without loss of time, he crossed the Rhine with a select body of troops, and advanced rapidly towards Italy, hoping to effect his passage before the snows had blocked up the roads. The year, however, had too far proceeded in its course towards winter, for the monarch to make much progress; and he was forced to pause at Shlestadt, in Alsace. This delay was nevertheless productive of no evil consequences. The torpid slowness natural to the Emperor Leo far more than outdid the necessary halt of the King of France; and, at a moment when activity was the great requisite to success, days, weeks, and months were wasted in idleness by the court of Constantinople.

Not so with Charlemagne: the first melting of the snows saw him once more across the mountains, and in full career against his enemies. Pavia had been secured by the troops he had formerly left there; and, traversing the country with immense speed, he left behind him Treviso, though strongly garrisoned for the revolted chiefs, advanced upon Friuli, and attacked the faithless Lombards before they knew that he had passed the Alps. Immediate destruction overtook the conspirators, and the death of Rodgaud, their leader, followed. Whether he was taken in arms, and executed afterwards, or was slain in battle, is by no means clear; but whichever way it occurred, his fate was undeserving of pity. He had broken the oaths which he had voluntarily plighted, and he had abused the confidence of a generous monarch. The clemency of a conqueror—a virtue then rare—he had repaid with ingratitude; and the power and property which had been left him, he had used as weapons against him who had spared them. He had risked all for ambition, was conquered, and died.

In leaving behind him so large a city as Treviso, strongly fortified and garrisoned, while he struck the decisive blow at the chief of his adversaries, Charlemagne seems to have followed a system of warfare, which has appeared new and bold when executed by an extraordinary general even in our own day. But the moment he had disconcerted the plans of Rodgaud, the monarch turned from Friuli, and, with the brilliant celerity which characterized all his exploits, marched directly upon Treviso, where Stabilinus, the uncle of the fallen duke, had shut himself up, resolved to hold out the city to the last. The strength of the place and the desperation of its defenders promised to render the siege as long as that of Pavia; but an Italian priest, of the name of Peter, who happened to be in the fortress, agreed to betray the gates of the Lombards to the Francs, and before Easter, Treviso also was taken. No severity followed; and although the priest who had delivered up the town was rewarded in a manner which the magnitude of the service he had rendered, more than his own honesty, deserved, no reason exists for believing that Charlemagne punished the revolt of Stabilinus in proportion to the value which he set upon the conquest.

The submission of all the other Lombard nobles was prompt and complete; but the monarch who had once so confidently trusted, and had been so speedily betrayed, now took more rigid precautions. The cities which he had found absolutely in revolt he consigned to Frankish governors, and provided with Frankish troops; those vassals who share in the conspiracy was not ascertained by any open act of rebellion, he wisely left unpunished, permitting them either to attribute their escape to his ignorance of their crime, or to the clemency of his nature. The garrisons throughout Lombardy were strengthened and increased; and, before the spring could be said to have fully commenced, the whole country was reduced to obedience, restored to tranquility, and secured by every provision for its government and defence.

The rapidity with which he had executed all these great acts, was not more than necessary to the monarch of the Francs; for during the very same year he was called upon for a display of his extraordinary powers of activity, both in resolution and performance, such as Europe has seldom beheld. But small space of time was allowed him for securing his Italian dominions against fresh commotions. At Treviso, the news reached him that the Saxons were again in arms upon his northern frontier; and before he could pass the Alps, which he accomplished with inconceivable rapidity, he found that the fortress of Eresburg had been once more attacked and taken, and that the castle of Sigisburg was besieged.

Not a moment was lost by the sovereign of the Francs; but, traversing his own country with the speed of lightning, he added what reinforcements he could gather to his Italian army, and, to use the words of the annalist of Metz, entered the territory of his pertinacious enemies like a mighty tempest. The garrison of Sigisburg had already repulsed the Saxon force which had attacked it; and the presence of Charlemagne himself, who, before the Saxons were fully aware that he had quitted Italy, was sweeping the whole country, from the Rhine to the Lippe, with the rapidity of the wind, spread terror and consternation through the land.

Once more subdued, the Saxons met him in great numbers, on the banks of the Lippe, supplicating peace and pardon; and again offering hostages, they declared their resolution of embracing the Christian faith. Charlemagne, with unwearied clemency, instantly acceded to their demand; but, determined to take greater measures of security, he added several fortresses to those he had before built, and employed his troops in again restoring the often demolished castle of Eresburg. While thus employed, the Saxons presented themselves in immense numbers, with their wives and children, for the purpose of receiving baptism; and the French monarch, imagining that the greatest step which had yet been taken towards their civilization, and the tranquility of his own dominions, was now gained, left them in peace, and returned to France.

Thus ended the warlike operations of a year of extraordinary activity, during the course of which, Charlemagne had carried on the strife in person, on the shores of the Gulf of Venice and on the banks of the Weser, had crossed the Alps and the Rhine, and had led an immense army more than three thousand miles in different directions. Such exertions, wonderful in themselves, are the more remarkable, when the arms of the Francs at that time are taken into consideration, and when it is remembered, that heavy cavalry, and men loaded with iron, were thus marched over a vast extent of country, at a time when every obstacle impeded the free communication of different parts of the world.

The war dress of Charlemagne himself was wholly composed of steel, consisting of the casque, breast and back plates, together with greaves, gauntlets, and cuissards, formed likewise of iron plates. Nor were inferior warriors less cumbrously defended; for though the arms of the earlier Francs were light, in comparison with this heavy panoply, yet we find that, in the days of Charlemagne, each man in the army, whose means permitted it, was protected by a suit of armor similar to that of the monarch.

Such rapid and continued movements as those in which the Frankish king had been occupied in the field, and the many dangers to be averted, and difficulties to be overcome, which had constantly besieged his mind, might be supposed to employ his whole thoughts, and leave him no time for the more pacific affairs of government. But, during all these wars, though, of course, the absence of the sovereign necessarily left some opportunities of abuse in the administration of justice, and in the civil polity of his realm, the arrears of business were much less than might be imagined.

The general government of the state remained, as I have before observed, in the hands of the monarch, who, without any minister to divide the fatigues, or support the responsibility, devoted every spare moment to its affairs, and soon learned to carry it on in whatever part of the world he happened to be. But the local administration was distributed amongst provincial officers, having the title of Duke, to the care of each of whom twelve counties were entrusted. The Counts placed under these officers, were, in fact, the judges of the land, and had power to summon to their court, anyone within the territory subject to their jurisdiction. Neglect or refusal to obey this summons, was visited with a severe penalty. At the same time, the Counts themselves were forced to render justice, by their station; and any denial or perversion of right, was punished by loss of land and rank. The distant menace of such punishment, however, would have been little effectual in procuring the constant and clear administration of the law, had not ambulatory magistrates been appointed to proceed through the kingdom, to render judgment themselves in particular cases—to take cognizance of the conduct of the Dukes and Counts—and to see justice impartially executed. These officers were called *Missi Dominici*; and, though I do not find it anywhere expressly stated that their times of visitation were uncertain, and, consequently, their reception by the Counts unpremeditated, yet many reasons exist for believing such to have been the case.

Their interference proved, of course, a great safeguard to the people; but still, as the provision of forage for the troops, as well as the maintenance of bridges, highways, prisons, passage-boats, and, in short, all the internal regulations of the country, both civil and military, were in the first instance entrusted to the Counts and Dukes, peculation and exaction were undoubtedly practiced, notwithstanding the active vigilance of the monarch.

Although the general administration of law was thus provided for, many cases, especially affecting the great vassals of the crown, or affairs of high ecclesiastical property, were reserved for the decision of the King himself, or the Count of his palace. These causes Charlemagne appears never to have neglected on any account; and, in all his wars, the suitors might follow to his tent, and obtain an immediate decision. Thus, in the heart of Saxony, he judged the cause of the Bishop of Treves and the Abbot of Pruim; and in the course of that very year in which he accomplished the two expeditions into Lombardy and Saxony, he heard and determined an extraordinary number of general pleas.

Amongst other affairs brought under his immediate notice about this time, was that of the Pope and the Archbishop of Ravenna, whose dispute, it appears, was not easily concluded; as the prelate of the Exarchate undertook a journey to France for the sole purpose of justifying himself in the eyes of Charlemagne.

Whatever was the decision of the King, in regard to which we have no clear information, it would seem that the award was not very unfavorable to the archbishop, who, after his return to Italy, conducted himself with such overbearing insolence, as to give more offence to Adrian than ever. In consequence, the great amity which had hitherto existed between Charlemagne and the supreme pontiff was diminished for a short time, and the papal epistles breathe a tone of complaint and discontent, very different from the usual tenor of Adrian's communications with his great protector. Before long, however, either Charlemagne removed the cause of dissatisfaction, or the pontiff perceived the impolicy of alienating such powerful friendship, by fruitless importunity and impotent resentment. The acerbity of Adrian's style soon mellowed again into more genial expressions—his language became once more that of praise and benediction; and Italy remaining in peace and security, left the monarch of the Francs to oppose his whole force to the inveterate enemies who still hovered upon his north-eastern frontier, eager for revenge.

Time for collecting his energies, and opportunity to apply them undivided, was now, indeed, absolutely necessary to Charlemagne; for though, at the end of the last year, he had left the Saxons with a more reasonable prospect of peace than had ever terminated any of his former campaigns, that prospect was soon destined to be obscured.

The immense tract of country occupied by the Saxons, the warlike habits of the people, and their fierce and indomitable courage, while it made even their temporary subjection by the Francs extraordinary, in reality left little hope of their permanent tranquility. The apparent cause of their easy and continual overthrow by the armies of Charlemagne was their division into various tribes, and their want of that unity of purpose, which can only be obtained by the action of a general and continuous government. The War-King of today was no longer War-King tomorrow; his military projects ended with his command; and the nation had to adopt new schemes, and habituate itself to a new leader, while no fixed principles in the art of war served to counterbalance the constant change of commanders. Had one man of great and comprehensive genius appeared, who could have held in his hands for a length of time the united energies and resources of the people, he might at any period have found means to oppose to the monarch of the Francs, a more equal and steady resistance than had hitherto been attempted.

Such a man was now rising into light; and, though greatly inferior to Charlemagne in talent, in firmness, in civilization, and in magnanimity, his powers were sufficient to give an entirely new character to the Saxon war. He was a chief of the Westphalians; whether duke of the whole of those who took that name, or only of a tribe, is obscure and unimportant. His name, which has come down with honor in every history of Germany as that of one of the greatest patriots of that time, was Witikind; and to personal courage, warlike abilities, and great powers of exertion, he added, as is proved by his influence on the minds of his countrymen, the force of eloquence and the talent of command.

During the greater part of the wars which had preceded this epoch, we have seen that the campaigns on both sides had been little better than devastating incursions into the territories of the enemy, wherein the Saxons had ever committed the first aggression, and fled before they could be strongly opposed. On the other hand, the Francs ravaged in retaliation, and retired as soon as submission and promises of future peace had been wrung from the enemy. Previous to the accession of Charlemagne, means of retribution, but not of coercion, had been employed; but he, finding that no reliance was to be placed on empty vows, had acted on a different principle; and at the termination of each campaign, had taken new measures to repress the Saxons, by building fortresses beyond his own border, by which precaution, though as yet he pretended to no dominion over them, he learned the first movements which preceded an incursion upon his territory, and broke the force of the torrent at its source. In return for continual aggression and violated promises, he held out frequent menaces of total and permanent subjection, on the next breach of tranquility; and in his last expedition, after having brought his enemies to his feet, he had commenced the erection of a fortified town within their limits. Far from showing any indignation at this proceeding, the Saxons—who, with the common craft of barbarians, were always profuse to meanness in their acts of submission when conquered—had not only given hostages, but, as before mentioned, had demanded baptism, which they knew would be pleasing to the victor.

Not so, however, Witikind, who, unconscious of any right but liberty, while he robbed and destroyed the property of his neighbors, viewed with insurmountable wrath the least infringement of his own. The measures of defence which Charlemagne was in a manner compelled to take, he looked upon as an ambitious aggression upon the liberties of the Saxons; and no sooner had the winter of AD 777 placed a barrier between his nation and the monarch of the Francs, than he stimulated his countrymen once more to violate their lately renewed engagements.

Before any active efforts could be made, the precursory movements of the Saxons were communicated to Charlemagne, and, with his usual promptitude, he marched directly to the point of danger. The plans of Witikind being thus disconcerted by the rapid energy of the French king, that chief, finding himself without any force to oppose the immense army suddenly led against him, fled into Denmark to seek aid and support from Sigifrid, the Danish monarch then reigning.

In the meantime, the whole Saxon population thronged to Charlemagne, and, protesting their innocence of the plots of Witikind, as well as their perfect submission, demanded eagerly the maintenance of peace. Charlemagne, though probably not deceived by the declaration, once more agreed to withdraw his army, but, at the same time, only did so upon the express condition, that if the Saxons again violated their faith, they should lose both their country and their liberty. I use the words of Eginhard, and shall not attempt to investigate far whether this was a condition which a conqueror had a right to demand, or which was any way obligatory upon the conquered. It must, indeed, be considered more as a threat than a condition; and it appears to me that no measure was unjustifiable that might, in the failure of all other means, procure peace for France from a nation which, for two hundred years, had kept her frontier provinces in a state of constant strife and desolation.

By this time—although, in those days, the wings of Fame were slow and feeble—the renown of the monarch of the Francs had penetrated to all the quarters of the earth; and, even while repressing the turbulent Saxons in the north, the deputies of another nation, and of a different religion, came from the very opposite extreme of Europe to solicit succor and protection.

These were a body of Saracens from Spain and a few words must be said in explanation of the state of the country from which they were sent, as, on their representations, a new war and new conquests were undertaken and completed.

FROM THE BEGINNING OF THE SPANISH WAR, TO THE INCORPORATION OF SAXONY WITH THE FRENCH DOMINIONS.

FROM 777 TO 780.

A twofold traitor to his religion and his country had, about the year 710, courted the Arabs from Africa into Spain. Whether revenge or ambition was the motive, is a question of little import here; it is sufficient that Count Julian betrayed his country and his God. A divided people and a feeble king on the one hand, and a daring commander with a veteran host on the other, decided the fate of the Gothic throne, and, by the close of the year 714, Spain, with the exception of a few remote districts, was subdued by the Arabs, from the columns of Hercules to the chain of the Pyrenees. The government of the conquered country was entrusted to the lieutenants of the caliphs; and the spirit of war had then so strong an influence on the Arab race, that few of the Spanish governors contented themselves, without adding something to that which their predecessors had acquired.

The Pyrenees were thus soon passed; and, a short time before the close of the Merovingian dynasty in France, a considerable portion of the southern districts of that country was under the Saracen dominion. The celebrated Abdurrahman, seeking to extend his power still farther, fell before the arm of Charles Martel, and the Saracens, retiring from France, contented themselves with their territories in Spain.

For the space of fifty years, the Iberian Peninsula remained dependent upon the throne of the caliphs; but domestic dissensions soon began to diminish the vigor of the race of Mahomet. A powerful faction sprang up against the children of Omar, who had for so long possessed the great Oriental throne. Two bloody battles decided the fate of the caliphate; and a cruel system of extermination destroyed the major part of the unfortunate Omaides.

While the house of Abbas, however,—the greatest which ever swayed the scepter of the East,—established itself firmly in the heart of the Mahommedan world, one of the rival race of Omar escaped to Spain, where the party of his family was predominant, and about the same period at which the Merovingian dynasty ended in France, and Pepin assumed the throne of that country, Spain separated from the dominion of the caliphs, and placed herself under a monarch of her own. This state of independence, of course, was not established without a contest; but the officer sent against Abdurrahman, now caliph of Cordova, was defeated and slain, and the power of the new sovereign was confirmed by victory. The subjects, over whom he was called to reign, were divided between Jews, Christians, and Mahommedans of the two sects of Abbas and Omar. Clemency and protection were, in general, shown to the Christians, and favor and regard to the Jews; but, according to the common course of human feeling, the very suspicion of being one of the party of Abbassides—the heretical usurpers of the caliphate—was enough to call down every species of severity and intolerance.

Besides those Christians who had submitted to the Arab yoke, and lived contented under the dominion of their conquerors, a portion of the ancient Gothic race still remained unsubdued in the heart of the Asturias, strong in bold, free, and independent hearts, but weak in number and in means. Such were the inhabitants of Spain, when, in the heart of Saxony, the monarch of the Francs was visited by one of the Saracen Emirs of Aragon, praying for protection and redress, and offering to hold the whole of his territories from Charlemagne, rather than from the crown of Cordova.

In all revolutions, such as those which had lately taken place in Spain, the natural tendency of private ambition is to divide the state, rather than to consolidate it. Selfishness, joined with talent, has, in all political convulsions, the greatest room for exertion; and each man who possesses the power, the activity, and the courage to struggle, aims at individual independence, if not at general dominion. In many instances this took place in Spain; and we find a multitude of petty princes rendering themselves wholly or partially free from the domination of the monarchs of Cordova. Whether this desire was the motive of Ibn al Arabi, as the Saracen who visited Charlemagne is termed by the analysts, or whether he was one of the hated Abbassides, whom oppression had driven to revolt, does not appear.

His vengeance or his ambition, however, took larger views than that of his fellows, when it led him a thousand miles across a strange and Christian country, to seek support from the conquering monarch of the Francs. To that monarch he held out a prospect of easy victory, extended dominion, and vast advantage; and his petition met with immediate attention.

Charlemagne undertook to invade Spain; and it must be here remarked, that this was the first war in which that great warrior ever engaged, with the sole view to conquest. The war of Aquitaine had been the act of a sovereign to correct and repress a revolted vassal,—that of Saxony, to defend his frontier, and punish the aggressors on his land,—the invasion of Italy, to fulfill the duties of an office he had long before accepted, and to deliver and protect a devoted friend. But the Saracens had committed no new infringement of the French territory,—no old and dear ally was to be defended by his expedition,—and, making every allowance on the score of Christian zeal, and the desire of protecting the oppressed Goths of Spain, this remains still the most unjustifiable war in which Charlemagne was ever engaged. But the desire for conquest and aggrandizement, like every other passion of human nature—and even more than any other—increases by habit and indulgence. Charlemagne had been educated to war, and pampered by victory; yet, through his life, his moderation is much more conspicuous than his excess.

In order that no long march might fatigue his troops and delay his progress, Charlemagne passed the winter in Aquitaine, collecting all his forces on the frontier he meant to violate. In the spring, as soon as the defiles of the Pyrenees were passable, he led one large division of his army through the mountains into Spain, and advanced rapidly upon Saragossa. At the same time, a considerable force, raised in Burgundy, Austrasia, and even Lombardy, passed the mountains of Roussillon, and made themselves masters of Catalonia. Their progress and success were rapid and extraordinary; and, after taking possession of Barcelona, Huesca, Gerona, and other neighboring towns, they advanced across the country, and joined their monarch at Saragossa.

Though the whole of that part of the country is highly defensible— though the Arabs of that day possessed more military skill and warlike energy than perhaps any European nation—and though the cities of Aragon and Catalonia were both strongly garrisoned and fortified, yet little or no resistance was offered by any place except Pampeluna. From these circumstances, and from a number of active military operations, which were almost immediately after undertaken by the Goths of the Asturias, it is more than probable that the Mahommedan monarch, embarrassed with doubtful friends and internal enemies, wore unprepared with any sufficient means to oppose the formidable army of the invaders. Whether the resistance of Pampeluna itself was at all vigorous, is not distinctly stated in any contemporary account; but it may be inferred that the struggle was severe, from the marks of triumph and precaution which followed its fall. A medal was struck, to commemorate the capture of the city; and the walls Mere razed to the ground, to guard against the consequences of future revolt.

The rest of Navarre and Aragon was soon reduced to submission. Ibn al Arabi and his companions were restored to their dominions, whatever those dominions were, and, giving hostages and tribute, rendered themselves in some degree vassals of the crown of France. The pledges, either offered by Abu Taurus, one of the Saracen Emirs, or exacted from him, were his brother and his son; and it is but reasonable to suppose, that the degree of protection granted, was in proportion to such a high price as the exile of two near and dear relations.

Garrisons were now placed in particular cities, to secure the country which had been won; every measure of precaution and defence was adopted; and what has been called "the Spanish March", comprising a broad band of country, extending along the southern foot of the Pyrenees, was added to the dominion of Charlemagne.

It is not easy to say, whether the acquisition and preservation of this territory by the Frankish monarch was designed from the first by cautious policy, or merely originated in the spirit of conquest. In a political point of view, however, it was infinitely well judged. The passages of the Pyrenees, which had ever been a refuge for the turbulent and treacherous Gascons, were thus secured. A barrier was placed between them and their old allies, the Saracens of Spain. The keys of the southern frontier of France, which had been heretofore in the hands of the Arabs, were thenceforth entrusted to Charlemagne's own subjects; and while the complete and final reduction of the whole of Aquitaine to law and submission, was ultimately ensured, his Pyrenean provinces, from the Gulf of Lyons to the Bay of Biscay, were secured from invasion.

Although the conquest of the Spanish March had been easy and nearly unopposed, Charlemagne was not suffered ultimately to fix his power in so important a district without a struggle. The time he was forced to employ in perfecting the various arrangements for incorporating the acquired territory with the rest of France, and in providing for its government, both civil and ecclesiastical, gave room for preparation on the part of the Saracens. A large army was collected, and poured down into Aragon. The Francs were attacked near Saragossa, but after a battle of several hours, in which many thousands of the Mahommedans were slain, victory declared in favor of the French monarch; and his new dominions in Spain were secured. After this success, Charlemagne proceeded calmly to complete that regular organization in the state of the province, which he always endeavored to introduce into every country he conquered. But before long, the news from his northern frontier became of such a nature as to call him back from the scene before him, with all the rapidity which never failed to attend his movements on every occasion of importance.

Dangers of the most pressing kind were represented as threatening the provinces on the Rhine; and the monarch's march was immediately directed towards the Pyrenees. Dividing his forces into two bodies, he advanced in person, at the head of the first division, and, for the sake of greater speed in his own progress, left all the baggage with the rear guard, which was strong in men, and commanded by some of the most renowned chieftains of his army. The names of Eggiard and Anselm have come down to us, together with that of Rolando, or Orlando, the nephew of Charlemagne, as the commanders of the second division, which had to suffer much from unforeseen hostility.

It must be remembered that Lupo Duke of Gascony, on delivering up his rebellious uncle Hunald, had been suffered to retain his duchy, which, from its position among the Pyrenean mountains, fully as much as its tenure, was but slightly dependent upon the crown of France. Lupo was ambitious as well as treacherous, and was filled with the same turbulent and rebellious spirit which had animated his ancestors. The sovereignty of the French monarch was alone tolerable so long as it was distant and unexercised; and tranquility was only to be expected while powerful armies enforced obedience, or suspended authority left the shadow of independence. To a man of such a character the acquisition of a large territory on the southern side of the mountains by Charlemagne was anything but agreeable. He saw himself surrounded on all sides by the dominions of a monarch against whom he eagerly sought an opportunity of revolt; and, with the mad miscalculation of his own powers which had ruined every other member of his family, he prepared to offer an outrage to his sovereign which could only be productive of temporary advantage to himself, and could never be forgiven by the king. It is probable that he had only suffered Charlemagne to enter Spain without molestation because he had no power of opposing him. But when he found that the ravages of the Saxons called the monarch imperatively to the north, and that the rear-guard of his army, loaded with baggage and treasure, was separated from the rest of the troops, he resolved upon an undertaking for which punishment seemed remote, and in which success was probable, and rapine sure.

The Pyrenees, extending in a continuous line from the Bay of Biscay to the borders of the Mediterranean, rise in a long straight ridge, the superior points of which are but a few yards lower than the summit of Mont Blanc. In the highest part of the chain there are occasional apertures; and from the main body of the mountains long masses of inferior hills are projected into the plain country on either side, decreasing in height as they proceed, till they become imperceptibly blended with the level ground around. Between these steep natural buttresses, narrow valleys, sometimes spreading out into grand basins, sometimes straitened into defiles of a few yards in width, wind on towards the only passes from one country to another. The roads, skirting along the bases of the hills—which, to the present day, are frequently involved in immense and trackless woods—have always beneath them a mountain torrent, above which they are raised, as on a terrace, upon the top of high and rugged precipices. A thousand difficulties beset the way on every side, and nature has surrounded the path with every means of ambush and concealment.

Mounted on heavy horses, and loaded with a complete armor of iron, the soldiers of Charlemagne returned from their victorious expedition into Spain, and entered the gorges of the Pyrenees, without ever dreaming that an enemy beset their footsteps.

The monarch himself, with the first division of his host, was suffered to pass unmolested; but when the second body of the Francs, following leisurely at a considerable distance, had entered the wild and narrow valley called the *Roscida Vallis* (now Roncesvalles), the woods and mountains around them suddenly bristled into life, and they were attacked on all sides by the perfidious Gascons, whose light arms, distant arrows, and knowledge of the country, gave them every advantage over their opponents.

In tumult and confusion, the Francs were driven down into the bottom of the pass, embarrassed both by their arms and baggage. The Gascons pressed them on every point, and slaughtered them like a herd of deer, singling them out with their arrows from above, and rolling down the rocks upon their heads. Never wanting in courage, the Francs fought to the last man, and died unconquered. Rolando and his companions, after a thousand deeds of valor, were slain with the rest; and the Gascons, satiated with carnage, and rich in plunder, dispersed amongst the mountains, leaving Charlemagne to seek for immediate vengeance in vain.

The battle must have been fierce and long, and the struggle great, though unequal; for, during the lapse of many centuries, tradition has hung about the spot, and the memory of Rolando and his companions is consecrated in a thousand shapes throughout the country. Part of his armor has there given name to a flower; the stroke of his sword is shown upon the mountains; the tales and superstitions of the district are replete with his exploits and with his fame; and even had not Ariosto, on the slight basis which history affords, raised up the splendid structure of an immortal poem, and dedicated it to the name of Rolando, that name would still have been repeated through all the valleys of the Pyrenees, and ornamented with all the fictions of a thousand years.

The news of this disaster soon reached Charlemagne, and he immediately paused on his march, to seek vengeance for the death of his followers. But the Gascons had dispersed amidst the impenetrable fastnesses of their mountains; no present enemy was to be found; the Saxons were ravaging the territories of France; and the monarch, with the joy of all his Spanish triumphs clouded, was obliged to continue his journey towards the north. Other circumstances, however, clearly establish that the perfidious Duke of the Gascons was afterwards taken, and forfeited his life as a punishment for his treason, although it is difficult, if not impossible, to ascertain at what precise period this retribution was accomplished.

It was some consolation to the French monarch to find, that the evil consequences which this signal defeat of a part of his army might have produced, did not follow. Notwithstanding the death of so great a number of their conquerors, the Saracen inhabitants of Navarre and Catalonia did not attempt to throw off the yoke which had been imposed upon them. The Spanish March remained for the time in tranquility, and Charlemagne pursued his journey towards the north.

The events which called him from the scene of his late conquests were such as admitted no unnecessary delay. His absence during the winter in Aquitaine, and his march into Spain, had removed from the Saxons, the terror of his immediate neighborhood, and had given both time for preparation, and opportunity of revolt. Such an occasion was not lost by a nation whose habit was to wander, whose delight was war, and whose occupation was pillage. Witikind returned from Denmark almost immediately after Charlemagne's departure; and soon, by his eloquence, roused the whole mass of his countrymen to throw off the indifference with which they had beheld the precautions taken by the monarch against their future irruptions. The visit of the Saxon chief to the savage courts of the north, had not tended at all to civilize his mind, or to open his eyes to the general principles of equity. Still forgetting the aggressions his own nation had committed, to him the forts built by the French king appeared as fetters on the Saxon people. The act of repelling or chastising their irruptions, he viewed as ambitious encroachment, or triumphant insult; and, animated himself by a wild spirit of liberty and a desire of vengeance, he found his purpose seconded amongst his countrymen by the predatory habits of ages, and the warlike character of barbarism.

In a short time the whole of the Westphalians were in arms; and, while Charlemagne was still in Spain, they were ravaging all the German provinces of France, even to the very banks of the Rhine. Often as they had invaded the Frankish territory, and little as they were accustomed to show mercy, their present irruption left all their former ones far behind in cruelty and depredation. Nothing was spared,—neither age, nor sex, nor condition. The child was murdered at the breast, the priest at the altar, the peasant by his hearth. Fire and death accompanied them on their way, and ruin and desolation spread out behind their footsteps. Finding that they could not pass the Rhine in safety, they ravaged the whole territory from Cologne to Coblenz. The monks fled from their monasteries, the citizens quitted the towns; nothing resisted their approach, nothing survived their passage; and all was confusion and destruction, rapine, massacre, and flame.

Such were the tidings that every day met the ear of Charlemagne, as he advanced from the south of France towards the north; and, finding that he could not lead forward his heavier forces with all the celerity that the occasion instantly demanded, he dispatched his lighter troops from Auxerre, with orders to make all speed, and, if possible, to overtake the Saxons on the territory of France, that their aggression might be punished where it had been committed. The troops chosen for this purpose, were all either of the eastern tribes of Francs or of the German tributaries, whose lands and dwelling-places were the first on every occasion to fall a prey to the Saxon invasions. Every personal inducement to speed, therefore, was added to the injunction of the monarch; but ere their arrival, the enemy, sated with blood and gorged with plunder, were once more returning to their native country.

Thus the Frankish army, notwithstanding the rapidity with which it always moved, did not succeed in coming up with the retreating Saxons, till they had traversed the greater part of Hesse; but at the moment the plunderers were crossing the river Adern, they found themselves assailed by the forces of Charlemagne. The very act of pursuing gave impetus to the Francs; while national hatred, and individual revenge, added the energy of passion to the vigor of constitutional courage. At the same time, the Saxons were already retreating, an act which too often degenerates into flight. They had accomplished their object; were loaded with spoil; the sloth of satiety hung upon their actions; their own country was before their steps, and escape was too near for resistance to be vigorous.

Thus, while they were embarrassed with the passage of the river, the Frankish cohorts poured in upon them. A feeble resistance but added to the slaughter; and very few survived to carry to their own country the tidings of their successful irruption, their retreat, and their defeat.

To fight and conquer in two far separated countries, within the space of a few months, was common to the Francs under the command of

Charlemagne; but a long campaign in Spain, and a march of nearly twelve hundred miles, had so far exhausted the year, that no farther movement could be made against the Saxons till the return of spring.

The other events which may be traced to this year, now call our attention to the civil government of Charlemagne,—an object, when considered in reference to the age in which he lived, far more interesting and extraordinary than all his great military operations. During the active scenes in which he had been lately engaged—the continual movement and incessant occupation in which he had existed—no part of his vast territories was neglected; and his eyes were alternately turned with careful attention to Italy, to Germany, and to France.

Ascending the throne in a barbarous period, when internal policy was perfectly in its infancy, and the whole mechanism of society rude and irregular, Charlemagne could not be expected to change, by the simple power of his own mind, the constitution of his whole race, rekindle in an instant the extinguished light of past ages, or hurry into maturity the whole fruits of coming years. The performance of such a task was not within the grasp of human faculties; but what he did do, when joined with the circumstances in which he was placed—surrounded on every side by darkness, superstition, and prejudices, and having to vanquish them all— shows him as great a conqueror in the moral as in the physical world; and raises him to the highest pitch of human grandeur, by evincing that he not only overcame the barbarians of his time, but also overcame the barbarism itself.

Whatever were the warlike undertakings in which the monarch was engaged, and whatever were the immense demands upon his time and attention, no evil to his fellow creatures which was brought before him, ever passed without notice and correction,—no effort to purify and improve the state of society was forgotten. We find instances to justify this assertion in every part of his reign; but at the present period, a great occasion for exertion and remonstrance presented itself, and was not neglected, although that remonstrance was necessarily directed against an authority for which he strove to inculcate respect, and towards which he always set the example of due reverence.

While in the midst of his preparations for the war in Spain, information was by some means conveyed to him, that the odious traffic in slaves was permitted in Rome; and not a few complaints reached him, about the same time, concerning the irregularities of the Italian clergy. To both these points his attention was immediately directed, and a strong remonstrance was addressed by him to Pope Adrian, pressing the reformation of the abuses which were said for exist. Adrian immediately replied, and, in the most positive terms, assured Charlemagne that no such trade in slaves was carried on between the Romans and the Saracens, as had been asserted. The Lombards, he said, it was true, were in the custom of selling slaves by means of the Greeks who frequented their ports,—a custom which he had in vain attempted to prevent, The lives, also, of the priests under his own inspection he boldly defended, and declared that their accuser had calumniated them basely by the charge he had brought against them.

Whether this explanation proved satisfactory to the monarch or not, does not appear; but the terms of Charlemagne's letter sufficiently evince, that he still considered Rome as under his sovereign dominion; and the reply of Pope Adrian equally proves his submission to the jurisdiction of the Patrician. Various other matters of civil polity occupied the attention of the monarch of the Francs about this time and he had an opportunity of displaying his clemency and moderation in a manner which changed a doubtful vassal into a firm and attached friend. Not long after the return of Charlemagne from Spain, Hildebrand, Duke of Spoleto, who had been one of the first in the conspiracy of the Duke of Friuli, but who had remained at once unpunished and unpardoned, trusting to the character of the sovereign, visited his court in France, and, with magnificent presents, renewed the homage he had cast off. His rebellion, which had never proceeded to open warfare, was immediately forgotten in this voluntary act of confidence. His gifts were accepted, but returned by others in full proportion and, after being entertained with splendor at the court of the monarch, he was dismissed to his own land a grateful and faithful subject.

Before joining the forces, which were in active preparation, for renewing the war against the Saxons, Charlemagne also issued a new capitulary, containing a variety of important laws on various subjects, some regulating the proceedings of the church, some affecting the duties of the various judges, and some regarding the people in general. The absence of all classification is the great want observable in these laws, and is the strongest symptom of the barbarism of the age. Various efforts, however, to overcome that barbarism are likewise to be noticed. Though considerable power is still entrusted to the clergy, several rules are laid down, for the purpose of enforcing regularity in their lives. The privilege of screening offenders found worthy of death, which has been so often claimed by the church, is formally rejected by the voice of the monarch; while a law against the exportation of arms, shows how much Charlemagne was obliged to look upon his nation as a military people.

As soon as the season permitted, Charles was once more at the head of his army; and, entering Saxony, he passed by the spot where the idol Irminsul had once stood, but which was now covered by a growing town, and advancing towards the Lippe, prepared to take signal vengeance of his incorrigible enemies. At first the Saxons displayed a strong disposition to trust to the force of arms, rather than once more appeal to the clemency they had so often abused; and at a place called Bucholtz, the situation of which is now unknown, their army was drawn up, to oppose the farther progress of the French monarch. The sight of the multitude of their enemies, however, shook their courage as the battle was about to close, and while only a few had fallen on either side, the Saxons fled precipitately, leaving the path open to Charlemagne. This flight was but a prelude to submission; and, proceeding rapidly through the country, the French sovereign, according to his custom, abandoned his more hostile intentions on the prayers and promises of his enemies. More unconditional submission, however, was demanded of the Saxons after their last aggression, and Charlemagne began to treat them as a conquered people, after having in vain attempted to put a stop to their irruptions while they retained their independence. About this time, the general division of the whole country into bishoprics, abbacies, and presbyteries, took place. Such of the clergy of France as zeal or ambition prompted to accept the dangerous trust, were appointed to the new cures thus created; and Charlemagne only left the country to return the next year and complete the arrangements which he had begun for incorporating Saxony with the Frankish monarchy.

The greater part of the annals of that day were composed by monks and ministers of the church, who, of course, attempted to magnify the affection of the Frankish king towards the body of which they were members, with the purpose of holding out both an example and an incitement to others. Nevertheless, it is evident, that Charlemagne was inspired by a sincere love for the Christian religion, and an eager wish to spread its pacific doctrines amidst his barbarous and intractable neighbors. Nor was it, as has been often falsely said, by the sword that he sought to convert. With the sword he overcame his enemies, and punished the pertinacious assailants who had so often ravaged his dominions and slaughtered his subjects. But the very desire of sparing the sword, made him the more eager in the propagation of that religion, which he hoped would remove the causes that compelled its use; and the work of conversion he entrusted, not to soldiers, but to the ministers of the Gospel. If he did, indeed, mingle on any occasion the means of worldly policy with the purer methods of religious persuasion, it was in the shape of gifts, presents, and menaces,—inducements more within the comprehension of the barbarians whom he sought to civilize, than any that could be afforded by reason and argumentation.

Though personally successful to a great degree, and seeing his power and reputation increasing in every manner, Charlemagne was visited in his dominions by many of those calamities which, from time to time, in the course of nature, affect whole countries and nations. Tremendous earthquakes shook his Lombard kingdom, during the year of which I speak, cast down many of the finest buildings, and spread death and ruin through the land. A pestilence devastated the country and the cities and a severe scarcity added to the horrors of the time. Terror and dismay reigned through the whole of France; and prayers and alms were the resources of the king and the peasant, the warrior and the churchman, in order to turn away the Almighty wrath, and obtain mercy from on high.

Thus passed the winter of the year 779-80, and early in the spring he returned to Saxony, and completed the subjection of the country. He had warned the Saxons, in 777, that in case of any new outrage, he would exercise the full power which he possessed, and deprive them of their independence; and he was now proceeding in the execution of that threat. It is to be remarked, however, that the total subjugation of Saxony, as far as we can discover from the contemporary writers, was by no means (as has been since represented) a blow struck at once, in the pride of victory, and the spirit of aggrandizement, conceived long before, and pursued through a series of unrelenting wars. On the contrary, it was slow and gradual, as Charlemagne found himself compelled to take progressive measures against his savage neighbors,—measures suggested by the great principle of self-defense, and executed with calm and clement reluctance.

I may be permitted to collect into one view the facts connected with this warfare, as they are spread through the preceding pages, when it will be found, that had he been so inclined, a thousand opportunities of taking possession of Saxony presented themselves, which he never showed any inclination to use, farther than his own security rendered necessary. In his first campaign against the Saxons, though he destroyed the idols that he found on his march, he granted peace to the nation as soon as they demanded it, merely taking twelve hostages, and raising a fort at Eresburg, to guard against their future incursions. On their next irruption, he left another body of French troops at Sigisburg, and required a more comprehensive oath before he withdrew his forces. During this time he had never desisted from his endeavor to civilize the Saxons, by sending missionaries among them; and his desire of converting them to Christianity appeared so evident, as to become a means of fraud in the hands of the barbarians themselves. The next cause of warfare was the Saxon attack upon the garrisons he had placed in the two castles; and being once more conquered, the assailants again supplicated peace, and many, to obtain it, demanded to be baptized. Charlemagne added a third fortress to those he had before constructed, and once more retired from the country. Finding that he had scarcely passed the frontier when his enemies actively prepared to attack him again, the monarch of the Francs frustrated all their schemes, by marching into the heart of the land before their plans were mature. Witikind, the instigator of the war, fled; and the nation completely submitted, generally seeking baptism as the strongest proof of their pacific intentions. Charlemagne trusted them once more; but he gave them full warning, that if they again violated the treaties they had entered into with him, he would not only inflict the temporary chastisement of a hostile invasion, but would use the right of conquest, which he had hitherto disregarded, and deprive them of that independence which they so constantly abused to his detriment. No sooner had he entered Spain, than the treacherous people, who crouched to the earth at his presence, took instant advantage of his absence, to destroy his provinces and massacre his subjects. The indignant monarch returned, and, marching through Saxony as a victor, he now annexed that country to his former dominions as a conquered province.

The next year he advanced at once to the junction of the Elbe and the Oder; and, having spent some time in taking precautionary measures against any invasion by the neighboring nations of the north, he proceeded to enact a variety of laws for the regulation of the barbarous people he had subdued; which laws have been made the subject of extravagant praise for a few points of superior excellence, and of ridiculous censure for severity, susceptible of great extenuation, if not justification. The same want of classification is observable in their construction, which affects most of the capitularies of the age; and a tinge of barbarism spreads over them all; but I doubt much, whether barbarous laws are not necessary to a barbarous nation; and whether Charlemagne, believing such to be the case, did not, like the great Greek legislator, frame for the people he had conquered, not the best laws which the mind of man could devise, but the best which could be adapted to the circumstances of the country. Charlemagne had found by long and painful experience that the only principle which could restrain the Saxons was fear and, accordingly, the code which he addresses to them is that of terror. Death is awarded for a thousand crimes, but especially for offering human sacrifices, and for refusing, or abandoning, or insulting the Christian religion.

The Saxons during the last two or three campaigns had almost universally received baptism; but in many instances, they returned to the most hateful rites of idolatry, which was always the sure precursor of outrage and irruption. Both from political and religious motives, it had become the great object of the French monarch to force this the most obdurate race of pagans in Europe, to listen to the voice of Christian teachers, which nothing but the fear of death could induce them to do: and for that purpose he used the terror of extreme punishment, as a means of enforcing attention to the doctrines of peace. But, at the same time, there cannot be a doubt, that he had no intention the severity of the law should have effect; for it was enacted by the self-same code, that the unbaptized who received baptism, and the relapsed who returned and underwent a religious penance, escaped the infliction of the punishment. By this means he forced the Saxons to hear, at least, the doctrines of the Christian church, and to become accustomed to its forms,—the first great step, without which conversion could never be obtained. By this means, also, he at once put a stop to the human sacrifices which continually disgraced the land; and he offered to all the power of escaping punishment, and gaining security.

It is true, as a general principle, that laws should never he enacted unless they are intended to be enforced; but this was an individual instance, where the object was but temporary. If he could compel the Saxons to hear the truths, and habituate them to the influence, of the Christian faith, Charlemagne never for a moment doubted that their sincere conversion must follow. That conversion once obtained, and the laws were not cruel, for they were ineffectual. In the meantime, however, their operation would be great before the Saxons discovered that they were not rigidly enforced. At all events, it is evident that Charlemagne believed that his object would be gained by terror, long ere the rude pagans, for whom he legislated, perceived that punishment was remote. For this great purpose, he framed the laws to which I refer, and made use of the only influence which he knew to be strong with the Saxons,—the influence of fear; while, at the same time, the natural benevolence of his own heart induced him to guard severity by mercy j and to add a law, which, while it offered the means of escape from the harshness of the others, tended to the same object.

Such considerations shield the Saxon code from the bitter censures which have been directed against it by some writers; but, at the same time, the lavish praises which it has received from others are equally inapplicable; for, though it was intended in mercy, and directed with wisdom, it was arbitrary in character, and in principle unjust.

No sooner was the regulation of Saxony completed, than the monarch turned his eves in another direction, and prepared to avert a storm that was approaching from a different quarter. Though constitutionally fond of war, and now habituated to conquest, Charlemagne, in general, took every means to prevent the necessity of having recourse to arms. Sometimes, it is true, he suffered himself to be dazzled with the prospect of brilliant expeditions; and, as in the case of the invasion of Spain, the prayers of others for protection and assistance, by offering a fair excuse to his natural inclination, occasionally overcame the better spirit of generous moderation which taught him to refrain. But wherever the probable war was likely to be one in which, as a sovereign, he was to act against a rebellious vassal,—one, in short, of revolt and punishment,—Charlemagne, if the danger could be foreseen, ever endeavored to stop it in its progress, before folly had been hurried into crime, and while pardon was compatible with justice.

Such views now called him into Italy; and as soon as the state of Saxony appeared finally settled, he took his departure for his Lombard dominions.

FROM THE INCORPORATION OF SAXONY, TO THE HOMAGE OF THE DUKE OF BAVARIA.

FROM 780 TO 782.

Although the sceptre of Lombardy had been snatched from the hand of Desiderius, and though he himself remained in the ecclesiastical seclusion from which he was never destined to be withdrawn, many members of his family still existed at large, spread over various parts of Europe; and the desire of vengeance, naturally fostered by affection for a fallen relation, and humiliated pride, was only restrained by the terror of the conqueror's arms. Adalgisus, the son of the dethroned monarch, continued to reside at Constantinople; and though, at the time, no efficient aid was granted to him by the imperial court, yet a favorable opportunity only seemed wanting to a renewal of the attempt to recover possession of Italy.

One of the daughters of Desiderius had married Arichis, Duke of Beneventum, and viewed, with unabated and inextinguishable hatred, the dominion of the Francs, in a land which had once been the portion of her family. At the same time, the high qualities and warlike character of her husband, rendered revolt probable, and success not unhopeful.

A second daughter of the dethroned King of Lombardy shared the ducal seat of Tassilo of Bavaria, whom I have before had occasion to mention as a relation and vassal of Charlemagne, and upon whose proud spirit the weight of homage lay an uneasy load, which he endeavored to make light by neglect, while he only waited occasion to throw it off for ever.

The mission of Saint Sturmius, in the early part of the French monarch's reign, had effected a reconciliation between the King and his cousin, upon whose head the open violation of his vows to Pepin had brought down the more terrible anger of Charlemagne. After that period, the immense power and the continual activity of his liege lord, had withheld Tassilo from making an attempt, to which triumphant success could alone secure impunity. It would appear, however, that about the present time, instigated by the revengeful spirit of his wife, and by his own proud desire of independent sovereignty, he engaged with Arichis, Duke of Beneventum, and with Adalgisus, their brother-in-law, for the purpose of wresting Italy from the grasp of Charlemagne, and of establishing an armed union sufficient to resist the power of their mighty opponent.

These schemes were carried on in darkness and secrecy, for the conspirators well knew that the watchful eyes of Charlemagne could only be blinded by the most cautious prudence; but, at the same time, long, slow, and careful preparation was necessary, to afford the slightest prospect of success. With hostile purposes laboring at the heart, and great and powerful designs advancing towards consummation, it is very difficult so to guard every action, that some suspicious circumstances will not betray, to an attentive observer, the plans which occupy the breast. Neither Tassilo nor Arichis were capable of such perfect dissimulation, as entirely to cover their schemes from the view of the French monarch. The first continued to absent himself from the court of the sovereign; and the proceedings of the latter, which were more bold and open, were from time to time communicated to Charlemagne by the wakeful attention of Pope Adrian.

At the period of the pestilence referred to in the last book, the Frankish monarch, according to the spirit of the age, had, with sincere faith, vowed a pilgrimage to some of the holy shrines in Italy, the execution of which vow, now concealed the political object he proposed to obtain at the same time. This objet, and the effort which he made to conceal it, were of a very different character from the usual policy of courts. His presence in Italy had become absolutely necessary; but he sought not to march with armies to chastise rebels, while there was a possibility of reclaiming them by milder means; and he determined to use all his own influence, both as a sovereign and relation, and to employ all the growing power of the church of Rome, in order to recall Tassilo of Bavaria to his duty, before he suffered his full knowledge of the incipient rebellion to appear.

This purpose, as well as that of overawing the Duke of Beneventum by his presence, and of guarding the kingdom of Italy from the civil commotions by which it was threatened, acted, beyond doubt, as a strong inducement to lead Charlemagne towards Lombardy. But there were also other motives, which were equally powerful with a monarch, whose native feelings of piety were strong and sincere, and whose devotion, though tempered and elevated by a vast and vigorous understanding, found no course open but through the common superstitions of the day. To offer up his prayers at spots which the church had pronounced holy, and to see his children baptized by the living representative of the Apostle, were probably amongst the motives, rather than the pretences, of Charlemagne's journey into Italy. Nor did the desire of seeing the royal consecration—which, in his own case, had been practised, to give weight to his right of succession— repeated in the persons of his sons, Louis and Carloman, add slightly to the inducements.

Leaving Pepin, his natural son, and Charles, the heir of the French throne, at Worms, Charlemagne set off for Pavia, late in the year 780, accompanied by his Queen and the rest of his children. On his arrival in Italy, the monarch found that country in a state of turbulence and agitation, which offed little prospect of any permanent tranquility. The disorganization which had taken place after the fall of the Roman Empire still operated in its consequences. The instability of all institutions, which a countless succession of invasions and subjections had induced, was now followed by a frantic thirst for change, and an impatience of all regularity. The jarring elements of a mixed population, consisting of thousand different tribes and nations, assimilated ill together; and, in society, a chronological gradation of conquerors and vanquished gave a gradual increase of hatred from the Roman to the Frank. The nobles were each waiting in gloomy expectation for some new revolution, which might call them into activity, and give them independence. The people, suffering under all, were careless of whose yoke they bore. The inhabitants of the

Tyrol had resisted, and both blinded and cast out the bishop, whom the pope had sent to claim the feoffs which Charlemagne had granted to the see of Rome; Terracin, Naples, and Calabria were more or less attached to the Eastern empire; the Duke of Beneventum was secretly leagued with the enemies of the Franks, the Greeks infested the outskirts of the land; and the Saracens commanded the seas.

Such was the state of the country when Charlemagne arrived in Italy. The loss of their separate existence as a people was undoubtedly one cause of discontent amongst its mixed population; but the monarch of the Francs had already determined to divide Italy from his hereditary dominions, and to raise it into a distinct kingdom, as the portion of one of his sons. In this determination, it is probable that he was influenced nearly as much by the habits of his nation, and by the prejudices of education, as by the desire of soothing the pride of the Italians, in rendering their country once more a separate state.

When the territory they possessed had been much smaller, the kings of France had been invariably in the custom of allotting it, with capricious irregularity, amongst their children. This had been always practised at the death, and sometimes during the life of the monarch, though, in the latter case, we do not easily discern under what limitations the power so entrusted by the father was exercised by the son. Now that countries and kingdoms had been added, in the short space of twelve years, to the vast dominions he had received from his progenitor, the idea naturally presented itself to the mind of Charlemagne, of apportioning to his children different districts of that immense and increasing empire, which already required energies almost superhuman to rule and consolidate as a whole. The division that he proposed on the present occasion was destined to convey the sovereignty of Italy to his second son, Carloman, while Aquitaine became the portion of

Louis, at that time the youngest of his family; and the rest of the monarch's hereditary dominions were reserved to form a kingdom for the eldest of his legitimate children, Charles. Saxony, at the same time, remained unappropriated, and might be left to provide for those future claims which the sovereign's age, and the fecundity of his wife, rendered likely to arise.

All the children of Charlemagne were still in their youth, and, therefore, the motives of their consecration could only be, in the first place, the solemn ratification of his design, in order to guard against contention at a future period; and, in the next place, the desire of satisfying both the Italians and the people of Aquitaine by the certain prospect of regaining, in a great degree, their territorial independence.

While thus busily employed in endeavoring to render his dominion as easy as possible, even to the prejudices of the people who had fallen under his sway, Charlemagne took every means to guard against external enemies. One of his principal cares in Italy was to secure that kingdom from the attempts of the Greeks; and so formidable was the aspect which his power assumed, that the policy of the court of Constantinople began to change towards him. Various circumstances, however, had occurred in the East to alter entirely the views of the imperial government.

Leo IV, a monarch feeble in body and in mind, had befriended Adalgisus, the son of the dethroned Lombard, and had loaded him with promises, which he found easy to utter, but laborious to execute. Still, he had undoubtedly designed to serve him; and, at all events, the recent memory of dominion in Italy, did not suffer the Emperor to see the increasing power of Charlemagne in that country, without jealous, though impotent, hatred. Such feelings had influenced the policy of the empire during the whole reign of Leo, but his death, which occurred in September,

AD 780, immediately changed the aspect of the eastern world. By the choice, or with the consent, of his father Constantine, Leo had espoused a beautiful Athenian girl, of the name of Irene,—a name equally famous for talents and for crimes. Charms of person and art of manner, together with much original and much acquired talent, completely ruled a feeble and dying monarch; and Leo, at the gates of the tomb, left to his young and beautiful wife the sole care of his child, Constantine VI, and the government of that vast, but decayed empire, which was all that remained of the world of the Caesars.

Before ambition had time to nourish crime, or opposition could call it into energy, Irene displayed nothing but genius for empire, and powers fitted for command. There were, however, various weaknesses in her character, which sometimes strangely opposed, and sometimes as strangely blended with, her policy. Amongst these weaknesses was superstition; and this principle acted with others in rendering her views, both in regard to Italy and to France, very different from those either of her husband or of his predecessor. The Athenians, her countrymen, had always been amongst the most strenuous supporters of that worship of images, the proscription of which by Leo III and Constantine V had been the cause of the revolt of Italy from the dominion of the East. Irene herself was one of the most devoted adorers of the saintly statues; and, consequently, beheld in the conduct of the Popes who had anathematized their condemners, nothing but a generous indignation and a holy zeal. During the life of her husband, forced to conceal her full sentiments, she had contrived at least to moderate the iconoclastic spirit which Leo IV had derived from his ancestors; and immediately that the reins of government had fallen into her own hands, she showed the most evident intention of restoring the worship of images, and of retaliating their persecutions upon the heads of the iconoclasts. Thus the great cause of separation between the East and the West was removed; and, both powerful and politic, Irene no longer treated the people of Italy as rebellious subjects. She regarded the monarch of the Francs, also, in a very different light from her predecessors; and sought his friendship rather than his enmity, especially while her reign was continually threatened by the factions of her husband's brothers.

Italy, it must be remarked, was not so wholly separated yet from the empire of the East, as to preclude the possibility of a reunion. No new emperor of the West had been chosen: the monarch of the Francs was but Patrician of Rome, an office which had existed under the Emperors; and whether Irene contemplated or not the chance of winning back, by the restoration of image worship, and an alliance with Charlemagne, the territories which the iconoclasts had lost, and which Pepin had maintained in their independence, her conduct was that which alone could do away the violence and folly of an hundred years.

Such was the aspect which the East assumed, shortly after the journey of Charlemagne to Italy; and one of the first acts of Irene's administration, after the death of her husband, was to court the friendship of the French monarch. Early in the spring, Charlemagne quitted Pavia, where he had passed the winter; and proceeded to Rome, in order to confer with the pontiff, on the measures necessary for the purpose of recalling the Duke of Bavaria to his duty. Peace and persuasion were the counsel of the Pope; and peace and persuasion were equally the means desired by Charlemagne. It was, therefore, determined that legates from the Holy See should he sent, together with ambassadors from the monarch, representing mildly, yet forcibly, the folly of rebellion, and the necessity of tranquility and submission; and endeavoring to induce the Bavarian prince to renew, by some voluntary act, the homage which his conduct had rendered doubtful.

The persons trusted with this important mission executed it well. Tassilo found his designs discovered, but being unprepared for resistance, and assured of the clemency of the monarch, he yielded at once to the remonstrances of the envoys, and promised to present himself speedily at the court of his cousin; which promise he accomplished before the end of the year; and, on the same occasion, repeated his vows of homage, and gave hostages for his future conduct.

In the meanwhile Carloman, the second son of the French king, was rebaptized by the hands of Pope Adrian; and, in memory of the first great protector of the Holy See, his name was changed from Carloman to Pepin. He was then solemnly consecrated with his brother Louis, the last as King of Aquitaine, the first as King of Italy. Although Charlemagne, in thus creating his son King of Italy, evidently looked upon the whole Peninsula as submitted to his sway, yet the title of the kingdom of Lombardy was not totally abandoned by those whose interest led them to shrink from a recognition of this extended power. We find, indeed, that though in general the historians of Charlemagne henceforth speak alone of the kingdom of Italy, yet the Popes, in their letters to that monarch, address him as King of Lombardy; in which difference of style, perhaps, may be seen a part of that same system of gradual encroachment by which the pontiffs accumulated titles, to be supported by the manufacture of deeds. Charlemagne himself still maintained his sovereignty over the whole of Italy, with the exception of the small part which adhered to the Greeks. He transferred that sovereignty to his son, who ruled it also for many years; but the Popes, determined step by step to establish the independence of their dominion, still called the monarch King of Lombardy; and though in actions they yielded implicitly to his sway, in words, which were to descend to after times, they did not acknowledge him as monarch of the whole Italian peninsula. An after pontiff, it is true, invested him with the imperial title in gratitude for personal favors; but the sway of an emperor left the vassal a king, while the yoke of a king pressed the vassal into a very inferior grade so that the position of the Popes, as vassals of the Frankish monarch, was elevated rather than depressed by his advancement to empire.

The creation of a separate Italian kingdom by Charlemagne in favor of his second son placed, of course, a great barrier against the designs of Irene, if the empress did indeed contemplate the reunion of Italy to the crown of the East. But her plans in regard to an alliance with the King of the Franks could not now be changed on that account, for, previous to the partition of Charlemagne's dominions, her ambassadors were already on the way to demand Rotruda, the eldest daughter of that monarch, in marriage for her son Constantine VI.

Constantine and Mamulus, two officers of her household, were charged with a mission, which, as Rotrada had not yet arrived at a marriageable might produce beneficial effects at the time, and could bring about no consequences that might not be averted in the course or the years intervening between the treaty and the marriage if a change of circumstances should require a change of policy. The Greek ambassadors reached Rome early in the spring, and found Charlemagne in that city. The proposal of an union between his daughter and the young Emperor of the East, was then formally made to the French monarch, who willingly concluded an alliance which promised peace upon his eastern frontier during the time required for confirming his sway over his new dominions in the north.

Rotruda was in consequence solemnly pledged to the bed of Constantine; and after the interchange of those mutual oaths of amity, which, by their constant infraction, have rendered treaties contemptible, the eunuch Elisaus was left with the young bride, to instruct her in the language and the customs of her future court; and the ambassadors returned to Constantinople to bear the consent of Charlemagne to the Empress Irene.

The visit of the Frankish monarch to Italy had been successful in restoring tranquility to that part of his dominions. The discovery of the schemes of the conspirators, and the return of the Duke of Bavaria to his duty, had effectually disconcerted the plans of Arichis of Beneventum; while the death of the Emperor Leo, and the alliance between the court of Constantinople and the monarch of the Francs, crushed the hopes of Adalgisus, and tore another limb from the conspiracy which had been formed against the power of Charlemagne. At the same time that the treaties now existing with the Isaurian dynasty of the East removed a fertile source of irritation from Italy, the inhabitants of that country were gratified and tranquilized with the idea of becoming a separate kingdom, instead of being joined as a conquered province to a superior country; and a great number of the nobles, won by the confidence and clemency of Charlemagne, forgot the bitterness of subjugation, and attached themselves sincerely to their conqueror.

With these prospects, the monarch of the Francs prepared to return to his native country. On his homeward journey, an event of apparently less importance than those in which he had lately mingled, awaited him at Parma, which event, however, tended, more than any other, by its consequences, to the development of some of the brighter and nobler points of his character. This was the visit of a single private individual from a distant, and then unimportant island, whose previous history, and state at the time, must be considered, in order to comprehend how Charlemagne could derive great benefit, and his best schemes receive accomplishment, from his connection with an English priest.

STATE OF GREAT BRITAIN

In the decline of the Roman empire, the necessities of the state had demanded imperatively the concentration of all her small remains of power; and the legions which had gone forth to acquire or maintain sovereignty on the distant borders of her immense dominion, were one by one recalled, to defend the hearths of Rome itself. Amongst the provinces conquered and abandoned, was Britain; and whether, after Constantine had usurped the purple, and withdrawn his troops from the British shores to support his usurpation, the Britons themselves at once threw off the Roman yoke for ever—or whether Victorinus again ruled the country for the Emperor,—it is evident, that early in the fifth century, these islands were left to the government of the inhabitants themselves, a wild, unskillful race, who added to the rudeness of a barbarous, the vices of a conquered, people. A period of darkness and bloodshed succeeded; and a thousand savage kings employed the arms which the Romans had left them, in murdering each other.

Scarcely forty years after the departure of the Romans had elapsed, when the Saxon savages of the north, who had begun already to infest the shores of France, first landed in England. Too few to effect a conquest, the soldiers of Hengist and Horsa, who commanded the three vessels which brought them thither, readily engaged with their chiefs in the service of some of the British kings, and were employed in repelling the invasions of the Irish and the Picts. Fresh reinforcements were demanded and obtained from Saxony; and tired of being the defenders of the Britons, the Saxons soon found a pretext for becoming their enemies. Partly by alliance, and partly by aggression, Hengist established himself as an independent sovereign in Kent; and the Saxon dominion began to extend itself in England.

The successful expedition of a small body of their countrymen soon brought fresh swarms of Saxons to the British shore. Ella and Cerdic followed with more extensive armies than their predecessors; and, after deluging the land with blood, obtained possession of a great part of the country. A number of British kings struggled bravely against the invasion; and Arthur, a chief of sufficient importance and success to have his actions immortalized in fable and doubted by history, beyond all question greatly retarded the progress of the Saxons by his valor, though he facilitated it by his barbarous contentions with his own countrymen.

A multitude of obscure battles, uncertain in their event, and the long and severe struggle of a divided and decreasing nation, against a continual influx of invaders, ended in the establishment of eight distinct kingdoms, of which Mercia, extending in a broad band from the Humber to the Severn, was the last in date, but one of the first in importance. The Britons, confined to Wales and a part of Cornwall, retained their language and their customs; while the Saxons, acquiring the taste for territorial possession, abandoned their predatory excursions, and only exercised their barbarous cupidity, in aggrieving and pillaging each other.

This state of things continued for some years. The natural rudeness of the inhabitants of Britain augmenting by a constant existence of strife, till about the year 596, Pope Gregory the Great was instigated, by the sight of some English slaves at Rome, to conceive and attempt the conversion of the Pagan islanders. The celebrated Augustin was sent with a band of missionaries, to effect this noble purpose. The marriage of Ethelbert, King of Kent, to a Christian princess, of the Merovingian race, favored the object of the messengers of Christianity. They were received, were suffered to teach, obtained converts; and the first principles of civilization were given to the barbarous conquerors of England.

At the same time that Christianity was introduced into Britain, a slight tincture of literature was also afforded; and the first Saxon compositions on record, are attributed to the period of the conversion of Kent. The kingdom of Northumbria was brought over to the faith with more difficulty; but the very cause of that difficulty,—the investigating and intellectual character of the King, Edwin, and perhaps of the whole people,—was also the cause of the rapid progress of religious impressions, and of their permanence, when once adopted. Such literature as the Church of Rome possessed, now spread fast in Northumberland; and, at length, in the person of Alfred, called the Wise, a great protector of the milder arts appeared. He had been educated by Wilfrid, one of the most learned priests of the day; and, with a clear and philosophical intellect, appreciated and applied the knowledge he obtained. The love of letters extended amongst his subjects; and the cloisters of Northumberland became the repositories of ancient learning. Security and leisure, the two great foster parents of science, were to be obtained alone in monastic life; and several of the Saxon kings of Northumbria, abandoning the scenes of bloodshed and turbulence which surrounded the throne, found peace and happiness in the studious seclusion of the monastery.

Amongst the people at large, civil wars and disturbances of all kinds greatly retarded the spirit of literature in Northumbria, after the reign of Alfred the Wise; but the same spirit remained concentrating all its powers in the cloister; and while France, under the declining race of her Merovingian kings, was every day losing the remains of Roman learning, the priests of England retained the elements of knowledge, and the love of science.

CHARLEMAGNE VISITED BY ALCUIN

Three great epochs of darkness are distinctly marked in the history of France. The first immediately succeeded the conquest of Gaul by the barbarians, when the arts of the Romans received their most severe blow. The second preceded the fall of the Merovingian and the rise of the Carolingian dynasty, when wars and civil contentions had worn away all that barbaric conquest had left. The third followed considerably after the period of which I now write, and took place just before the accession of the Capetian line, when the folly of Charlemagne's descendants, the invasions of the Normans, and the complete anarchy of the times, destroyed all which the great monarch had succeeded in restoring.

The second of these epochs still existed in full force at the accession of Charlemagne himself; and in his grand and general views for the consolidation of his power, his magnificent intellect, and his benevolent heart, immediately led him to conceive the project of raising his empire above the surrounding world, by superior civilization, and of binding all its component parts together by a community of taste, of knowledge, and of cultivation. To obtain his object, however, was difficult, even in the outset; for, where could he seek for people qualified to instruct the ignorant nations over which he was extending his sway? The Italians were now almost as uncivilized as the Francs; and Greece, where literature still lingered, was infectious with vices, and jealous of communicating her better stores. Barbarism spread around the monarch on every side; and, at the first view, it appeared as if it would be necessary, not so much to revive, as to create, a literature for France.

On his return towards his native country, however, after having calmed and regulated his Italian dominions, Charlemagne was visited at Parma by an English priest, named Alcuin, who had come to Rome, charged by the Archbishop of York to receive for him the pall which was occasionally sent from the Apostolic See to various bishoprics, as a symbol of the archiepiscopal dignity. The renown of the monarch had drawn the priest to Parma; but the eloquence and learning of the Saxon had as powerful an effect on the mind of Charlemagne. He now found that the cloisters of England contained men able and willing to cooperate in his great design of civilizing and instructing the nations under his dominion; and Alcuin was accordingly invited at once, to visit France, and to combine with the monarch in framing a plan for reviving the light of past ages, and dispelling the darkness of the present.

Such an occupation was, of all others, that which best suited the talents and inclination of the Saxon priest. Passionately fond of knowledge, though the learning which he himself possessed was tinctured with the sophistical rhetoric of the lower empire, and in a degree obscured by the gloomy superstitions of the Roman church, Alcuin was zealous in his desire to extend his information to others, and ardent in his aspirations for a more polished and humane state of society. Nevertheless, charged as he was at the time with a mission of a totally different character, and subjected by the rule of the church to the will of a superior, he could not at once meet the wishes of the French sovereign, and all that he could promise was, to visit France if he could obtain permission. The desire of so great a monarch, however, was not likely to be rejected by the Archbishop of York; and, after having distinguished the object of his favor by every mark of honor and regard, Charlemagne returned to France, satisfied with having taken the first step towards improving the state of society, and mitigating the rudeness of the age.

After his arrival in his native country, he held a general diet at Worms, at which Tassilo, Duke of Bavaria, having received assurance of personal safety, appeared as a vassal of the French crown. His oaths of fidelity and homage were renewed; and, having been entertained for some time with splendor and hospitality by his sovereign, he gave twelve hostages for his very doubtful faith, and returned to his own territories.

The whole empire now slept in peace; and Charlemagne closed the year without any warlike movement,—an event which occurred but seldom during his long protracted reign.

FROM THE SUBMISSION OF THE DUKE OF BAVARIA TO THE BAPTISM OF WITIKIND, AND THE SUPPRESSION OF THE REVOLT OF BRITANNY.

FROM 782 TO 785.

The winter after the monarch's return from Italy, in ad 781, passed by in peace; nor, indeed, had he cause to apprehend war from any other quarter than from Saxony, whose treacherous and versatile inhabitants could never be relied upon, whatever promises they had made of obedience, whatever pledges they had given of tranquility. The monarch of the Francs had taken every measure which could be devised to ensure the permanence of his control, after the last expedition which he had been forced to undertake against them. The construction of fortresses, and the presence of armies, had not been the only methods he had employed. The introduction of the Christian religion was, as I have pointed out before, both an object and a means in the complete subdual of the people; and this he had left no effort unexerted to effect. He caused a number of churches to be built, and sent missionaries and prelates to superintend the religious instruction of the people, while he took care that neither pomp nor splendor should be wanting, to win the cooperating power of imagination, which, amongst a savage nation, is easily gained by that which addresses the external senses. Nor had the endeavor to conciliate, by every means of kindness and confidence, been neglected; and, that the Saxons might feel as little as possible the weight of a foreign domination, he had chosen the Dukes who were to reign over the different provinces t of Saxony from amongst the people themselves

The Saxons had submitted with apparent willingness, had been baptized, and had attended the court and camp of the French monarch with every appearance of satisfaction and contentment. Aware, however, of the uncertain nature of the barbarian character, Charlemagne did not choose to leave a land which had cost him so much labor to reduce to subjection, for any great length of time, without his presence; and in the spring of the year which followed his journey to Italy, he advanced into Saxony, and, encamping at the source of the Lippe, applied himself to establish as firmly as possible the basis of his newly acquired power

During his stay, he was visited by the ambassadors of several distant nations, amongst whom were missives from Sigifrid, King of Denmark, and from the Chagan of the Avars, or inhabitants of Hungaria. Both these monarchs solicited the amity of the Francs and their king; but, at the same time, Sigifrid had on all occasions afforded a refuge to Witikind, the great instigator of the Saxon irruptions, so that Charlemagne had just cause to doubt the sincerity of his friendly expressions. That great monarch, however, seems ever to have disdained to persecute a fugitive enemy. Adalgisus himself remained secure at the court of Irene, whose son was the betrothed husband of the French king's daughter; and, in the present instance, Charlemagne, without noticing the asylum granted to the Saxon chief, received the ambassadors of Sigifrid with the same pacific assurances which they bore from their sovereign.

After dismissing the envoys with honor, and completing his arrangements for the internal government of Saxony, the French monarch returned to France. But scarcely had he quitted Germany when a Slavonian tribe, called Sorabes, inhabiting a district between the Elbe and the Sale, upon the immediate frontiers of Saxony, took advantage of the monarch's absence, the confusion of a lately conquered country, and the invariable indifference, if not hatred, of a subdued people, to pour in upon the Saxons, ravaging also a part of Thuringia, which had long been dependent on France.

The invading force was so small, that the personal presence of Charlemagne did not seem called for, and he dispatched Adalgisus, his chamberlain, Geilo, his constable, and Worado, count of his palace, with orders to march the united army of Francs and Saxons, which was probably not far from the spot, to check the progress, and punish the aggression of the Sclavonians.

In the meantime, issuing once more from his retreat in Denmark, Witikind had again appeared amongst the Saxons. The same energy of character, and the same powerful eloquence which he had before displayed, produced the same effect. The Saxons rose in every direction, expelled the ministers of the Christian religion, and, feeling now that the patience of their conqueror must be at length completely exhausted, they prepared for a war of a more fierce and resolute character than any of those they had hitherto sustained against the Francs.

The officers commanding the army, which was proceeding against the Sclavonians, had no sooner entered Saxony, than they found the whole country in revolt; and wisely judging that the success of the insurrection in that province was likely to be far more fatal than the petty irruption of the Sorabes, they instantly determined to turn their arms against Witikind and his followers.

Whether the Saxons, who had composed part of their original force, voluntarily quitted them to join the party of the revolt, or whether, judging them unworthy of reliance, the generals left them behind, does not clearly appear; but it is certain, that only the oriental Francs marched towards the spot, where the insurgent Saxons were mustering. The army of the Francs was thus greatly weakened; but, at the same time, Theodoric, a cousin of Charlemagne, holding a provincial command on the banks of the Rhine, collected in haste all the troops of his government, and proceeded with prompt vigour to suppress the rising of the Saxons, before it had reached a still more dangerous height. The information which had caused his movement into Saxony, guided him towards the spot where his presence was necessary; and, marching on with all speed, he soon came up with the forces of Adalgisus and his companions, advancing with the same purpose as his own. The two armies united composed a very formidable host, and hurrying on together, they approached a mountain called Sonnethal, or Sinthal, near the banks of the Weser, on the northern side of which hill Witikind was encamped with the Saxons, whom he had induced to break their vows.

As soon as the news of his position was obtained, it was determined between Theodoric and the commanders of the other army that a simultaneous attack should be made on both sides of the insurgent's camp. For this purpose, Adalgisus, Geilo, and Worado, were directed to cross the river with their forces, while Theodoric, during the time required for their march round the mountain, constructed an entrenched camp on the southern side, in order to secure a retreat in case of defeat. At an appointed hour the attack was to commence; and the united army of the Francs, with the advantages of discipline, experience, and well concerted operations, would undoubtedly have completely overthrown the crude forces of the Saxons, had not that unhappy spirit of jealousy, which has in all ages ruined so many noble enterprises, mingled with the counsels of the Frankish chiefs.

Theodoric, the relation and friend of Charlemagne, was already renowned as a general; and the commanders of the other army were fearful that, if they admitted him to share in their attack upon Witikind, the glory of the victory which they felt sure of winning, would be solely attributed to him. Having received a separate command from their sovereign, they were not absolutely obliged to obey the orders of the duke; and, consequently, instead of waiting for the appointed time, they determined immediately after separating from Theodoric, to attack the Saxons at once. They accordingly advanced directly towards the enemy's camp; and despising an adversary whom they had so often beheld fly from the presence of Charlemagne, they felt confident of conquest, and took no precautions to ensure success.

Witikind had drawn up his army to receive them; and the Saxons had no choice but death or victory. So often had they ravaged the territories of France—been conquered and pardoned so often had they submitted, and again revolted; so often had they bound themselves by treaties and vows, and violated the most solemn and sacred engagements; so often had they abused the confidence, and mocked the religion of their conquerors, that they could hope for no safety but in triumph. They fought with courage, and were led with skill.

In the Frankish army, on the contrary, the misconduct of the leaders was, of course, followed by the misconduct of the troops. They attacked with insolent confidence, and careless confusion. Each spurred on his horse irregularly against the enemy as fast as he could come up; but, instead of finding fugitives to pursue, and plunder to be taken, they met with warriors, resistance, and death. Pouring in upon the centre of the Saxons which had the advantage of the ground, the Francs left the flanks of their army exposed. Witikind saw their mistake, their confusion, and their danger; and immediately caused the wings of the Saxon army to wheel upon his imprudent enemies. The French, disordered, with desperation, but fought in vain. The havoc was tremendous, and the battle of Sinthal was a massacre as well as a defeat. Two of the generals, whose crime and folly had thus exposed the army committed to their guidance, fell with their soldiers. The third, Worado, or Wolrad, fought his way out, and survived; but, besides the generals, four counts, and twenty of the noblest and most distinguished warriors of the Francs, remained dead upon the plain; while a few fugitives, flying over the mountains to the camp of Theodoric, brought to that general the first news of his companions' treachery and punishment.

The tidings of the defeat of Sinthal soon traveled into France, and Charlemagne himself, at the head of a large army, immediately passed the Rhine, and advanced, with the speed of lightning, towards the scene of the revolt. By this unhappy battle the glory of his arms had been tarnished, but the consequences which he anticipated were still more dreadful than the fact. For nine years he had been labouring to deliver France from the continual scourge of the Saxon irruptions. Fear had been the only engine which repressed them for a moment; and now, after so long a period of successful warfare, during which he had accomplished the security of his own dominions only by the subjection of theirs, all that he had done was entirely rendered void by one great defeat, which, restoring confidence to the people he had formerly subdued, held out a long prospect of wars and insurrections for the future. This expedition he resolved should now be one of chastisement, as well as repression. When conquered, and at his mercy, the Saxons had bound themselves, by the most solemn vows, never to bear arms against him again, and on the security of those vows he had shown them clemency; but now, that every engagement was broken, and infidelity had been encouraged by victory, he determined to punish as well as to conquer, and to wage the same exterminating warfare against his faithless and pertinacious enemies, that they had on all occasions waged against him.

His very name, however, was sufficient to carry dismay into the hearts of the Saxons. The courage which had animated them fled, their victorious army dispersed at his approach, like a morning mist before the sun; and their triumphant chief, abandoned by his followers, was obliged to seek safety in flight. At the same time, the nation flocked to meet the French monarch, glossing their infidelity with all the excuses which terror and cunning can suggest, and offering once more the treacherous vows with which he had been so often deceived.

Indignant at their baseness, and desirous of striking such terror into their hearts as would do away the consequences of their late victory, and make the impression of their punishment more deep than that of their success, Charlemagne unhappily forgot the clemency which was one of the most beautiful traits of his character. He pardoned the nation, it is true, and sheathed the fiery sword, which he had drawn with the purpose of wasting the whole land; but he demanded that those who had taken an armed and active share in the insurrection, should be given up to his vengeance. This was pusillanimously conceded by the rest of the Saxon people, and, as a terrible example for the future, the French monarch ordered four thousand five hundred of the most criminal to be executed in one day.

There was, beyond doubt, much to palliate this tremendous act of severity. The dreadful evils which the Saxons had incessantly inflicted on France, their unceasing treachery, the broken vows and ruthless disregard of all engagements, of the very men who suffered, were all motives which may be admitted to qualify the awful sternness of the deed; but still humanity revolts from so terrible an act of punishment; and though Charlemagne was far more justified than many who have been less censured for similar acts, yet the death of the Saxons has left a stain upon his name, which has been magnified by the partialities, and distorted by the theories, of men equally unable to appreciate his virtues or his faults. As in the case of almost all severe measures, the effect he intended to produce was not at all accomplished. Witikind had again fled into the north at the approach of Charlemagne; and, though the monarch of the Francs did not absent himself far or long from the confines of Saxony, before the next spring, the whole country was once more in revolt. The successes of the former year had given fresh hopes and expectations to the Saxons; and the death of their countrymen was far from impressing them with that terror, which the Frankish monarch had expected. Accustomed themselves to sacrifice their prisoners, the minds of the Saxons were perfectly made up to undergo the same destiny after a defeat; and, whereas a much lighter infliction, if it had taken some new and strange form, would probably have spread consternation through the whole country, a fate, however horrible, to the contemplation of which their minds were habituated, inspired but little fear, and produced a small effect. The memory of a battle gained against the Francs, however—an event which centuries had not seen—was not easily obliterated; and the consequences of the impulse thus given to the national hopes, was the raising of two armies, such as had never taken the field against Charlemagne before.

The monarch was early informed of the gathering storm, and speedily prepared to meet it; but a domestic grief, the death of Hildegarde, his Queen, which took place in April, retarded his movements against the enemy. Various other cares also occupied him till the middle of May; but about that time he quitted Thionville, where he had passed the winter, and advanced rapidly upon Dethmold, where the army of Witikind had taken up its position. We have no means of calculating the number of either force; but it is probable, from the expression of Eginhard, who calls the Saxon host "an innumerable multitude", as well as from the fact of their having stood, for the first time, the charge of Charlemagne, that the troops of the insurgents were numerically superior to those of the monarch. Charlemagne had no advantage but that of attack. He had come from a long and weary march, in a summer, the heat of which was so uncommonly intense, that several instances are mentioned of persons having died from its effects. The Saxons had chosen their own position; they were led by one of their greatest chiefs, were animated by the memory of victory under his command, and were stimulated by vengeance, superstition, and despair: nevertheless, the French monarch hesitated not a moment, but attacked them at once on their own ground; and, after a short, but terrible conflict, succeeded in almost annihilating their army.

Few are said to have escaped alive of all the Saxon host; but, of course, such a struggle could not take place, without great loss also on the part of the Francs. A hostile country and another powerful army were before the steps of Charlemagne; and his forces were too much weakened by the battle which he had just won, to admit of his advance, without much risk of his retreat being cut off. Retiring, therefore, upon Paderborn, he awaited the arrival of fresh troops, which were in preparation throughout France; and, immediately after their coming, he once more marched forward, to encounter the second army of the Saxons, which occupied the banks of the Hase, in Westphalia. Scarcely a month had elapsed after his former victory, when he achieved another that completely destroyed the hopes of being able to contend with the Frankish monarch in general conflicts, with which the success of Witikind in the former year had inspired his countrymen. The army which opposed the passage of the river, was as totally defeated as that which had encountered Charlemagne near Dethmold; with this difference, however, in the event, that in the first battle fought, the greater part of the Saxons died where they stood, and in the second, a considerable number surrendered.

No severity of any kind seems to have been practised by Charlemagne towards his prisoners; and on the part of the Saxons, all thought of opposing the monarch himself, appears to have been abandoned, though the whole country continued still in revolt. The next two years were consumed in a desultory warfare, equally destructive to both parties; though, as the Saxons were the weaker of the two, the same extent of loss was more detrimental to them than to their enemies.

Witikind and Albion, who had commanded the two great armies of the insurgents, though conquered, were not subdued and while Charlemagne, determined to crush the revolt at any cost, marched through one part of the country, punishing insurrection and compelling submission, the rest of the land rose up behind his steps, and did away all that he had effected in his passage.

During those two years, only one event of importance chequered the monotonous character of the war. This was a victory gained on the banks of the Lippe by Charles, the eldest legitimate son of the French monarch. In order to overawe Westphalia, while he himself marched in a different direction, Charlemagne left a part of his army under the command of the Prince, then but twelve years old. The Saxons, hoping to strike a deep blow at the monarch in the person of his son, hastened to attack the young commander; but their efforts still proved unsuccessful. Both armies consisted entirely of cavalry, and, after a severe conflict, in which a great number of Saxons fell, victory remained with the Francs, and Charles returned to Worms, crowned with the earliest laurels that the annals of the world record. Whatever was the Prince's share in the victory—for it is not probable that Charlemagne committed such great interests solely to the inexperience of twelve years—the fact of Charles having, even nominally, commanded, shows at what an early period the Frankish youth were inured to arms, and may aid conjecture in regard to the cause of that people's long preponderance as a military nation.

At length, in the year 785, after having passed the winter in the heart of Saxony, and spent the most severe season of the year in traversing the land from side to side, and repressing revolt wherever it appeared, Charlemagne found the whole country once more completely subdued, Witikind and Albion had fled, and were now wandering on the other side of the Elbe, endeavoring to excite the people of that already devastated country to fresh, though fruitless revolt. But the French monarch now determined to try, by persuasion and kindness, to win the hearts of his two most constant and intractable opponents.

His first step was, through the intervention of some of their countrymen, to represent to them the inutility of farther resistance, and to invite them to his presence, with promises of security and favor. Neither of the Saxon chiefs, however, prone as their own nation was to the breach of all promises, would confide in the mere word of the French monarch; and Charlemagne offered hostages for their safety, if, by appearing at his court, they would but afford themselves an opportunity of comparing civilization and Christianity with the state of society and religion to which they had shown themselves so pertinaciously attached. With this proposal Amalvin, a Franc of distinction, was dispatched across the Elbe, and the first direct communication being opened between Witikind and Charlemagne, the negotiations were easily concluded.

The French monarch animated but by one view in the whole transaction granted the Saxon chieftains whatever assurances of safety they demanded; and Witikind at length, satisfied of his sincerity, traversed the country, and visited his great conqueror at Bardingaw in Saxony. This visit, although its duration was but short, excited a strong desire in the bosom of the rude Saxon chieftain to see more of the splendid court and civilized people, whose monarch, he had too many reasons to know, was as irresistibly great in war as he now found him generous in peace. Such an inclination was doubtless encouraged by Charlemagne himself; and, after his return to France, he again received Witikind and Albion at Attigny, on the Aine. From that moment, a great change took place in the opinions of his two opponents. What means of conversion were used, and whether the minds of the Saxons were brought to conviction by the reasoning of Christian prelates, or whether their imaginations were dazzled, and their sight deceived by the pomps and pious frauds of the Roman Church, we can only vaguely discover from very doubtful legends. The chronicles state the meager fact, that Witikind and Albion, after having opposed the Christian faith in their native land for many years, were solemnly baptized at the Palace of Attigny, where Charlemagne himself appeared as the sponsor for his conquered enemies. Doubtless, no art was left unemployed by the zealous advocates of the church to win the Saxon chiefs to the renunciation of paganism; but all that is positively stated in regard to Charlemagne himself is, that, after having honored them highly during their stay, he dismissed them to their own land, loaded with costly presents. The whole of Saxony now at once embraced the Christian religion; the churches which had been burnt were rebuilt, and others were constructed. The priests who had fled returned to their altars, and universal thanksgivings were ordered by the Catholic Church, for the establishment of the faith of Christ, amongst the obstinate idolaters of the north. This state of things did not, it is true, prove of any long duration; but we here find a sort of epoch in the Saxon war, to which it seemed as well to conduct the reader, without pausing to notice in their chronological order, a number of domestic events, of more or less importance, which, during these years of active warfare, occurred in the life of Charlemagne

Two of these events are worthy of particular notice, from the influence they may be supposed to have had upon his afterlife. Soon after the death of Hildegarde his queen, Bertha, the mother of the French monarch, also took her destined place in the inevitable tomb.

THE THURINGIAN CONSPIRACY

Kings are surrounded by so many temptations to forgetfulness, that their griefs are generally of short duration. But Bertha was regretted long and deeply, by Charlemagne; and, if virtue, rectitude, talents, and active benevolence, be qualities which should attach, Bertha was well deserving of the tears which her son bestowed upon her loss. His sorrow, also, was justified, by a long retrospect of affection; for we learn, that the harmony existing between Charlemagne and his mother, was never known to be interrupted, except on the one occasion of the divorce of Desideria. That cloud itself had soon passed away; the evil consequences which she had anticipated, were averted by his extraordinary powers; and Bertha lived to see her son the greatest monarch of his age and race.

The sovereign of the Francs was, by natural temperament, soon led to supply the place which the death of Hildegarde had left vacant; and in the choice of another wife, he fixed upon Fastrada, the daughter of Rodolph, a Frankish noble of high repute. We are led to conclude, that the personal beauty of the new Queen, was not accompanied by great powers of mind, or by fine qualities of the heart; and her conduct soon produced consequences the most painful that could affect a monarch from the actions of his wife. These were murmurs amongst the people, and ultimately the revolt of a part of his subjects.

All accounts represent Fastrada as oppressive and merciless; but what was the precise nature of the cruelty she is accused of exercising, and how a monarch of such firmness of mind as Charlemagne, could entrust a dangerous portion of authority to the hands of a woman, are points on which history is silent, and in regard to which, all inferences must be derived from collateral evidence..

It appears, however, that towards the end of the year 785, one of the Eastern Francs of noble birth, called Hartrad, conceived the design of exciting the part of the country in which he lived, to insurrection; and determined by stratagem to get possession of the person of the King, and murder him, or to throw off the yoke of France, and declare his province independent.

Either from discontent at the conduct of the Queen, general ambition, or that love of change so universal in the minds of the weak, a number of other Counts joined in the conspiracy, which soon began to assume a formidable aspect. For some time Charlemagne had known that treasonable efforts were in meditation against his government; but the information he had received was either so vague, or the schemes of the conspirators so immature, that he suffered them to proceed till the commencement of the ensuing year, keeping nevertheless a strict watch upon their movements. At length, the chief of the discontented nobles, Count Hartrad—on the coming of a royal messenger, charged to demand that his daughter, who had been long betrothed to one of the Western Francs, should be given to her husband—took occasion to throw off the authority of the King, and to call together the abettors of his treason.

His summons was instantly obeyed; but when the conspirators appeared in arms, it was found that, as usual on such occasions, they had sadly miscalculated their strength; and that their forces were still so scanty, as to render perseverance in their design, utter madness. The consequence of this conviction was their immediate dispersion in order to seek places of concealment. But they had now too openly proclaimed their treason for justice to remain inactive any longer. A considerable number were arrested in the different spots where they had taken refuge, and were afterwards tried at Worms before an extraordinary court, to which a number of the bishops had been summoned. On the present occasion this commixture of Christian prelates with the lay judges of the land, did not seem to temper greatly the severity of the punishment awarded. None of the conspirators, it is true, were put to death; but such as were proved most guilty, were condemned to that fearful infliction, the loss of sight, a sentence then common. Others were degraded from their rank, and the whole were doomed to permanent or temporary exile.

REVOLT OF BRITANNY

Another war, within the actual limits of France, demanded the attention of Charlemagne, immediately after the revolt of Hartrad; and it may be necessary, for a moment, to look to the state of Britanny, in which it took place, in order clearly to understand its cause and object. On the first invasion of Gaul by the Franks, no resistance of so determined a nature was offered to their progress, by any of the various tribes or nations who adhered to the Roman government of that province, as by the Armoricans,—a people inhabiting one of the western districts of France, but the extent of whose territory at that time, it would be difficult to define. The struggle was kept up between them and the barbarians, long after it had been yielded by the rest of the inhabitants of Gaul; and their courage and vigor, though obtaining no support from the country in whose defence they fought, at least served to win the admiration and respect of their adversaries. At length, abandoned by Rome, and assailed on all sides by enemies, the Armoricans chose rather to enter into a general league with the Francs, than still contend for a falling state, which had already cast them off.

What were the precise terms of this league, and how far the

Armoricans were absolutely amalgamated with the Francs, cannot be discussed in this place, but it is more than probable, that long before the accession of Charlemagne, a complete assimilation of the two nations had taken place.

However that may be, in a part of the territories formerly inhabited by the Armoricans, a, new people had established themselves, sometime previous to the period of which I speak. These fresh settlers consisted of fugitives from England, where the invading Saxons had compelled each native Briton to choose between domestic servitude, eternal strife, and foreign exile. Those who preferred the latter, soon colonized a large part of the sea coast of France, extended their territories, consolidated their power; and having, both by their own strength and the dissensions of the Merovingian monarchy, extorted the privilege of governing themselves, they maintained their own laws and language, and existed a separate people within the French dominions. A tribute alone marked their dependence; but even this they often neglected or refused; and though Charlemagne had taken precautions to prevent their encroachments on the neighboring country, they yet judged so ill of his authority, that they chose his reign as the time for making a great effort to assert their immunity from their customary mark of vassalage.

Although Charlemagne, conscious of his own power, viewed their efforts to shake off his sway with contempt, yet it was contempt in no degree mingled with that blind arrogance, which neglects the means of safety, in the confidence of strength. The revolt of Britanny, however, was not a matter of sufficient importance to call for the personal presence of the monarch; and, while he himself devoted his attention to the internal regulations of the state, and the punishment of the Thuringian conspirators, he directed Audulphus, his seneschal, to lead an army into the refractory province, and reduce it to subjection. This was easily and rapidly accomplished. The Bretons were in no state to maintain the independence which they claimed; and, after the capture of all their fortresses by the Francs, they threw themselves on the clemency of the monarch, which was never appealed to in vain. Audulphusreturned in triumph to the court, bearing with him the trophies of his victorious expedition. The Bretons gave hostages for their future obedience; and several of their nobles even presented themselves at the diet which was then sitting at Worms.

FROM THE PACIFICATION OF SAXONY, TO THE DEFEAT OF ADALGISUS AND THE GREEKS IN ITALY.

785 TO 788.

Through the whole of Charlemagne's northern dominions, peace was now fully established; but the storm which his presence had for a time averted from Italy again threatened to break upon it with redoubled force. Sufficient time had elapsed for the weak Duke of Bavaria, under the influence of a violent and vindictive wife, to forget the engagements he had entered into, and the oaths he had taken. The Duke of Beneventum, also, who had espoused another daughter of the dethroned King of Lombardy, was, like Tassilo, instigated both by his wife's revengeful spirit, and his own ambition, still to pursue his schemes of casting off the almost nominal dependence which he owed to the crown of France. Irene, too, the Empress of the East, had by this time adopted views adverse to those of Charlemagne. She had tasted fully the sweets of power; the passion for dominion had developed itself in her heart; and the nascent desires of rule which began to manifest themselves in her son, led her to dread the speedy loss of that authority so dear to her own bosom, if she suffered the youthful Constantine to strengthen himself by such an alliance as that which she had formerly proposed with the French monarch.

It is not proved, indeed, that the Empress supported the Duke of Beneventum in his schemes of ambition, or that she pampered the pride of Tassilo of Bavaria into treason and revolt, but it is clear that she kept up a correspondence with both. Nor does it seem unlikely, although the actual rupture of the alliance between France and Constantinople is attributable to Charlemagne himself, that Irene was in the highest degree unwilling to complete it, and that her intrigues hurried it to its termination. It is sufficient, however, here to say, that the marriage proposed was entirely broken off within a short period of the time of which I now write, and that, long before its absolute relinquishment, Irene showed the most decided signs of hostility towards the court of France.

Whatever part the Empress acted in these transactions, it is evident that a very extensive conspiracy existed in Italy, embracing almost every portion of that country and the Tyrol, and extending itself to Bavaria. At the same time, its ramifications spread to nations over which Charlemagne had no control; for the Bavarian Duke, well aware of the vast power of him whose authority he sought to cast off, and whose wrath he was about to encounter, had negotiated with many of the barbarous hordes in the vicinity of his dominions. From them he had obtained promises of aid and support in the moment of strife; and, had time been given for accomplishing the preparations meditated by all the conspirators and their allies, an united force would have been created, which the whole genius, skill, and vigor of Charlemagne could scarcely have found means to overcome.

The watchful care, however, of the French monarch left no part of his vast dominions unobserved, and his active energy encountered and crushed the evils by which he was threatened while they were yet immature. The designs both of the Duke of Bavaria and the Duke of Beneventum became known to him while regulating the internal policy of Saxony, and receiving the hostages of the revolted Bretons. His determination to place himself in the midst of the scene of danger was immediately taken; and, late in the year 786, he departed from Worms, and marched directly upon Italy.

His first halt was at Florence, where he arrived at Christmas, and, after a brief pause, with a view to refresh his troops, he proceeded thence to Rome. He was joyfully received by Pope Adrian, who was bound to him, on every account, by friendship and by a similarity of mind, as well as by the remembrance of benefits and the existence of mutual interests. The coming of the great king was therefore always a subject of rejoicing at the court of the prelate, and never more so than at a moment when the muttering voice of the great Italian volcano threatened the country every hour with convulsion and ruin.

Charlemagne lost not a moment ere he turned his whole attention to the regulation and pacification of Italy. His first care was to deliberate with Adrian and with his own nobles upon the state of Beneventum, and upon the necessity of its subjugation,—a step without which the tranquillization of Italy seemed remote, if not impossible. But motives such as seldom actuate monarchs and conquerors induced him to pause, and guard against himself, lest any causes but stern and absolute necessity should influence him in hurrying on towards the certain evils of warfare. Even supposing that neither siege nor battle were to follow, yet the dreadful ravages which his army would unavoidably commit on a hostile occupation of the country, weighed heavily upon the monarch's mind, and cost him much hesitation ere he determined to pursue his march towards Beneventum.

The halt of the Frankish forces, and the deliberations which ensued at Rome, gave full time for the news of Charlemagne's approach to reach the Beneventine Duke, who, aware of his own designs, and totally unprepared to resist so powerful an army as that which threatened his territories, saw nothing but destruction before him. To appease the monarch of the Francs, without absolutely abandoning his former plans, Arichis immediately dispatched his eldest son, Romuald, to Rome, charged with many presents, and fair speeches; and directed to supplicate Charlemagne to desist from his hostile advance. He was also commanded to promise, on the part of his father, entire obedience to the will of Charlemagne, and that great king gladly welcomed his coming, till he discovered that the young Prince of Beneventum had no specific act of homage to offer—no inviolable engagement to propose.

Perceiving instantly that the object of Arichis was to gain time, and to turn him from his course till Beneventum could be prepared for resistance, Charlemagne detained Romuald in his camp, and, instead of pausing to deliberate any farther, advanced rapidly towards the Beneventine territory. Arichis now found that the Frankish monarch was not to be deceived; and, having rather hastened than retarded his own fate by his duplicity, he quitted his capital and fled precipitately to Salernum, which, in addition to strong fortifications, possessed the great advantage of offering the means of escape by sea. Sincere submission, or still farther flight, were now the only expedients left for his choice, and he immediately determined upon the former. His second son Grimwald was accordingly dispatched towards the monarch, with proposals no longer intended to amuse, but to satisfy. By these Arichis offered to yield both his sons as hostages, and to give any other security for his future good faith that the sovereign himself would point out, at the same time supplicating, in the humblest terms, that the Frankish army might be stayed in its rapid and destructive march.

This new embassy met the monarch at Capua; and, influenced rather by the humane desire of sparing the Beneventines, than by any confidence in the promises of Arichis, Charlemagne accepted the submission of the Duke. Twelve hostages were given by the people of the dukedom in pledge of their own fidelity; and the second son of Arichis, named Grimwald, was alone detained by the French king, who afterwards carried the youth back with him into France, and educated him by the noble lessons of his own society and his own example. The eldest son, Romuald, he generously sent back to his father; but he exacted, as a mark of his undisputed authority, that the Dukes of Beneventum should, in future, bear upon some part of the coin of their dukedom the name of their sovereign lord.

Charlemagne, it would appear, remained a considerable time at Capua, awaiting the return of messengers whom he dispatched to Beneventum for the purpose of receiving the oath of fidelity prescribed both to Arichis and his people. During this halt he received the ambassadors sent by the Empress Irene to treat with the French court in regard to the proposed marriage of her son. What were really the instructions given to these envoys, we do not know, but neither party were any longer desirous of an alliance the aspect of which had been entirely changed by the lapse of six or seven years. Charlemagne, however, as before mentioned, took the odium of the refusal upon himself. The ambassadors were coldly entertained; and, after asking the opinion of his council on the subject of their mission, the monarch dismissed them, filled either with real or apparent dissatisfaction.

As soon as these affairs were ended, and the tranquillity of Beneventum was secured, Charlemagne retraced his steps to Rome, and proceeded to investigate all the various branches into which the plot of Arichis had spread itself throughout Italy. During these transactions, he left the news of his proceedings to reach Tassilo, Duke of Bavaria, and work their proper effect upon his weak and versatile mind, before he took measures to punish that vassal's renewed breach of faith. The tidings of the complete subjection of Arichis, his brother-in-law, and ally, were thus carried to the court of the Bavarian prince, long before his means of resistance were in any degree prepared; and, at the same time, he had good reason to fear that the inquiries which the monarch was, even then, engaged in making into the darker points of the conspiracy, would soon bring his criminality to light more glaringly than ever.

Confident in an alliance with the Huns or Avars, together with various other northern nations, and only requiring time to mature his endeavors, Tassilo determined upon exactly the same step by which Arichis had endeavored to blind the eyes of Charlemagne. He, accordingly, at once sent messengers to Rome, in order to deceive his cousin by a pretence of contrition for his past offences, and to delay him by long negotiations, which he believed, from the distance between Rome and Bavaria, might be easily protracted till the necessity of temporizing was done away by the power of resistance.

In order to give additional efficacy to his own representations, his envoys were commanded to pray the intercession of the Pope between the offended sovereign and the contrite vassal, and Adrian, believing his professions to be sincere, willingly undertook the dignified and appropriate office of mediator. He exerted himself with zeal; and, although the designs which Tassilo had entertained were laid open more and more, yet the monarch's real attachment towards the Roman pontiff, and deference for his opinion, soon mitigated the anger which his subject's renewed treachery had justly excited. Charlemagne accordingly declared that he was ready to receive any security which the ambassadors might have to propose for their master's future fidelity. But, on communicating to them the success of his intervention, the Pope learned, with surprise and indignation that the envoys had nothing to offer without sending to Bavaria for farther instructions.

Some more efforts were made to deceive and gain time, but the object of the Duke and his treacherous duplicity were now evident, both to the pontiff and the monarch; and, while Adrian lanched the thunders of the church at him who had dared to use its most sacred attribute for the purpose of deception, Charlemagne hastened, with the speed of light, to chastise his rebellious vassal, and guard his peaceful dominions.

Carrying with him a considerable number of the Lombard nobles, who had been convicted of conspiring against the state, he left his son, Pepin, in Italy, with a tranquillized territory, and a considerable army, which he was directed to lead towards Bavaria by the way of Trente. The monarch then hurried his own march towards France, dispersed the Lombards whom he had brought from Italy, through a country where they could work no evil, and called a diet of the nation at Worms, to consult for the public safety, and raise the necessary forces for the maintenance of the royal authority. In this assembly, he displayed to his people all that he had done during his absence; and, explaining to them the danger of his situation and of their own, easily obtained all the supplies he could desire.

Two armies were instantly raised, and as speedily in motion. The one, composed of the transrhenane Francs, mingled with several bodies of Saxons, was thrown forward immediately to Phoringen, upon the Danube; while Charlemagne himself, followed by the Francs of Gaul, advanced into the territories of Augsburg, and reached the banks of the Lech, which then marked the frontier of the feudal duchy of Bavaria. It is more than probable that indignation, as well as caution, had given wings to the movements of Charlemagne, and had hurried him forward to the boundary of his unworthy cousin's territory. There, however, the same generous compassion, which had withheld him from entering the country of the Duke of Beneventum, again caused him to pause, and give time for fear, rather than punishment, to produce submission.

The Duke of Bavaria found himself, not only detected, but surprised. He had endeavored in vain to deceive a great and magnanimous mind; he had again raised his hand against a forgiving relation, and a clement lord; and now, before he could believe that his treachery was fully known, he found himself surrounded with armies, irresistible by numbers, courage, and skill, and long inured to victory and success.

At the same time, Tassilo discovered that he could in no degree depend upon his own people for support; as his nobles, more faithful than himself, remembering the oaths of homage they had taken to Pepin and his children, showed no disposition to join in the Duke's schemes of rebellion. His allies were afar; and one course alone was left,—submission.

With his proud heart burning at the degradation which his treachery had called upon him, Tassilo appeared at the camp of his cousin as a suppliant and offered every pledge for his future conduct. The clemency of Charlemagne was still unwearied: "he was gentle by nature" to use the expressive words of Eginhard; and he once more extended his forgiveness to his criminal relation, though the tranquility of his dominions obliged him to demand sufficient hostages for the observance of his vassal's renewed engagements. Twelve of these were given by Tassilo, together with his son Theodon, a hostage of much more consequence than any of the others, not alone on account of his superior birth, but also, because, inheriting all his mother's hatred towards the Francs, he had been a sharer in all his father's treasons.

Trusting to these pledges, Charlemagne now withdrew his armies, and retired to Ingelheim, where he spent the winter in striving to cultivate and improve the moral situation of his people. This constant and rapid change of occupation and endeavor, is one of the most singular points in the character and history of Charlemagne. The moment that his great and comprehensive mind was withdrawn from one object of import, it was directed, without pause, to some other mighty undertaking. The affairs of peace and war, of policy and literature, the grandest schemes for consolidating his power, and extending his dominions, and the noblest efforts towards civilizing his subjects, and dispelling the darkness of the world, seem alternately, yet with scarce a moment's interval, to have occupied the attention of the French monarch, in the midst of a barbarous nation, and a barbarous age.

CHARLEMAGNE'S EFFORTS FOR THE REVIVAL OF LETTERS

In pursuance of the purpose he had disclosed to Alcuin, Charlemagne, during the short time he had lately spent at Rome, had collected a number of grammarians and arithmeticians, the poor remains of the orators and philosophers of the past, and engaged them to accompany him from Italy to France, "where", to use the words of the Monk of Angouleme, "the study of the liberal arts did not at that time exist".

As soon as he had terminated his expedition against Tassilo of Bavaria, the monarch applied the whole energies of his mind to promote the cultivation of literature in his dominions; and spreading the teachers he had collected in Italy through the various provinces of France, he offered the means of instruction to all his people. The sole sources of knowledge which had existed previous to the present period, were the few schools held by some of the bishops in their houses, and by some of the abbots in their monasteries. These, however, had been hitherto exclusively devoted to ecclesiastics; and at the time to which I now refer, the first effort was made to extend the benefits of such establishments to the whole community. The monarch dictated an encyclical letter to all the clergy of France, calling upon them to aid in spreading knowledge and information, and he himself began to establish schools in various parts of his dominions, at which the laity as well as the clergy might procure instruction. His example was speedily followed by the church: the ecclesiastical seminaries were either opened to the rest of the people, or other establishments were founded for their instruction, in the various dioceses of the empire; the excellence of knowledge was inculcated from the pulpit, and the chair; its pursuit rewarded by favor and advancement; the natural inappetence of ignorance was counterbalanced by every stimulant that could be devised, and both the desire of information, and the means of procuring it, became general throughout France.

In the cultivation of his hereditary dominions, the monarch did not neglect the improvement of those territories which he had acquired since his accession; and nothing was forgotten which could contribute to the instruction of the northern people whom he had conquered, and who in every point of civilization were far behind the Francs themselves. However, as the principles of a mild religion were still but little known amongst them, the first object of Charlemagne was to plant in their hearts that primary germ of all amelioration; and the propagation of Christianity amongst the Frisons and other people of Saxony, met with its full attention from the unwearied zeal of the French monarch. Bishops and preachers were appointed to every part of the country; and eloquence and piety were sure to be singled out, for the dangerous but glorious distinction, of turning the dark pagans of the north to the light of a purer faith.

Such were the occupations which filled the hours of Charlemagne during the brief period which he was permitted to devote to the arts of peace. That period, however, soon drew towards a close; for neither active vigilance could overawe, nor invariable clemency disarm, the hatred of some of his enemies; and even in the midst of his most pacific employments, continual intelligence reached him of the meditated treason, both of Arichis of Beneventum, and of Tassilo, Duke of Bavaria. Neither of those perverse vassals remembered the oaths of fidelity which danger and necessity had extorted, as anything else than as acts of degradation and incitements to enmity; and both prepared to seize the first opportunity of revolt. Arichis, finding himself unable to stand singly in opposition to so great an adversary, took advantage of the position of his territories upon the Italian coast, to negotiate in private with the Greek empire. Upon condition of receiving dignity and assistance himself from the Empress and her son, he promised to seat Adalgisus on the throne of Lombardy; and to open the way for Greece towards the conquest of the rest of Italy.

The hope of regaining that country by means of an alliance with Charlemagne, if ever it did exist in the bosom of Irene, had now passed away, while the desire of recovering that portion of her predecessor's empire remained as strong as ever, heightened by the wish to snatch it from one who had insulted the imperial court by the refusal of his daughter. A thirst for revenge was certainly felt by the young Emperor, whose hopes and passions had been excited early towards the bride that was afterwards denied him; and the breaking of the marriage might be perfectly consistent with Irene's views, and yet the rejection of her alliance by the Francs be regarded by her as an insult, which she was bound to resent. At all events, such was the tone of offended dignity which she assumed; and willingly listening to the proposals of Arichis, she sent ambassadors to assure him of aid and protection, and to concert with him the means of accomplishing their mutual designs.

Man's most cunning policy, however, serves but to work out the unseen purposes of Heaven; and when the shrewdest schemer of the earth has plotted a device, which no human power can oppose, Fate causes his foot to stumble over some minute circumstance, and lays him and all his projects prostrate in the dust. On their arrival in Italy, the missives of the Empress found the Duke of Beneventum and his eldest son both dead; while the inhabitants of the duchy, divided into different factions, threatened to overthrow all the schemes which had been adopted by their former lord. After long discussions, the great majority of the people agreed to petition Charlemagne to establish in the ducal seat, Grimwald, the second son of Arichis, who some time before had been delivered as a hostage to the monarch of the Francs; and, in consequence of this determination, while the ambassadors of Irene were honorably conducted to Naples, messengers were dispatched to France by the Beneventines, in order to ascertain the pleasure of the King.

In the meanwhile, Pope Adrian had watched, with a jealous eye, all the proceedings which have just been detailed, and had sent envoy after envoy to Charlemagne, in order to warn him of the negotiations with Greece. His suspicion of the Beneventine dukes did not end with the life of Arichis; and fearful that the machinations of that prince might be renewed under the reign of Grimwald, he opposed, with every argument in his power, the nomination of the young Lombard to the dukedom of Beneventum. He assured Charlemagne, by letter, that the people of that state had bound themselves by promises to the ambassadors of the Empress, to pursue steadily the schemes of Arichis, if they obtained Grimwald for their governor. He informed him also, that the Greek commander of Sicily was still at Gaeta, carrying on his intrigues with the Beneventines, who, on their part, were using every exertion to induce the rest of Italy to revolt; and he added a thousand incentives to suspicion, many of which, probably, originated in his own fears. In short, the terror of the pontiff made him doubt even the judgment of Charlemagne; and his hatred of the whole Lombard race, urged his opposition to Grimwald to the bounds of indecent vehemence.

Sometime had now passed, however, since that young prince had begun to accompany the army and court of the French monarch; and, while Grimwald himself, by the sight of splendid actions, and the continual example of great and generous qualities, acquired a guiding principle for his own conduct, and a sincere love and admiration for his magnanimous sovereign, the King of the Francs had an opportunity of seeing and judging the behavior of his hostage, and of appreciating the fine but undeveloped, properties of his understanding and his heart. This examination had been sufficient to fix the determination of Charlemagne. In spite of the remonstrances and warnings of the Pope, he instantly named Grimwald to the dukedom which his father had held; and sent him back to his dominions, where he was received with universal joy.

Adrian, on reflection, found that perhaps he had carried his opposition to an unjustifiable extent; and began to fear, that the unwise and fruitless endeavor he had made, to bias the judgment of the French monarch, might weaken his influence for the future. He accordingly attempted to palliate his conduct, and explain away his more violent assertions, as soon as he found that Charlemagne had decided against him. But the behavior of Grimwald himself, was the strongest reproof which the intemperate zeal of the Roman pontiff could meet with. Far from entering into the views of the Greek court, the young Duke instantly evinced his determination of keeping the most inviolate faith with his sovereign and benefactor.

Notwithstanding this change in the policy of Beneventum, Irene's schemes still continued; and Charlemagne soon learned, that armies were preparing in the East, for the invasion of his Italian territories. But other dangers surrounded him at the same time, from the persevering treason of the fellow conspirator of Arichis, on whom his menaces had produced no farther effect than temporary alarm, while his clemency had been totally thrown away. Scarcely a day passed, that the court at Ingelheim did not receive news of warlike preparations making in Bavaria; and the Bavarian nobles themselves, strongly attached to Charlemagne, gave him private intimation, that Tassilo was calling from Pannonia—so long the source of barbarian torrents—new tribes of plunderers, to ravage the fertile countries of the south, and occupy the arms of his sovereign, while he effectually threw off the homage he had so often deceitfully rendered. Even at the court of Charlemagne himself, the son of the Duke of Bavaria, though a hostage for his faith, joined in the intrigue while his father, imagining that the efforts of the Eastern empire would soon call the King into Italy, hurried his hostile preparations, to take advantage of the monarch's absence.

Charlemagne now found, that no time was to be lost and, while in person he remained on the Rhine, to repel or avert the storm which threatened to burst upon him from Hungary and Bavaria, he dispatched an army into Italy, under the command of an officer, named Winegisus, in order to cooperate with the Dukes of Spoleto and Beneventum, in the defence of the Italian peninsula. The Duke of Spoleto was still the same Hildebrand who had taken so considerable a share in the conspiracy of the Duke of Friuli, but who had afterwards, as mentioned in the forgoing pages, obtained pardon and favor, and had, by twelve years of faithful service, obliterated the memory of his fault, and merited the confidence of his sovereign. Of the young Duke of Beneventum I have already spoken; and it is probable, that the very suspicions which the Pope had lately cast upon him, made him the more eager, on the present occasion, to distinguish himself in the service of his sovereign.

Having taken these precautions in regard to Italy, Charlemagne resolved to cut short at once the proceedings of the Duke of Bavaria, and to bring the conspiracy to an issue. For this purpose he concealed studiously all knowledge of Tassilo's renewed treason, but summoned him, in the common feudal form, to appear as his vassal at the usual assembly of the nation, which was this year held at Ingelheim. The embarrassment into which such a summons threw the Duke of Bavaria was very great. Condemned by his own conscience, yet unprepared to resist the command of his sovereign, if he obeyed, he exposed himself to punishment—if he refused, he proclaimed his crime. Trusting, however, to the secrecy of his negotiations with the Huns or Avars, he determined to assume the boldness of innocence, and to present himself at the court of the monarch. Accordingly, on the meeting of the diet, he appeared with a splendid train of vassals and retainers, but he appeared only to meet the reward of his crimes. He was instantly arrested, and accused of various acts of treason before the assembly of which he had come to form a part. The tribunal, consisting of his peers, was one in every respect competent to take cognizance of his crime; and his trial, as well as that of his wife and children, was proceeded in without delay. Witnesses from their own country flocked in, to bear testimony against them. That, since the last pardon which the King had granted him, Tassilo had again conspired to throw off his allegiance, was proved by a mass of evidence, which he could in no degree invalidate, while the implication of his whole family in his treason was made equally manifest. Sentence of death as a traitor was immediately passed upon the Duke himself by the unanimous voice of the assembled nobles; and all present clamored for the instant execution of a man whom they looked upon as a disgrace to their order and their nation.

The awful fate thus suddenly and unexpectedly presented to him, overcame pride and firmness, dignity and courage, in the breast of the unhappy Duke of Bavaria; and, casting himself at the feet of the monarch whose clemency he had so often abused, he petitioned for life in the most abject terms. Charlemagne, ever averse, when he consulted his own heart, to that cruel anomaly, judicial bloodshed, once more interfered to mitigate the sentence, though every principle of justice required him not to pardon the criminal. That ceremony, which amongst the Francs was the invariable sign of loss of temporal rank, and eternal seclusion from the world, was performed upon Tassilo and his son. Their heads were shaved, as a mark of degradation; and both princes being confined to a cloister, found it, we are told, as calm a retreat in after years, as it then appeared a happy asylum from the immediate sight of an ignominious death. Luitberga, the wife of Tassilo, and the daughter of Desiderius,—whose persisting animosity had met ready instruments in the idle pride and wild ambition of the Duke— after having witnessed the downfall of her father, and aided in the overthrow of her husband and her son, was compelled to assume the veil, and, left in the leisure of reclusion, to weep over her faults, or madden over her failure, as wisdom or passion might dictate. The rest of the Bavarians who had joined in the conspiracy of the Duke were punished with exile; and the country, deprived of its separate form of government, was divided into counties, under magistrates appointed by the French monarch.

While these events took place in France, and while the final regulations of Bavaria required the presence, and occupied the time of Charlemagne, his generals in Italy had to encounter the army of the Eastern Empire. Before the disposition of Grimwald could be known at Constantinople, Adalgisus, the son of the former King of Lombardy, had set sail with John, one of the officers of the Empress, accompanied by a considerable fleet. Having been joined on the passage by Theodore, governor of Sicily, they landed with their united armies on the Italian coast. Scarcely had they touched the shore, however, ere the young Duke of Beneventum, much to their surprise, appeared in arms to oppose their farther progress; and, having effected his junction with Hildebrand, Duke of Spoleto, and with Winegisus, and the army of the Francs, Grimwald advanced at once to encounter the Greek forces. All parties were eager for battle, Adalgisus and Theodore being as desirous of fighting before Charlemagne could arrive, as that monarch's generals were of distinguishing themselves during his absence. In consequence, no sooner did the two armies appear within sight of each other than the engagement began. The strife was severe and long, but at length victory declared herself in favor of the Francs, and the Greeks were obliged to fly to their ships, leaving four thousand men dead upon the field of battle, and a thousand prisoners in the hands of the enemy.

Theophanes implies that John, the general who accompanied Adalgisus, was killed after the battle was over. That he fell on this occasion is evident; but I know no other writer that alludes to the barbarous cruelty with which the Greek charges the generals of the Francs; and it may be doubted whether national and party spirit did not take advantage of some vague report to found a calumnious assertion.

This was the last effort of Adalgisus to recover the throne of his father; and so entirely did he disappear, after the period of this expedition, from the busy stage of the world, that many of the Frankish annalists represent him as dying in the battle by which he strove to win back the Lombard crown.

Thus ended, also, the war between Charlemagne and Irene—a war which sufficiently proved the weakness of the Greek Empire. Irene, busied in the intrigues of internal policy, forgot her hostility to Charlemagne in her struggles with her own son; while the monarch of the Francs suffered the remains of the Greek power to exist in Sicily and Calabria, either from pity, contempt, or some political motive which has not come down clearly to the present times. The consequences, however, of the treasonable machinations of Tassilo and Arichis were not yet fully developed. They had allied themselves, as before mentioned, with other powers besides that of Greece, and had roused a people in Europe which had slumbered for many years after a long period of devastation. This nation, even after his fall, remembered its treaty with the Duke of Bavaria; and the rapidity with which it proceeded to perform its engagements, showed that the hand of justice had but struck him in time.

GEORGE JAMES

FROM THE CONDEMNATION OF THE DUKE OF BAVARIA, TO THE DECREES OF THE COUNCIL OF FRANKFORT.

788 TO 794

The people who now prepared to attack the empire of Charlemagne, though called by most of the writers by the name of Huns, were not the same nation, which, under Attila, had menaced the existence of the Romans, and ravaged the territories both of the East and West. They sprang, however, in all probability, from the same origin, occupied nearly the same country, and comprised the remnant of many of those tribes which had once been united under the famous scourge of God.

When Attila, after his last successful invasion of the Roman state, retired before the bribes of the weak Valentinian, the eloquence of Leo the Great, and the diseases which affected his army, he met, in the bed of luxury, the death which he had escaped in a thousand battle fields. The various hordes which, consolidated under the dominion of the Huns, had fought and triumphed together, having been bound to each other by the talents of Attila alone, were separated the moment that his spirit had fled. The desire of dominion being no longer directed by one powerful mind against other nations, spread disunion amongst themselves; and the swords which had so long conquered their enemies, were now turned by the savage tribes against each other. The great battle of Netad, where they contended for sovereignty over each other, destroyed many, and dispersed the rest of the Hunnish confederates; and, scattered in different bodies over the north, they were insensibly amalgamated with other people. That tribe which remained perhaps the most distinct, turned its steps under the command of Irnac, one of the sons of Attila, towards the Lesser Scythia, where it was encountered, and probably afterwards subdued, by the other hordes, which wandered continually through the wide pasture grounds of the north; so that it, as well as the rest, becomes speedily lost to history. At the same time, the Gepids, who claimed, and perhaps had won, the battle of Netad, took possession of Upper Hungary and Transylvania, and soon after possessed themselves of part of Pannonia and Noricum, all of which territories were destined to be wrested from them by a new influx from the source which had given rise to themselves.

It is not my purpose to inquire here, which of the Tartar nations that poured, during many years, a barbarian torrent upon the West, gave origin to the tribe afterwards calling themselves Avars, nor to investigate whether the people which acquired that name in Europe, really formed a part of the original Avars, whose possessions extended to the most eastern point of Asia, or whether they belonged to the primary stock of the Huns themselves. Suffice it, that shortly after the dispersion of the hordes of Attila, a warlike and powerful people, calling themselves Avars, first approached the northern part of Europe, driven from their native country by the growing power of the Turks. At that time, the feeble empire of the East was in the habit of employing various barbarian nations in her wars; and the Avars sought and obtained service under the Emperor Justinian, who, in the weak craft of his dotage, loaded them with presents, in order that their arms might be turned against various other tribes, more inimical to the imperial crown. Success crowned their efforts, and increased their reputation and power; and, advancing on their way, they conquered almost the whole of European Scythia, and incorporated with themselves several of the scattered tribes which had formed the Hunnish confederation.

At length, finding themselves strong, and the Eastern Empire weak, they boldly threatened the nation they had proposed to serve; but the firmness of Justin, and the wisdom of his precautions, rendered them humbler in their expectations; and turning their arms against the northwest of Europe, they first attacked the Frankish monarchy on the confines of Germany. Defeated by Sigibert, King of Austrasia, they again tried the fortune of battle; and though the Frankish annalists claim victory for their monarch, he was obliged to purchase the absence and friendship of the invaders. They then leagued with Alboin, King of the Lombards, for the destruction of the Gepids, who were, by that time, the only remaining tribe of great importance, which had formed part of the empire of Attila. On this occasion, the Avars, with the most profound dissimulation, obtained from the necessity of the Lombards, a treaty, by virtue of which, all the country, and one-half of the spoils of the conquered people, were to be theirs, in the event of success.

The Lombard arms proved successful in battle against the Gepidae, whose country was immediately overrun by the Avars. What remained of the vanquished nation was incorporated with their conquerors, and the whole territory they had inhabited became the property of the wandering Scythians. Thus Hungary, now so called, was possessed by the Avars, who, joining with themselves a multitude of Hunnish tribes, accumulated the immense spoils which both they themselves and their equally barbarous predecessors had torn from the other nations of Europe.

From this period, the Avars, under their monarchs, called Chagans, pursued a long system of aggression and negotiation towards the empire of the East, which always ended to the advantage of the barbarians. They extended their limits towards Lombardy; and touched upon the very verge of Bavaria; and in the height of their power, they leagued with Chosroes the Persian, and advanced to the gates of Constantinople. Various changes afterwards took place in their state; and a fixed residence, the accumulation of an immensity of plunder, habits of luxury, and the desire of repose, gradually took from the Avars, or modern Huns, the first fierce necessity of warfare, which expulsion from their own country had occasioned, and which, while it lasted, produced strength and conquest. Much of their eastern frontier was now lost, almost without a struggle on their part, by the rise of other barbarous nations, especially the various tribes of Bulgarians, and we do not find them making any great military exertion, either to defend themselves, or to aggrandize their territory, till the year 662, when, at the instigation of Grimwald, King of Lombardy, they ravaged the dukedom of Friuli. From that time history is nearly silent concerning them, till, at the period of which I now write, we find Tassilo, Duke of Bavaria, calling them to his aid in his ambitious, but impotent, struggles against his sovereign.

Before the arrest and condemnation of that unhappy prince, his negotiations with the Huns had been carried to a conclusion; and two armies of Scythians were already prepared; the one to pour into Lombardy, and divert the forces of Charlemagne to that quarter, and the other to enter Bavaria, and support the rebellion of the Duke. Whether the discovery of his treason, and the condemnation of Tassilo, were known in Hungary or not, when the Pannonian armies began their march, we are not told; but, notwithstanding his fall, the Huns kept their engagements to the letter; and early in the year invaded both Friuli and Bavaria.

Their irruption into the first named province, was instantly repelled by the vigor and conduct of the Frankish governors and in a sharp conflict which took place on the occasion, the arms of the Christians were completely victorious. In Bavaria, where they probably calculated on more certain success, from their alliance with the Duke, they were equally unsuccessful. Tassilo no longer held the reins of government; and the inhabitants of the country, whose attachment to the monarch of the Francs have had occasion to notice, instantly prepared to resist the invaders. Two envoys from Charlemagne, also, named Grahamannus and Audacrus, were present with a small body of troops; and directed the movements of the Bavarian forces. The two armies encountered each other in the open country, near Ips, on the Danube, and the Huns were here defeated and driven back, with even greater loss than they had suffered in Friuli.

They must have become aware, by this time, that the original object of their expedition was now unattainable; and that the fate of their ally, the Duke of Bavaria, was sealed. But personal revenge supplied a motive for farther exertions, and a fresh army was immediately raised by the Avars, to avenge the loss of their countrymen, and wipe away the disgrace of defeat. Once more passing the Danube, the forces of the Huns entered Bavaria, but were encountered anew by the Francs and Bavarians; and, after a more severe and total defeat than before, were forced to fly in confusion, leaving an immense number of their companions dead upon the field of battle, and still more swallowed up in the waters of the Danube.

To this active warfare between the Francs and the Huns succeeded one of those cold suspensions of hostility, which augur anything but peace. On the one part, the Avars were alarmed and astonished at the event of the war—so different from that which a thousand traditions of success had taught them to expect—and ceased their irruptions in order to collect their forces, and measure the strength of their adversary. On the other hand, Charlemagne also paused, to consolidate his dominions, and to guard and regulate that territory, which the revolt and fall of his vassal Tassilo had brought more immediately under his own superintendence.

Accordingly, as soon as he found that his presence in the centre of his dominions was no longer necessary for the protection of the whole, he proceeded through Bavaria in person, fixing the government as he intended it to remain for the future, and fortifying the frontier against any new aggression. When this necessary duty was completed, the monarch returned to Aix-la-Chapelle, where he spent the winter in regulating the affairs of the church, and the internal police of his kingdom. We cannot, of course, trace the whole of the monarch's efforts for the perfect establishment of order and tranquillity, in realms which for centuries had been torn by anarchy and strife. Nor can we always discover the motives for various laws, originating in a state of society, with the general situation of which we may be fully acquainted, and yet be ignorant of many of the inferior details. It is but fair, however, under such circumstances, to look upon those laws with a favourable eye; and where it is necessary to have recourse to indirect conclusions to consider the general character of Charlemagne's designs, and to suppose the same motives which we discover in the rest of his actions, to have influenced those where no other cause is apparent.

The regulation of the church, and the preservation of its purity, both in doctrinal points and in the lives of its servants, was always a great object with a monarch, one of whose chief engines of civilization was the Christian religion; and the principal acts which we find attributed to him in the present year, have chiefly this tendency. Such was the composition, by his command, of a book of homilies by the famous Lombard historian, called Paul the Deacon, and the order for these homilies to be read in all the churches. A general council was also held at Aix-la-Chapelle, for the purpose of reforming abuses in the Gallican church; and a capitulary was issued, in which, as well as various regulations respecting the clergy, are to be found many useful and many curious laws. Amongst the last, are prohibitions against divination, either by dipping into the Evangelists, and applying the first passage met with as a prophecy,—a mode then common,—or by any other method; against the practice of baptizing bells; and against the custom of keeping hounds, falcons, or jesters by bishops, abbots, or abbesses. The more peaceful occupations of Charlemagne, however, were never suffered to continue very long, and, indeed, could seldom be protracted beyond that season of the year, when the severity of the weather, and the scantiness of forage, kept his armies from the field. A new cause of warfare soon called the attention of the monarch, both from the internal regulations in which he was engaged, and from the unconcluded hostilities which he had been carrying on against the Huns.

The more immediate aggression of a Slavonian tribe, called Weletabes, or Wiltzes, inhabiting the northern part of Germany, near Brandenburgh and Pomerania, from the Elbe to the Baltic, induced the French King to march at once against them. This aggression, it is true, was rather directed against the allies and tributaries of the Francs, than against the Francs themselves; but it is not unworthy of observation, that, with wise zeal, Charlemagne strove to make his friendship valuable to the nations round about, by the promptitude and certainty of his efforts to protect them, and on all occasions showed more active vigor in defending a friend or an ally, than even in repelling an irruption upon his own territory, or avenging an insult to his own crown. Many personal causes, in the present instance, contributed to render it imperatively necessary for Charlemagne to act vigorously against the Weletabes. Their contempt of his power had been displayed in a quarter where his authority had not yet been confirmed by time. The Saxons were the daily witnesses of their incursions upon the Abrodites, and other tribes dependent upon France; and the French monarch soon found, that the insolence of a petty people whom he condemned, might, if unpunished, produce the insurrection of a country from which he had much to apprehend.

In the spring of 789, he accordingly made every preparation for an early and active campaign. He called together a considerable army of Francs, mingled with these more trustworthy forces, a large band of Saxons, and commanded the Frisons to ascend the Elbe in their small vessels, while the Abrodites, and other nations who had suffered from the aggressions of the people he was about to punish, made great efforts to second his design with all their power. As soon as these arrangements were completed, Charlemagne passed the Rhine at Cologne, and, traversing the whole of Saxony, reached the banks of the Elbe. Here, however, he paused. The country before him was wild and unexplored, the inhabitants, warlike and active, while in the rear of his army lay a nation—extending over a space of several hundred miles—whose subjection was forced, whose hatred he had little reason to doubt, and whose perfidy was known by long experience.

The loss of a battle, scarcity of provisions, or a thousand other emergencies, might compel him to retreat with precipitation; and no deep political sagacity was required to show, that the Saxons would rise on the slightest misfortune which might befall him, and endeavor to obstruct, or prevent entirely, the repassage of the Elbe. To guard against this danger, Charlemagne paused on the banks of the river, and employed his army during several days in constructing two bridges across it, one of which he fortified strongly at either extremity with a fort of wood and earth, which, being sufficiently garrisoned, secured a retreat in case of discomfiture. The monarch then advanced into the heart of the enemy's territory, and a long and desultory warfare succeeded, in which no general battle was fought, and the subjection of the country effected, rather by persevering efforts than by any one decisive blow.

The chiefs of the various tribes composing the nation of the Weletabes, yielded to the superior discipline of the Francs, and, one after another, sacrificed their independence, by taking the oath of homage prescribed by the victor. Hostages of their faith were demanded and given, and, whether from soon learning to appreciate the benefits of a civilized government, or from having at once felt the impossibility of successful resistance, the Weletabes adhered firmly to their vow, and never attempted to shake off the yoke which had been imposed upon them, till moved by the influence of a greater power.

Having thus terminated with ease an expedition which had appeared fraught with dangers and difficulties, Charlemagne repassed the Elbe, and returned to Worms, where he entered the year 790, celebrated as a year of peace. It is probable, however, that the twelve months which succeeded would not have passed so tranquilly if the Chagan of the Huns, or Avars, had not made the first advances towards a termination of the differences between France and Hungary, by sending ambassadors to the court of the French monarch, with the ostensible purpose of settling the respective boundaries of the two kingdoms on the Bavarian frontier. Whether the object of the Chagan was solely to amuse the King of France, till Hungary was again prepared for warfare, or whether the enchantments of self-interest on both sides, blinded the eyes of the two monarchs to simple justice, and created those unreasonable exactions which too often obstruct the arrangement of the simplest claims, cannot now be told, from the want of all minute information in the writings of contemporaries. The general facts, however, are clear. The ambassadors of the Chagan did not accomplish the purpose of their mission, if it was really a peaceful one, and retired from the court of the French monarch without any definitive determination of the points which they had been sent to discuss. After their departure, Charlemagne, in return, dispatched messengers to the court of Hungary, but this mission proved not more fruitful than the other, and soon terminated, leaving all parties more disposed to hostility than ever.

While these transactions were taking place, Charlemagne, as if to enjoy to the full the year of tranquility which he had snatched like a flower from amidst the thorns of war, visited various parts of his dominions, and inspected personally several of the buildings which were proceeding by his command throughout the empire. His first visit of the kind was to a new palace which he was raising at Seltz, and round which the infant stream of the Sale murmured amidst some of the most beautiful scenery in Germany. The church and monastery of St Ritharius also, were this year completed, under his especial care and direction; and we are told, that skillful artificers in wood and stone, in glass and marble, were sent by the monarch for the decoration of the building, while an immense number of extremely strong vehicles were dispatched to Rome, for the purpose of procuring materials from the ruins of the glorious past. Descriptions of the construction of a great many ecclesiastical buildings, begun about this time, have come down to us; and on no part of his general scheme for improving his dominions, does Charlemagne seem to have bestowed more pains, than on the cultivation of architectural science. Although, of that science, Rome now possessed scarcely any vestige, she still offered the choicest models and materials that France could procure; and the various journeys, both of Charlemagne himself, and of the workmen he at different times sent to Italy, greatly contributed to the improvement of art in his native country.

The advance of society in Gaul had been very great since the fall of the Merovingian dynasty; and the year of peace which now intervened, was in no degree lost to the people of Charlemagne. They had, indeed, much need of some pause in the gratification of their natural propensity to war, in order to permit the growth of those milder arts, which the monarch was so anxious to cultivate, notwithstanding the warlike character of his own mind. It is not, however, to be supposed, although each year had been almost uniformly passed by the Francs in hostile expeditions, that the useful branches of knowledge had hitherto made little advance during the reign of Charlemagne. On the contrary, we find, that their progress had been rapid and continual.

Unfortunately the state of commerce and industry at that remote period can only be learned from the vague mention of facts and events, to be found occasionally in the midst of an immense extent of desultory and irrelevant writing. Nevertheless, it is evident, even from these casual notices, that France had been rendered by this time the most cultivated country in Europe, (with the exception of the Eastern Empire), as far at least as regarded trade and manufacture. The stores of ancient learning, and the remains of ancient magnificence, were still the ruined inheritance of prodigal Rome; but even prior to the year of which I now write, we find Rome herself applying to the monarch of the Francs for skillful workmen and overseers, to superintend those architectural labors for which Italy had been once renowned, and demanding those materials for the construction and reparation of her buildings which the commerce of France could alone supply. Various collateral proofs of the extent of this commerce are derived from the letters and annals of the day, amongst which proofs one of the most convincing is, the fact of the great facility with which ponderous and unwieldy objects were transported for considerable distances. Thus we learn that entire marble columns, and immense stone crosses, were sent overland through the whole extent of France on many occasions, and were uniformly carried in vehicles of French construction. A regular system of port duties also was established, the collector-general of which we find distinctly mentioned; and it would appear, from the same authority, that the right of trading to France was considered of great importance to the neighboring countries,—so much so, indeed, that Charlemagne is reported to have threatened to prohibit the commerce between England and France as the severest punishment he could inflict on Offa, sovereign of the Anglo-Saxon kingdom of Mercia, who had given him cause for anger. These facts, as well as the laws concerning mercantile transactions, in which various articles of luxury are expressly mentioned as in common use, and as ordinary matters of traffic, tend to show that art had reached a greater height amongst the Francs at this time, than has been generally supposed. The vases and cups of gold and silver, carved and embossed with a thousand complicated figures—the silver tables, richly chased, representing cities and countries—the bracelets, rings, and ornamented belts—together with the praises bestowed on the workmanship,—prove that the arts of luxury, which always follow far behind those of necessity, were known, cultivated, and esteemed at this period.

In addition to this, the fact of tablecloths of fine linen having been then in use shows the perfection to which a branch of industry had been carried that always speaks a considerable degree of refinement in the nation by which it is practised. The skillful manufacture of iron, also, and the strict and severe laws which forbade the exportation of arms, afford another instance of the superiority of the Francs at that time to the nations round about them; and a thousand other circumstances might be adduced to show, that—however much literature and taste were still inferior to what they appeared in some of the ages which preceded, and in some which followed—yet the necessary and the convenient arts were carried to a height which we do not usually attribute to the eighth century. The advantages to be derived by states from the promotion of industry, and the cultivation of every species of knowledge, was never lost to the sight of Charlemagne; and he snatched each interval of repose, to secure all those facilities to commerce and manufacture, by which alone they can be brought to flourish and increase.

To afford to all the efforts of labor, by clear and comprehensive laws, both instant protection and adequate return, was one great purpose of his legislation; and we find a large proportion of all his capitularies dedicated to the object of guarding merchants from unjust exactions, as well as that of enforcing the performance of bargains, and ensuring justice in all mercantile transactions.

From his capitularies, also, we derive many small points of information, which, though seemingly unimportant, and sometimes even ridiculous, tend greatly to show the state of society in France at that time; and while the general scope and tendency of these laws offer the best representation of the monarch's mind, the minute particulars often furnish a more curious and interesting portrait of the manners of his country, and his age, than circumstances of far greater apparent importance could supply.

Where there exist many facilities for a traveler to procure refreshment and repose, we may generally conclude that the traffic of the country is great, and the state of civilization considerable. In this point of view, the fact that, in the reign of Charlemagne, taverns, where both meat and drink were to be procured, existed throughout France, is not insignificant; and the number of laws in regard to watching the bridges, and the highways, and guarding against those who were likely either to injure individuals, or to destroy public works, presents a singular picture of the struggle between the premature civilization of the sovereign's mind, and the lingering barbarism of his people.

The principal domestic occurrence attributed to this year of Charlemagne's life, is the provision of a distinct jurisdiction for his eldest son. Sometime previous to this period, he had apportioned to the two younger brothers, Pepin and Louis, separate territories, the government of which, under his own eye, educated them to the use of authority, and accustomed them to the responsibility of command. His eldest son, Charles, had remained at his father's court unportioned; and, though the dominions to which he was to succeed, were sufficiently vast to gratify even an ambitious mind, yet Charlemagne this year bestowed upon him the duchy of Maine, one of the richest and most beautiful provinces of France, as a foretaste of the sovereignty which he was afterwards to enjoy.

The conflagration of his palace at Worms and the continual news of warlike preparation on the part of the Huns, were the only events which disturbed Charlemagne's tranquillity during the year 790. But the first of these evils was not so complete as to oblige him to change his residence; and against the latter, he took those prompt measures of precaution, which he always employed with success, in averting or repelling attack. Finding that the Chagan of the Avars still continued to claim a part of Bavaria, and that the subjects of that prince made frequent predatory excursions upon the frontiers of the country, the monarch of the Francs, as winter approached, dispatched a considerable force towards the scene of contention.

INVASION OF HUNGARY

Whether he had at this time absolutely determined to carry the war into Hungary itself, or whether the measure was merely, as I have said, one of precaution, in order to guard his territory from attack, till the negotiations which were still pending should be terminated, does not clearly appear. It is probable, however, that, towards Charlemagne, the Avars, or Huns, made use of the same mixture of cunning and insolence, which they had displayed successfully in their conduct towards the empire of the East, on their first entrance into Europe; and it is evident that the discussions were protracted for a great length of time, and were not broken off till the end of the year. But Charlemagne was not to be turned from his purpose; and the moment the spring arrived, he was once more at the head of his armies, prepared to pursue the war with more than usual vigor. He well knew the great resources of the country he was about to invade, its natural and its artificial defenses, and the courage and resolution of its inhabitants;

and, though he both contemned the arrogance, which we find from all historians that the Avars displayed, and felt that confidence of victory which is often both a presage, and a means, of success, he prepared for a war of a more serious character, than any which he had hitherto undertaken, and had recourse to measures and precautions, which he had previously neglected to employ.

These precautions were to be taken for the security of the territories which he left behind him, as well as for the conquest of those which he invaded. The paths of conquerors are always on volcanoes, and each step may be shaken by an earthquake; for, in most instances, it requires a longer space of time than the life of one man, so far to amalgamate a subdued people with their victors, as to render any one footfall of ambition secure, in the whole march of hostile aggrandizement. Many have been the means employed, to assimilate nations more rapidly; and the most rational, as well as the most successful, has been that practised by Charlemagne, of endeavoring to overcome national prejudices and the bitter memory of subjection, by a community of interest, and a participation of endeavor and reward. This plan had produced the most happy consequences in regard to the Lombards, who, fighting side by side with the Francs, had become identified with them in victory and glory; and Charlemagne hoped, by the same measures, to bend the Saxons in the same degree.

A large body of that people was accordingly incorporated with his army, and destined to march against the Huns, probably with the double view of employing a number of fierce and active men, at a distance from their own country, and in a situation where they could not revolt, and of habituating them to the customs, the religion, and the discipline of the Francs. His whole forces were then disposed in three great divisions; and, having taken measures to ensure a regular supply of all things necessary for the expedition, he marched towards the frontier of the enemy. The plan of his campaign was one well calculated to secure success. The army which had been previously sent forward to Bavaria, together with the troops raised in that country, were commanded to descend the Danube in boats, which contained also abundant military stores and provisions. He himself marched forward with a large force, on the southern side of the river; and his generals, Theodoric and Meginfried, led the third division, composed of Saxons and Oriental Francs, along the northern bank of the stream. Although these dispositions would, in all probability, have determined the event of the opening war, Charlemagne omitted nothing which might procure a speedy and fortunate issue to his enterprise; and, before entering Hungary, he dispatched messengers to his son, Pepin, King of Italy, requiring him to march with the Duke of Friuli and the Lombard forces, upon the frontier of the Avars, and cooperate with the other troops, which he was leading against that nation from the West. Much of the success of an invasion, of course, depends upon the nature of the invaded country; and the territory of the Huns was defended in so peculiar a manner, that it may be well to consider for a moment the difficulties which opposed the progress of the French monarch. A more distinct account of the Hungarian dominions in that day, has come down to us, than the old annalists often furnish on any subject. But that account is so extraordinary in itself that each writer who has since touched upon the history of Charlemagne, has endeavored to explain, according to his own ideas, the description furnished by the Monk of St Gall, from the words of an eye witness. Some have magnified, and some have softened, the particulars of this account; but the fact, of the country of the Avars having been guarded by fortifications of a very ingenious and perfectly singular nature, is admitted by all. The whole country, we are told, was surrounded by nine circles of double palisading, formed of trunks of trees, twenty feet in height. The interstice of the double palisade was twenty feet in width, which was filled with stone and compact lime, while the top of the whole, covered with vegetable earth, was planted with living shrubs. At the distance of twenty Teutonic, or forty Italian, miles from the first circle, or *hegin*, as it is called, was a second internal one, fortified in the same manner, and thus the country presented fortress after fortress, from the outer palisade to the small inner circle, or ring, as the writers of that day term it, within which the accumulated wealth of ages was guarded by the Avars. The space between the various ramparts was filled by a woody country, so thronged with towns and villages, that a trumpet could be heard from the one to the other; and the means of egress from the inner to the external circles, or from the extreme boundary to the neighboring countries, consisted alone in very narrow sally ports, practised in various parts of the palisades.

Such is the description given by a person who wrote within a century of the events he narrates; who received his account from one of the officers of the monarch; and who addresses his work to an immediate descendant of Charlemagne. But, when we remember, that other parts of his work are full of errors and absurdities, and find that, amongst the annalists of the time, his statement is confirmed by little but vague allusions to extensive fortifications, and the still more vague traditions of after years, we shall feel inclined to reject the particulars as hyperbolical, if not totally false, while we admit the general fact, of the country having been carefully secured by strong artificial defenses of a singular kind.

In addition to these obstacles to the progress of a conqueror, the people of Hungary were known to be a hardy, bold, and persevering race, so that it required the exertion of all his vast resources to ensure the success of Charlemagne's enterprise. The preparations necessary for carrying on the war upon the extensive scale which these circumstances demanded, delayed the French monarch so long, that the month of September had commenced before he reached the banks of the river Ens, which at that time formed the boundary of Bavaria. From that moment, however, no time was lost ere he proceeded to put in execution the plan he had formed for his campaign. He immediately entered the country of the Avars; and no resistance in the open field seems to have preceded his attack of the fortresses which lay in his way. Three of these were immediately taken by the monarch, sword in hand, and he then marched onward with his usual rapid advance, laying waste he country, till he reached the banks of the Raab, which he crossed, and, following the course of that river, only halted at its junction with the Danube.

Here Charlemagne encamped for some days, and received the news of the success of his son Pepin, who, with the Duke of Friuli, had entered the territories of the Huns, and, encountering their army almost immediately, had totally defeated them, with immense slaughter. Every promise of success, therefore, had hitherto attended the expedition of the French monarch; but at this time one of the most terrible scourges which could afflict an army, almost entirely composed of cavalry, fell upon that of Charlemagne. A pestilential disease broke out amongst the horses with such violence, that before the sovereign could effect his retreat into Bavaria, nine-tenths of those which he had brought with him had perished.

Notwithstanding this disaster, the retreat of the Francs was not followed by any of those terrible consequences which might have taken place, had the Avars awoke from the panic, into which the rapid motions and immense forces of the French monarch had thrown them, in time to take advantage of the opportunity which accident produced in their favor. The Francs were suffered to retire unmolested, and carried with them an immense quantity of booty, as well as an innumerable multitude of prisoners. Thus far successful, it would seem that Charlemagne, at the time of his return, was fully determined to pursue the war he had commenced, to the utter subversion of the power of the Huns; but circumstance, that mighty disappointer of the best laid designs, intervened, and the monarch of the Francs never more set his foot within the confines of Pannonia as a warrior.

In accordance with his intention, however, of re-entering Hungary early in the spring, he proceeded no farther on his return towards France than Ratisbon, where he employed the winter in constructing a bridge of boats across the Danube, and in examining a new heresy which had arisen in the church. As this investigation tended not alone to the refutation of an idle schismatic, but brought on discussions attended with more important historical consequences, we must pause upon the subject longer than would have been otherwise necessary.

THE FELICIAN HERESY

Some short time before the precise period of which I write, Felix, who had been established Bishop of Urgel, a city within the limits of the Spanish march, had declared his belief, that Christ was merely the Son of God by adoption, and maintained his nature to have been human. This doctrine was first promulgated by him in a letter addressed to the Bishop of Toledo; but, not contented with the simple assertion of his own opinions, he endeavored to propagate them by various writings; and was, in consequence, brought before Charlemagne at Ratisbon. A council was immediately called by the King, consisting of such French prelates as happened to be in the neighborhood at the time. By these, the opinions of Felix were condemned as heretical, and he himself was sent to Rome for the judgment of Pope Adrian, to whom he confessed his error, and from whose hands he received absolution.

His doctrine, however, had gained ground; many of the Spanish bishops had embraced the Felician heresy; and it was found necessary to hold a more full and general synod at Frankfort, to consider the subject with greater solemnity and deliberation. In this assembly, Alcuin pleaded against the errors of Felix; and a solemn condemnation of the opinions of that prelate was again pronounced, and generally promulgated, together with Charlemagne's profession of faith. Disputations on points of doctrine almost always lead to the examination of new subjects, and the excitation of new disputes. It is probable, that had the Felician heresy never been examined, the council of Frankfort might never have been held; but, as it was, after deciding upon the first question, the assembled bishops proceeded to discuss the famous Nicene Council, (the second of Nice,) by the authority of which, the Empress Irene had restored the worship of images.

Either sufficient folly, superstition, or civilization, was wanting in the Frankish assembly, to adopt the pure idolatry of the Greek Church; and the Council of Nice was, consequently, declared by the Council of Frankfort to be useless and invalid, and its decrees were unanimously rejected. On this last occasion two legates were present on the part of the Pope, who had previously disavowed the messengers which had appeared in his name at the Council of Nice. Nevertheless, it can hardly be supposed, that the Roman pontiffs, whose separation from Greece had for its motive and justification the abolition of idol worship at Constantinople, would willingly countenance the rejection of the same idolatry in France.

No sooner had the Council of Frankfort decided upon this question, than the priests and learned men, who were gathered together by the patronage of Charlemagne for very different purposes, united to compose a long and studious refutation of the doctrines of the Nicene Council. The book, or rather books, thus produced, (called the *Libri Carolini*), though somewhat scurrilous, and not very argumentative, received the sanction of Charlemagne, were honored with his name, and were sent, together with an epistle, to the Roman pontiff by the hands of Angelbert, one of the ministers of the monarch.

The Pope replied to the French sovereign's letter, but not to his book; and, quietly allowing the subject to drop, left time and superstition to do their work, and lead the Francs from the toleration of images as useful memorials of faith, to their adoration as visible intercessors. Not long after this period appeared the false decretals, on which so much of the assumed authority of the Roman church has been founded; and it is not at all improbable, that the manufacture of these antedated decrees was first suggested to the policy of the Lateran by the bold tone of the Council of Frankfort. Undoubtedly, to put down such synods, or rather to command them, was the great object of those decretals; and it appears certain, that they were published between 794 and 800. Thus it is probable that Adrian attempted, without answering the arguments of the Gallic scribes, to annihilate such assemblies as that which had prompted them to write.

FROM THE CONSPIRACY OF PEPIN THE HUNCHBACK, TO THE FINAL SUBJUGATION OF THE SAXONS.

792 TO 804.

When Charlemagne first undertook to revenge the aggression which the Huns had committed in their irruptions into Bavaria, internal tranquility and external peace, offered the fairest opportunity for the endeavor, and the clearest prospect of success. But, before he could enter upon a second campaign, unexpected dangers assailed him on all sides. The first, and the most imminent of these dangers, as it menaced his own person, as well as the security of his dominions, arose in a conspiracy formed by several of his nobles, who had again occasion to complain of the cruelty of the Queen Fastrada. How that cruelty was exercised is not stated on this occasion, any more than on that of the conspiracy of Hartrad in 785; but it is easy to conceive many ways in which a harsh and imperious woman might bring the government of her husband into hatred with his people, though it is difficult to comprehend how such a monarch as Charlemagne permitted his power to be abused by anyone to whom it was partially delegated.

It is probable that the conspiracy was long in embryo, and that both real grievances, and restless ambition, added day by day to the numbers implicated. At length the discontent extended to a sufficient number of nobles to render success probable, and nothing farther was required but a chief to give dignity to the enterprise, and to direct the efforts of the conspirators. That chief was unfortunately too soon found, and found in the family of the monarch himself. In very early years, as I have before mentioned, Charlemagne had connected himself with a woman of inferior rank, named Himiltruda, but solely by the ties of illicit love. By her he had one son, named Pepin, who grew up with a shrewd keen mind, an irritable temper, and great personal deformity. Whether from any doubts in regard to paternity, or from some other cause, cannot be told, but Charlemagne so little regarded this child as one of his family, that he gave the same name which he bore to one of his legitimate sons. He educated him, however, and kept him at his court; but it is easy to conceive that, in a bad and irritable mind, the grief which his inferior share of love and authority must have produced, might easily be perverted to hatred towards his father, and malignant envy towards his more happy brothers.

The conspirators who had planned the subversion of their sovereign's throne, found it no difficult matter to bring Pepin the Hunchback, as he was called, to abet their schemes; and, as very frequently happens, the additional criminality of the child who revolted against his father, brought an aggravation of crime to all. To the plot for rising against their sovereign's authority, was added the design of taking his life, and that of all his legitimate sons. What share of private benefit was to accrue to each of the inferior conspirators is not known; but Pepin was to be raised to the throne of France, upon the dead bodies of his father and his brethren.

Pepin feigned an illness, in order to absent himself from the court; and the last arrangements were concluded for the proposed revolt and massacre; but it so happened that a certain monk, named Fardulphus, who had been brought by Charlemagne from Lombardy, shortly after the fall of Pavia, overheard by accident the unnatural resolution of the son, and the bloody designs of the conspirators; and instantly hastened to give information of their purpose.

His account was clear and distinct. The whole of the traitors were arrested and brought to trial; their crime was fully proved; and death was the sentence of all. The sword and the cord were the punishments inflicted on the conspirators in general. One only was spared, in whose case the ties of blood, and perhaps the belief that he had been made an instrument by more designing men, outweighed the cruel justice which demanded impartiality of infliction. Pepin was condemned to eternal seclusion in a monastery; and if we may credit the description of him given by the monk of St Gall, he carried to the cloister the same bitter and disappointed malignity, which had led him to conspire against his father and his king.

The sentence on Pepin and his accomplices was, of course, pronounced by a more impartial tribunal than the palace judgment seat of the offended monarch. The general assembly of the Prankish people was called, to take cognizance of the detected conspiracy, and, for the second time, awarded the extreme penalty of the law, for the crime of high treason.

Since the death of Charles Martel, a great change had taken place in the functions of this assembly, the constitution of which, during the first years of the French monarchy, probably varied with everything else, according to the character and power of the sovereign, and the circumstances of the times. Charles Martel, confident in his own superior vigor of mind and body, despising the clergy, who were then in almost as degraded a state as the kings, and fearful of fixing his authority on the support of the nobles, which had often proved the most unstable of all foundations, dispensed as much as possible with all assemblies of the people; and if he did not formally abolish them, suffered them to fall into desuetude. Pepin, on the contrary, with the object of a crown before his eyes, made use of the ancient meetings of the nation to obtain his purpose; but, jealous of the authority, which he had only shared with a view to confirm, he circumscribed afterwards the powers of the assemblies, and suffered them only to deliberate upon church discipline and general policy. Charlemagne, seated in the hearts of his people,—a nobler throne than the bucklers which raised his father to the acme of his fortune,—trusted the nation that trusted him; and, striving to wield the mighty sceptre of his own genius solely for the benefit of his subjects, neither feared nor encountered opposition to measures, which were conceived in the spirit of disinterested beneficence, and framed with wisdom far superior to his age.

Under his administration, the diets, or general assemblies of the people, constituted as before of all the nobles, both secular and ecclesiastical, exercised immense power. They formed the great council of state, destined to advise with the monarch on all questions of peace or war; and, indeed, on the whole conduct, of his empire. They framed the laws, and enacted the imposts for the following year; acted as the principal court of appeal for the whole people; and possessed all the prerogatives of the highest judicial as well as legislative body.

At these meetings in general, the ambassadors from foreign powers were received; and after the many conquests of Charlemagne, when the national assembly contained representatives from almost every continental country—from the shores of the Baltic to the British Channel, from beyond the Pyrenees to the depths of Pannonia—the splendor and singularity of the scene was such as to call forth many a glowing description from the pens of admiring contemporaries. At these assemblies, also, were presented those peculiar tributes, or fines, which vassals were required to pay by the tenure of their lands, and which were called *annua*, or *dona annualia*. Here, too, were received the general dues, collected throughout the kingdom, and the tribute, by which conquered nations acknowledged their dependence, while they retained their separate form of government.

In the first ages of the French monarchy, these assemblies were held, usually, only once in the year; but in the beginning of the second race of kings, (though at what period is not precisely known,) two meetings took place annually. The first of these, however, still remained the most important: regulating everything for the ensuing year that foresight could accomplish; while the second took heed of all which by accident, or from press of business, had been neglected in the first.

Such was the vast machine which Charlemagne employed, in the beneficent purpose of governing his people, for their own advantage. But, notwithstanding the great power which he ascribed to these assemblies, we find that he himself, without their concurrence, often made war or peace; and added laws to those which they had enacted. Thus, while he called the nation, for its own benefit, to participate in the exercise of the authority which his predecessors had assumed, he relinquished no particle of real power himself; and, indeed, the whole of his reign evinces, that if the monarch had confidence in his people, the people had confidence in their monarch; and that, showing his reliance on the nation by consulting them whenever it was possible, he was despotic through the affections of his subjects.

Nevertheless, although the diet served the king as a great and general council on all subjects of universal interest, and in regard to all permanent institutions, there were many sudden emergencies and minor details, on which it could not be consulted; and which, in after ages, have been generally submitted by sovereigns to particular advisers, forming their privy council.

On these occasions, Charlemagne either acted by his own judgment, or by the advice of some of the most prudent of his officers and attendants, who happened to be with him at the time. These he called to a private consultation, whether the question was warlike or political; but there does not appear to have existed any permanent and regular council, to assist the King in matters of general administration.

In regard to the dispensation of justice, however, a regular court was established in the royal palace, at which the King himself frequently presided. The principal officers of this court were called Counts of the Palace, or, in other words, Palace Judges. Of their functions in general, I have given a more detailed account before; and shall only repeat, that to them was a general appeal from all other courts throughout the country, though the right of judging in the first instance also belonged to them, if occasion required such a proceeding. Under the first race of French monarchs, one of these counts sufficed, and the duties were either small, or were neglected; but in the reign of Charlemagne,—who considered promptitude of decision as an essential part of justice—these officers were considerably multiplied. So much was this the case, that continual access could be had to judgment; and, to use the words of Mably, the business of a courtier was then not to offer flattery, but to administer the law. In aid of these counts, were a number of counsellors, called *Scabini Palatii*; and, with their assistance, the palatines held continual sittings in the royal residence, where causes of every kind were argued and decided, so that redress could never be retarded, nor offences remain long unpunished.

To this court, however, such conspiracies as those of Tassilo, Hartrad, and Pepin, were not submitted, although it would seem that their reference to a general assembly of the nation depended more on the impartial feeling of the monarch, than on the acknowledged incompetency of his palace court. It never appears that the national assembly was less severe in its judgment against traitors, than the most bigoted advocates of authority could have been; for, in all cases, we find that the indignant clamor with which the people doomed to death those who conspired against their King, showed at once how little the nation in general sympathized with the treason of individuals. Mercy, however, has always been one of the peculiar prerogatives of royalty; and Pepin, as well as Tassilo, though condemned by his countrymen, was pardoned by the voice of Charlemagne himself.

The service of the Lombard priest, who, by the loyal promptitude of his information, had saved the state, was not forgotten by the gratitude of the monarch. A year passed away, indeed, before it received its reward; but, at the end of that time, the abbacy of St Denis became vacant; and Fardulphus, so lately a poor and unknown clerk, was raised to one of the richest dignities in the Gallic church.

REVOLT OF SAXONY

To a mind like that of Charlemagne, the conspiracy of his subjects and the treason of his son, were in themselves profoundly painful; but other griefs and disappointments now fell thick upon the monarch of the Francs; and it seemed as if the whole labor of his life were to be done away at once, and to commence anew. Whether the secret negotiations of Pepin and his confederates had extended to Saxony or not, cannot be discovered, but scarcely had Charlemagne encountered the sad news of his son's treachery, and undergone the bitter task of judging his crime, ere he received intelligence that the people on whom he had spent so much time, and labor, and blood, to subdue and civilize, had suddenly broken the oaths they had taken, driven forth the teachers he had sent them, destroyed the churches he had built, and spilt the blood of his officers, wherever they could be found.

After the repeated defeats which they had received, while singly opposed to the monarch of the Francs, the Saxons had not ventured upon so bold an insurrection, as that which they now undertook, without having assured themselves of support. For this purpose, they had entered into a general league with all the Pagan nations round about; and having allied themselves with the Huns, whom they had been led to subdue, they no longer feared to renew the struggle, which, they imagined, disunion and want of allies had hitherto alone rendered ineffectual. The first symptom of their revolt was, as usual, a general return to paganism, and their first effort, an attack upon the troops which Theodoric, the cousin of Charlemagne, was leading back from the campaign against the Huns. A great part of the forces under his command consisted of Saxons and Frisons, and were consequently enemies, rather than fellow-soldiers. The rest, comprising several thousand Francs, taken by surprise, and overpowered by numbers, were cut to pieces to a man.

Such was the first news which reached Charlemagne after the discovery of Pepin's conspiracy; and scarcely had it been received, when another unexpected attack was announced to him. When the French monarch, as I have shown in the history of the campaign against the Avars, commanded his son Pepin, King of Italy, to lead his armies into Hungary, that young prince was already embroiled in hostilities with Grimwald, Duke of Beneventum, concerning the cities of Salernum, Acherontia, and Consia, which Grimwald, on receiving the investiture of the duchy, had promised to dismantle, but which he still held fortified and garrisoned. The young King of Italy, laying aside the affairs of his own government, instantly hastened, as before stated, to obey his father's commands, entered Hungary, defeated the Avars, and worked an important cooperation with the troops of Charlemagne. In return for this prompt and effectual obedience, Charlemagne, early in the winter, dispatched his son Louis, King of Aquitaine, with all the forces he could muster, to the aid of his brother in Italy. The King of Aquitaine, in hastening to share the glory of the war against Grimwald, had probably left the frontiers of his province somewhat exposed, so that the Saracens of Spain judged it a convenient opportunity to avenge the aggression which had been made upon their territory, and to recover a part of the ground which had been lost.

FRANCE INVADED BY THE SARACENS

An active and warlike prince then possessed the principal Mahomedan power in Spain; and placing at the head of his army Abdelmelec, an officer of a mind similar to his own, he ordered him to break in upon the Spanish march of Charlemagne, on the side of Gerona. This was accordingly done, and, with the usual rapidity of Saracen conquest, the Moors were at the gates of Narbonne before any force was ready to oppose them. The suburbs of that city were plundered and burnt, and the whole country round laid waste. The invaders then again turned towards Carcassonne, and were marching on in their desolating course, when they were encountered by the army of Wilhelm, Duke of Toulouse, one of the Counts of the March, who, with inferior forces, instantly resolved to give them battle. But, in this instance, the Francs met with an enemy equal to themselves in courage and skill, and superior in numbers. The forces of the Counts of the March were totally defeated; an immense number were slain; Wilhelm himself only escaped by a rapid flight; and the Saracens returned to Spain, loaded with booty and captives.

The breach of a great barrier he had taken immense pains to establish between Christian France and Mahomedan Spain—the total revolt of a country which he had spent half his life to subdue—the conspiracy of his own son against his existence,—such were the misfortunes that, almost at once, assailed the monarch of the Francs. But a glorious record of the greatness of his mind has been preserved by one who was an eye witness to his private life; and it may be boldly stated, on the authority of Eginhard, that, while Charlemagne never showed a sign of exultation in all his mighty successes, he never suffered a reverse to impair his confidence, or disturb his serenity.

Louis and Pepin, immediately on hearing of the conspiracy against the life of their father, hastened to his support and consolation; but finding the evil past, Pepin returned at once to Italy, with directions for carrying on the war against the Beneventines, while Louis, after a short stay, proceeded to

Aquitaine, in order to guard against any new irruption of the Saracens. No great operations took place in either of these wars for some time. That with the Beneventines proceeded with some degree of activity; but, while Pepin ravaged the territories of Grimwald, famine and pestilence wielded a more fatal sword in the heart of his own camp. The Saracen invasion, on the other hand, was not renewed; and Charlemagne was left free to carry on the war against the Huns and the Saxons.

His first effort was against the latter people; for the Avars had suffered too much from their recent defeats, to attempt a renewal of active hostilities for some time. Nevertheless, it may be necessary, before proceeding to conduct the Saxon war to its conclusion, to notice an undertaking of great magnitude, the expediency of which had been shown by the former campaign against the Avars, and which a prospect of renewed hostilities hastened in endeavor. In the course of the Hungarian war, Charlemagne had experienced so much benefit from the power of transporting his provisions, and a part of his army by water, that the great and magnificent scheme of establishing the same easy means of communication from one side of Europe to the other, suggested itself to his mighty mind.

It would be attributing too much to him, great as he was, to suppose that the first idea of the enterprise was suggested by any other thing than the desire of facilitating his military operations: but, at the same time, anxious as he always evinced himself for the revival of arts and sciences, the encouragement of manufactures, and the diffusion of commerce, it would be yielding too little credit to his greatness of mind to conceive, that such motives did not mingle with the course of his design, hasten it in its progress, and strengthen it against the difficulties of execution. Whatever might be the origin of his intention, and whatever collateral purposes might combine to urge the attempt, it is certain, that during his stay at Ratisbon, the project of joining the Danube and the Rhine occupied him deeply. The proximity of the two small rivers, the Rednitz and the Altmuth— the one of which falling into the Mein near Bamberg, communicates with the Rhine, while the other joins the Danube near Kelheim—seemed to offer great facility for its execution; and the state of the Danube in that day, very different from what it appears at present, held forth the greatest prospect of advantage. In the spring, Charlemagne had himself laid out the plan of the proposed undertaking; and ordered the works to be commenced but towards the autumn, he proceeded himself, by water, to the spot where they were in progress, ascending the stream of the Danube and the Altmuth, from Ratisbon to the proposed point of junction. The whole autumn was consumed by the monarch in superintending the execution of his design, and encouraging by his presence the host of workmen employed. As winter approached, he crossed the narrow space between the two streams; and, embarking on the Rednitz, by sailing down its course into the Mein, which easily conducted him to Frankfort, at once proved the advantages that might be derived from the passage, if the junction of the rivers could be effected. To this, however, obstacles were opposed, which were in that day insurmountable. Tremendous rains continued to fall during the autumn; and acting upon a light, unstable soil, destroyed during the night nearly the whole fruit of the labours of the day. As the season advanced, diseases broke out, and difficulties multiplied; and, at length, after having carried the works two thousand paces in length, and three hundred in width, the attempt was abandoned. The conception, however, was worthy of Charlemagne; and the vestiges of that great endeavor may still be seen near the little village of Graben, a splendid monument of that magnificent mind, which, in the midst of a barbarous age, devised so vast an enterprise.

At Frankfort, to which Charlemagne proceeded after this ineffectual attempt, was held the general council, some of the proceedings of which I have already alluded to; and there, also, died the Queen Fastrada, whose deeds had served to darken the splendor of her husband's character, and whose epitaph remains to show the emptiness of epitaphs in all ages.

It may be now necessary, without following any farther chronologically the war against the Saxons, to conduct the history of the struggle between them and Charlemagne to its conclusion; which may be done in a few words. As soon as the Council of Frankfort had terminated its sittings, the monarch of the Francs prepared to re-enter Saxony, and to repress the revolt which had taken place in that country. He divided his army into two parts, and, directing one under the command of his son Charles to pass by Cologne into the lower part of the Saxon territory, he himself led the other division, by the eastern provinces, towards a place called Sintfield, where a large Saxon force lay, with the intention of giving him battle. A sudden terror, however, seized them at the aspect of the monarch, and instead of having recourse to arms, they immediately surrendered themselves prisoners at discretion, implored and received the clemency they had so often abused, and gave hostages for the faith which was soon again to be violated.

Scarcely was the revolt suppressed than it once more broke out; and though no new chieftain sprang up to lead the Saxons, and to concentrate their efforts, they still waged a long and desolating warfare with the Francs, the history of which is but a catalogue of insurrections and repressions, without any incident of interest to render the detail either amusing or useful.

Charlemagne still pursued his purpose with unconquerable perseverance. If, from their proximity to France, their predatory barbarism, their utter faithlessness, their obstinate courage, and their savage cunning, as well as from the want of all natural barriers against them, and the impossibility of raising artificial ones sufficient to repel their incursions, the Saxons had been found by Charlemagne, at the beginning of his reign, the most dangerous enemies of his nation, he now felt himself far more called upon to subdue them utterly, since they had learned from the Francs themselves the art of war.

The conquest of the Saxons was not a matter of choice, but of necessity, involving at once the existence of the transrhenane provinces of France, the safety of all her northern allies, and her position amongst nations. To this war, therefore, Charlemagne in person devoted all his energies; and, at length, after having in vain attempted, by chastisement and by kindness, by force and by instruction, to tranquillize the whole of Saxony, he fell upon the extreme, but successful, measure, of transporting an immense number from the most turbulent tribes of the Saxons to a great distance from their native country. He accordingly entered Saxony early in the year 804, and, collecting his whole forces at the source of the Lippe, he detached several large bodies, which swept both banks of the Elbe of their inhabitants. Men, women, and children, were alike carried away, and spread over the face of France; and a great number were also transferred to Brabant and various parts of Flanders, where, at the time of the compilation of the Chronicle of St Denis, their language and many of their customs were still preserved.

Only one event took place during the course of these latter wars which is at all worthy of particular remark,—this was the first hostile collision between the Normans and the Francs. Some officers of Charlemagne accompanying his ambassador towards Sigifrid, King of Denmark, were met and slain by the piratical Northmen, and, as usual with savage nations, one aggression was immediately followed by another. The Normans, almost as soon as they had perpetrated the murder of the French ambassador, marched in a large body to attack the nation of Abodrites,—the firmest allies which the crown of France possessed amongst all the northern nations.

Thrasicon, Duke of the Abodrites, however, with Eberwin, an officer of Charlemagne, instantly opposed their progress with activity, vigor, and success. A severe conflict took place, in which many fell; but the principal loss was on the side of the Normans, who were routed and dispersed with terrible slaughter. These events took place sometime previous to the last severe measure by which Charlemagne terminated the Saxon war; but on the depopulation of the banks of the Elbe by the transportation of the Saxons, the good services of the Abodrites were not forgotten. The vacant country was bestowed upon that friendly tribe; and Charlemagne thus at once recompensed his most faithful allies, and placed a host of brave and warlike friends between his own dominions and the savage countries of the north.

It has been asserted—though without even a show of reason to support the assertion—that the conquest of Saxony by Charlemagne called the ferocious Normans upon the rest of Europe. Without applying to this idea the harsh term of absurd, a few words may suffice to show, that the subjugation of the Saxons, while it removed one immense swarm of predatory barbarians, did not in the least facilitate the progress of those which followed; but had, in fact, the most opposite effect.

That the Normans never invaded the South by land is sufficiently well known. All their expeditions were naval, made from their own coasts, and not at all depending upon what nation possessed the German territory; so that the Abodrites were a full and sufficient protection for the northern frontier of the Frankish dominions; and the subjection of the Saxons gave no facilities to the Normans in that direction. On the other hand, it is more than probable, that, had the Saxons not been subdued, the irruptions of the Normans would have been attended with far more terrible and desolating effects. The Saxons, under the government of the Frankish Emperors,— while in other circumstances they might have been the friends and allies of the Normans, proved their first enemies, and the strongest barrier to their progress in the north of Europe. Scarcely forty years after the death of Charlemagne the pirates of the north, landing on the coast of Saxony, suffered a most signal defeat from the Frisons and Saxons, whom the great monarch had conquered and civilized; and in 873 and 876, they were again and again overthrown in battle by the same Frisons. But had the Saxons not been so subdued and civilized, what would have been the probable result of their proximity to the Normans? Those two nations were, in fact, but two succeeding waves, in the long tide of barbarian invasion from the north. They were the last and most feeble of those waves, it is true; but had they been suffered to unite and roll on together, they might once more have overwhelmed Europe. Nor was it unlikely that they should unite. The great Saxon confederation offered a model, their proximity a means, and conquest and plunder an object akin to the habits and desires of both; while religion, manners, and national character, afforded a bond of union, and a strong assimilating principle.

Charlemagne conquered the Saxons, as the inveterate enemies of his nation; he attempted to civilize them, for the purposes of peace and security; and he strove to convert them, as a means of civilization. His objects, as a great king and a great patriot, were personal and national; but he no less conferred a signal and lasting benefit upon Europe at large, by subduing even one of those barbarian nations which had more or less desolated every land, and revelled in the blood of every people. That it was the natural tendency of all the northern nations to coalesce, for the purpose of conquest and plunder, is sufficiently evinced by the history of the Francs, the Saxons, and the Normans themselves.

FROM THE RENEWAL OF THE HUNGARIAN WAR, TO THE ELECTION OF LEO III

794 TO 796.

Having conducted the Saxon war to a conclusion, the history of Charlemagne may proceed with more regularity than it could possibly have done, embarrassed with continual repetitions of similar excursions and similar revolts. It is necessary, however, to retrograde in point of time, and to look back to the year 794, at which period the war already commenced with the Huns, or Avars, had been arrested in its progress, by the conspiracy of Pepin the Hunchback, and the insurrection of the Saxons.

While the monarch in person turned his arms against his more immediate enemies, and met the new danger the moment it appeared, internal dissentions, probably arising in their late defeats, sprang up amongst the Huns, which greatly facilitated the after efforts of the Francs, and soon afforded that nation a favorable opportunity of pursuing the war. During a temporary halt on the banks of the Elbe, in 795, Charlemagne received messengers from one of the chieftains of the Avars, named Thudun, expressing a wish to embrace the Christian religion, and offering to hold his territory of the monarch of the Francs. Though Charlemagne was not yet prepared to lead his armies against Hungary in person, his immediate answer was evidently favorable to the Hunnish prince; but the precise nature of the whole negotiation is not to be ascertained; and an obscure, perhaps impenetrable, veil hangs over the civil dissentions, which opened the way for the entire conquest of Pannonia. It became evident to Charlemagne, however, that internal strife reigned amongst his enemies; and every motive induced him to seize the favorable occasion which now presented itself. Thudun is represented, by all accounts, as one of the most wealthy and powerful of the Hunnish chieftains. He willingly submitted himself to France. The rest of the nations were in actual contention amongst themselves; and it was clear, that the moment had now arrived, for pursuing the unconcluded war with every prospect of success.

The subjugation of Saxony, as the enterprise most necessary to the security of his dominions, still occupied the monarch of the Franca himself; and, in consequence, he entrusted the important task of seizing the opportunity, and instantly renewing the war against the Huns, to Herric, Duke of Friuli; but, at the same time, he commanded Pepin, King of Italy, to hasten back from the south, and abandoning his strife with the Beneventines, to complete what Herric was about to commence.

The Lombards and the Huns had been continually at feud, and the accumulated animosity of many years, especially amongst the people of Friuli, soon procured for Herric, Duke of that province, an immense and willing army. Supported by this force, he invaded Hungary, swept the greater part of the country,—which, exhausted by civil wars, made little or no resistance,— and returned, bringing the most immense booty which had ever been captured by any of Charlemagne's armaments.

His steps were followed by Pepin, King of Italy, who, penetrating still farther, broke through all the fortifications of the Huns, whose monarch had been slain in the civil war, captured the royal fortress called the Ring, and carried off all that immense mass of wealth, which the Avars had accumulated, both by plundering the nations round about, and by wringing from the feeble empire of the East, the hoarded riches of centuries of prosperity. All the spoil was brought into France, and laid at the feet of Charlemagne; but that great monarch, after selecting some of the most splendid objects, as offerings to the church, distributed the rest of the enormous prize which had been thus captured, amongst his nobles and soldiers, so that the whole nation of the Francs "became rich, whereas they had been poor before".

At the same time, Thudun, who had betrayed his country probably with the sole purpose of his own aggrandizement, came willingly, with a number of his dependants, to receive baptism, and constitute himself a vassal of the crown of France. Charlemagne treated him with distinction and loaded him with presents, both as an inducement to himself to keep the faith he had voluntarily embraced, and as an incitement to his countrymen to follow his example, as far as regarded religion. Nevertheless it cannot be doubted, that the monarch of the Francs, though he might look upon the baptism of Thudun as an act of conviction, not of apostasy, could not regard his treason to his country in the same light, and, while he applauded the convert, must have despised the traitor.

For the purpose of affording religious instruction to the conquered people, Arnon, Bishop of Salzburg, was commanded to preach the Gospel in Pannonia; and both captives and populace were treated with every kind of lenity, in order that the consequences of this warfare—so different from those they were themselves accustomed to inflict—might not disgust the Avars with the religion of their conquerors.

That portion of the spoil taken by the Duke of Friuli from the Huns which was destined by Charlemagne for the Church of Rome, was carried to Italy by Angelbert, Abbot of St Richarius, or Centulensis, who was also charged to receive the oath of fidelity from the Roman people, and from Leo III, on his elevation to the chair of St Peter. On Christmas day, *AD* 799 Adrian, the tried and affectionate friend of the French monarch, had closed a long and active papacy, in the course of which, though he manifested several faults, he had exhibited many noble virtues and splendid talents. Though he did not possess the grand dignity of Gregory the Great, neither did he possess many of the petty absurdities which chequered the character of that extraordinary man. He was firm and courageous, keen and clear-sighted, humane, charitable, and consistent. He saw deeply into the characters of men, took extended and sagacious views, both in regard to the present and the future; and, had not a monastic education narrowed his mind, and the petty individuality of ecclesiastical policy contracted his feelings, it is probable that, free from the selfishness apparent in some of his negotiations, and the cunning contrivances which occasionally disgraced his pontificate, he would have been one of the greatest men of that or any other age.

When the news of the death of Adrian was conveyed to the ears of

Charlemagne, the monarch wept. He afterwards composed the epitaph of his early friend, which was sent to Rome, engraven on marble in letters of gold; but the noblest epitaph on the dead prelate was to be found in the tears of the hero.

The election of a new Pope had not in that day acquired the extreme importance which it received in after years, when the progressive encroachments of individual pontiffs, had raised the tiara above both the sceptre and the sword. It was a matter of sufficient consequence, however, to cause infinite intrigue and faction in Rome itself. On the death of Adrian, his nephews, who had been elevated by him to the highest ecclesiastical dignities of the Roman church, and who, beyond doubt, expected to obtain the apostolic seat in succession, were nevertheless excluded from the object of their ambition, and Leo, a Roman priest, the son of Arnulphus, was raised to the pontifical throne. No tumult, however, took place at the time; the wrath which the disappointed competitors felt profoundly, was covered with the specious mask of friendship; and the new Pope, secure in possession, instantly sent messengers to the great defender of the Roman See, to announce his election, and to do those acts of homage towards the Patrician, which were usual in feudal times on any new inheritor entering upon the feof of his predecessor. The forms of homage were ever various, according to the different terms of investiture, the different countries in which the territory lay, and the different circumstances under which the feof was granted. In the present instance, as the mark of his subjection, the Pope sent the keys of the tomb of St Peter, and the standard of the city of Rome; but, at the same time, he begged the monarch to dispatch some great man to Italy, who might, in his name, receive the oath of fidelity from the Roman people.

We must pause for a moment here, to consider this transaction, as it has been a matter of great difficulty and controversy amongst critics and historians. One party appeals to the positive testimony of Anastasius, that certain territories were bestowed upon the Church of Rome, and to the corroborative allusions of the *Codex Carolinus*; while the other relies on the acts of sovereignty exercised by Charlemagne in those very territories, and the acts of submission constantly performed by the Pope. The one party declares, that the gift was absolute, the other maintains that there was no gift at all; and those ambitious of the character of candour and moderation, assume, that Charlemagne gave, in a moment of liberality, what he chose to resume upon reflection. At the same time, both sides pervert the stubborn facts which are opposed, more or less, to every one of the hypotheses, which they uphold, and either corrupt the texts of the historians, mistranslate the passages which they dare hot admit, or violate all the rules of grammar, to give a forced interpretation to the most simple statement.

I have adopted, in the third book of this history, the opinion that the territories were granted to the Church of Rome, but that they were still held by feudal tenure from Charlemagne, in the same manner that other territories were held by his various vassals. My strongest reason for admitting this idea at first was, because it reconciled all the apparent difficulties which were opposed to every other hypothesis; and each event which I have since had occasion to notice, confirms my belief, that the monarch of the Francs, always reserving to himself the absolute sovereignty, had bestowed upon the Popes and their successors the Exarchate, the Pentapolis, and the Duchy of Rome, merely as feofs. Thus the donation stated by Anastasius, and alluded to by the Codex Carolinus, is admitted, and yet the acts of sovereignty exercised by Charlemagne explained, while the dispatch of the keys and the banner appears as an ordinary act of homage from the new vassal to his sovereign. Neither does the fact of the Roman people having sworn allegiance personally to Charlemagne, at all prove that the monarch had made no donation, as some writers have imagined, nor at all militate against the opinion, that the provinces specified were granted as feudal lands. On the contrary, we find that it was the common custom, in the cases of high feofs, not only for the great vassal himself, but for all his principal nobles also, to take an oath of fidelity to the general sovereign,—an instance of which may be found in the homage of Tassilo, Duke of Bavaria, mentioned in the former part of this work.

BUILDING OF THE PALACE AT AIX-LA- CHAPELLEU (AACHEN)

We must now turn for a moment to the internal occupations of the French monarch. With Adrian, the late Pope, Charlemagne had lived in that constant reciprocation of friendly offices, which we seldom find between men of so elevated a station; and it has been supposed, that the presents selected from the spoil of the Huns, though afterwards conveyed by the monarch's command to Leo, were originally reserved for his predecessor. Indeed, a gift had been conferred by the prelate shortly before his death, which Charlemagne was not likely to leave long unrequited. This consisted of the beautiful marbles and mosaics of the ancient palace of Ravenna, which had been sent to France by the pontiff, for the purpose of ornamenting the superb buildings then about to be raised at Aix-la-Chapelle. These specimens were, in every respect, invaluable, for although, as I have before shown, architecture, as a science, was by no means unknown in France at that time, and though the kind of mixed Roman, which has been sometimes denominated Lombard, was then making great progress in that country, yet no such works could be produced in any branch of art as those which were still to be seen at Rome and Ravenna, accomplished when the united powers of the East and the West had brought knowledge and skill to their highest perfection.

At Aix-la-Chapelle, situated nearly in the centre of his vast dominions, and in a salubrious climate, Charlemagne had fixed upon a spot for building a palace, in the neighborhood of some natural warm baths,—a Roman luxury, in which the Frankish monarch particularly delighted. All that the great conception of Charlemagne could devise, and the art of the age could execute, was done, to render this structure, and the church attached to it, worthy of their magnificent founder. But no account can be given; for nothing has come down to the present age which can justify anything like detailed description. Nevertheless, a number of circumstances in regard to this building are occasionally mentioned in the historians of the time, that convey an idea of vastness and splendor, which probably might have been lost had minute examination been possible. Immense halls—magnificent galleries—a college—a library —baths, where a hundred persons could swim at large— a theatre, and a cathedral— a profuse display of the finest marble—gates and doors of wrought brass—columns from Rome, and pavements from Ravenna,—such, we know, to have been some of the many things which that great palace displayed.

Workmen were gathered together from every part of Europe; and, though but small reliance can be placed upon the anecdotes related by the Monk of St Gall, it is evident, from every account, that the building must have been the most magnificent architectural effort which Europe had beheld since the days of the splendor of ancient Rome.

Besides the palace itself, we find, that an immense number of buildings were constructed around it, for the accommodation of every one in any way connected with the court; and adjoining, were particular halls, open at all times, and in which all classes and conditions might find a refuge from the cold of night, or from the wintry storm.

Within the walls, was that famous domestic college, on the maintenance, extension, and direction of which Charlemagne, amidst all the multiplicity of his occupations, found means to bestow so much of his time and attention. But every trace of his actions tends to prove, that his first and greatest object—to which even conquest was secondary, if not subservient—was to civilize his dominions, and to raise mankind in general from that state of dark ignorance into which barbarian invasion had cast the world. The great primary step which he had taken had been the restoration of general order, and the re-establishment of individual security by a variety of laws—perhaps not the best that could be framed upon abstract principles, but beyond doubt the best which could be adapted to the age and society in which he lived. By his care the disorders which had pervaded France, even under his father's reign, were speedily done away; and security opened the way for literature and art. These we have seen encouraged by the monarch in their advance; and by this time, his efforts were beginning to bear fruit. The schools which he had established in every different province and cure, throughout his dominions, had now made great progress. Alcuin had returned from England to fix his perpetual abode in France. St Benedict, the younger, had already distinguished the school established by his monastery, had gathered together a considerable library, and had rendered his success a matter of emulation. The college of Orleans, under the care of Theodulphus, bishop of that city, had by this time acquired a name in Europe; and while science had become an object of ambition throughout the whole of France, the means of acquiring it were multiplied in every province. So much, indeed, had been the progress made by the French people since the commencement of the reign of Charlemagne, that, whereas at his accession letters were unknown, and all was darkness, at the present period we find innumerable efforts in literature, comprising both poetry and prose, which, though rude and dusty with ages of forgetfulness, still show the human mind struggling up like a Titan from the mountains which had been thrown upon its head.

During the first ten or fifteen years after its establishment, the college of the palace had probably followed the court during its frequent migrations, notwithstanding the number of members, and the difficulty of transporting the library, which soon became considerable. Many circumstances, however, seem to show, that after the construction of the great palace at Aix-la-Chapelle, it became fixed in that place. The library, we know, was there concentrated; and several of the books thus collected, such as the *Codex Carolinus*, &c. have come down through a long line of emperors to the present day. Indeed, a great part of the most valuable literature of former ages, was preserved alone by the efforts of the French monarch for the revival of science; and the link of connection between ancient and modern civilization, owes its existence, as much to the endeavors of Charlemagne, as even to the papal preservation of antique Rome.

In speaking of the domestic college thus established by the Frankish King, I must not omit to notice a curious trait, of even childish levity, which mingled with some of his grandest efforts, for the improvement of his people. Amongst a number of very doubtful anecdotes concerning this institution, we find one fact mentioned, of which we have incontestable proof in the letters of the monarch himself, and which may well go to swell the long catalogue of the puerilities of philosophers, and follies of the wise.

This was the adoption of emblematical names by all the persons connected with the palace college; so that we find Alcuin himself writing to Charlemagne as David, and the monarch of the Francs addressing Angelbert, his chancellor, as Homer.

Notwithstanding this little absurdity, which may be conceded to the darkness of the age, Charlemagne gave an example to his subjects of that ardent and indefatigable zeal in the pursuit of knowledge, which alone could lead others on the path along which he sought to guide them. Even the most dry and fatiguing parts of studies, which now form the very rudiments of education, he went through, when he had arrived at manhood. Under Peter of Pisa, whom he brought with him into France, after the conquest of Lombardy, he studied grammar; and Alcuin, at a still later period, became his teacher of rhetoric, dialectics, and astronomy; in the latter of which sciences, the scholar soon excelled his master. Gifted naturally with great eloquence, Charlemagne assiduously cultivated a knowledge of various languages, spoke Latin with the same facility as his own tongue; and acquired a thorough acquaintance with Greek, though the soft sounds of that musical language were difficult of pronunciation to the lips of the Frankish King. At the same time, the national dialect of the Francs was not neglected by the monarch. Licentious and irregular, it was at once corrupt and barren; and Charlemagne applied himself earnestly both to purify and enrich it. The names of the months and of the winds, which had formerly comprised both Latin and barbarian terms, he changed to others of a Teutonic origin. A grammar of the language was commenced under his inspection; and he ordered the old and barbarous poems, which sang the wars and actions of the ancient kings, and which had previously been only transmitted by tradition, to be preserved in registers for the benefit of posterity.

About this time, also, the mode of writing underwent a change. The rude characters employed under the Merovingian race were disused, and the small Roman letters were introduced. As the spirit of improvement proceeded, new alterations were sought; and some years afterwards, to write in the large Roman capitals, became the mode of the day, the initial letter of each paragraph being always highly ornamented, and sometimes painted, many specimens of which have come down to the present time. Though at an advanced period of life when this method of writing first began to prevail, Charlemagne endeavored to learn it, and even caused models of the letters to be laid by his pillow, that during the waking moments of the night, he might practise the art which he sought to acquire.

Nor did the monarch remain satisfied with leading the way himself on the path of knowledge which he desired the whole nation to follow; nor content himself with bestowing on his children a careful and judicious education, both mental and corporeal; but, by constantly proposing in writing questions for solution, addressed to the various prelates and teachers of his realm, he forced them to exercise their talents and cultivate their minds, under the severe penalty of shame and ridicule. On the other hand, literary merit was never without its reward, for though, as far as we can discover, Charlemagne, wise in his generosity, seldom if ever gave more than one profitable charge at once to one man, yet those who distinguished themselves by talent and exertion, were sure to meet with honor, distinction, and competence.

Sometimes the nature of these recompenses must have rendered the conferring of them a painful duty on the part of the monarch, as it inevitably separated him from many of his best loved friends. Thus, in the year 796, to which I have now conducted the history of Charlemagne, his nomination of Alcuin to the abbacy of St Martin, of Tours, deprived him of that society in which he had been long accustomed to delight. Nevertheless, some compensation must have been derived by the monarch in this instance, from perceiving, that the sacrifice he had made produced great benefit of that particular kind which he was most anxious to effect. At Tours, Alcuin immediately established a school, which soon became the most famous of all those that had lately arisen in France. From it, as from a parent, sprang a multitude of others; and knowledge was progressively diffused over a large tract of country, which had previously been destitute of any sufficient means of instruction.

I have before pointed out, that France alone was not the sole object of the monarch's care in these respects; and while speaking on this subject, I may be permitted to cast my view a little farther forward than the precise epoch to which the military and political events of this reign have been conducted. In those countries which Charlemagne had added to his native dominions religion and civilization advanced hand in hand. We have seen, through the whole of his life, that the mitigation of the ferocious character of the Saxons was one of the principal objects of his endeavor; and never, either during the fresh revolts which broke out after the Hungarian campaign, or when the whole of Saxony was at length totally subdued, did Charlemagne relax for a moment in his efforts to soften their barbarism, and court them to a better state.

Schools of various kinds were established throughout Saxony; and though the particular institutions of many of these are now lost, yet we find the instance of one perpetually endowed by the French monarchal Osnaburg in Westphalia, where Greek and Latin were to be taught to all applicants. Such were the means he employed to raise his new territories from a state of barbarism; and the immense progress which we find the Saxons had made within the years after their subjugation justifies the policy of the monarch, and evinces the wisdom with which his endeavors were conducted. Other means however, were at the same time employed; the rich and extensive plains of Germany from a savage wilderness were turned into a polished and cultivated land. Cities and towns rose up on the path of Charlemagne, and a civilized population became generally mingled with the original citizens of the country.

Some of these cities still remain, and some have vanished away beneath the decaying footsteps of time; but while France herself, soon after the death of Charlemagne, relapsed into anarchy and confusion, and sank rapidly down from the height to which he had raised her, the change which the great monarch had wrought in Saxony was never done away; and Germany has yet to bless him as the guide which first led her from darkness unto light.

FROM THE RENEWAL OF HOSTILITIES IN THE SPANISH MARCH, TO THE DEATH OF THE QUEEN LUIDGARDE.

797 TO 800.

The successful irruption on the part of the Saracens, mentioned in another place, had not only served the temporary purpose of carrying terror and destruction into the heart of the ancient Septimania, but had also procured more solid advantages to the Mohammedan princes of Spain, by shaking the Spanish March, or defensible frontier which Charlemagne had pushed forward far within the limits of the original conquests of the Moors. Barcelona, Huesca, and the entire seashore of Catalonia had now fallen into their hands; and it would seem that this line of coast became the great place of refuge for all those predatory armaments with which the Saracens now swept the whole extent of the Mediterranean. Sicily, Sardinia, the Balearic Islands, and even the coasts of Italy were all in turn made the subject of attack; and Majorca and Minorca remained for some time in the hands of the Moors.

Charlemagne, as the greatest and most zealous of the Christian monarchs at that period in Europe, was applied to by the sufferers; and he was never appealed to in vain. Notwithstanding a fresh insurrection in Brittany, and the war which he was then still waging with the Saxons, the monarch of the Franks made the most immense exertions to aid his Christian brethren in their struggles against the aggressions of the infidel. The Bretons were speedily subdued; and while he himself remained to direct the operations of his army in Saxony, he dispatched a strong force to expel the Moors from the Balearic Isles,—an expedition which was crowned with the most triumphant success.

At the same time, domestic dissensions among the Arab princes of Spain encouraged him to renew the war upon the Catalonian frontier; and the desire of assisting the Gothic Christians of the Asturias in their struggle against the Saracens gave vigor to his determination, and promptitude to his endeavors. Issem, the son of Abderaman, the Moavite, had expelled his brother Abdallah from the Moorish territories in Spain, and had driven him into exile in Africa. A number of the Saracens, however, of Catalonia and Arragon, retained their affection for the exiled prince; and either from private ambition or from attachment to Abdallah, Zatun, who, on the capture of Barcelona from the Franks, had been named governor of that city, sought the French sovereign at Aix-la-Chapelle, and surrendered the territory which he had been appointed to defend.

Although this act of treachery was not committed without an express stipulation that the territories thus yielded were still to be entrusted to Zatun, yet, according to the Frankish accounts, his homage to Charlemagne was complete; and the opportunity now afforded of diverting a part of the Moorish forces from the war with the Spanish Christians, and of regaining the eastern portion of the Spanish March, was not lost upon the monarch of the Franks. His son Louis, King of Aquitaine, then in his twentieth year, a period of existence when the springs of enterprise and zeal are unoppressed by the heavy load which all the difficulties and obstacles of life soon cast upon them, was commanded to march into Catalonia, and take possession of the country, which the Saracen irruption had snatched from the power of France.

Louis, however, notwithstanding his youth, wanted entirely the active vigor of Charlemagne; and though he made frequent expeditions into Spain, obtained some successes, took Lerida, and finally recovered the Spanish March, Huesca baffled his efforts more than once; and a marked difference was to be seen in all his proceedings, from the rapid and sweeping energy which had borne forward his progenitors to conquest and to empire. It has been frequently asserted, that the young King of Aquitaine either advanced in person to the assistance of Alphonso, the Christian monarch of Spain, or sent a large detachment to his aid: but as neither the annalists of Charlemagne nor the especial biographers of Louis himself make any mention of such a circumstance, it must not be admitted as an historical fact. Nevertheless, it cannot be doubted that a great and effectual diversion was operated in favor of Alphonso by the warfare carried on by Louis in Catalonia; and much of the success of that great monarch, in his struggles with the infidel strangers, who, locust-like, had invaded his land, may be attributed to the divided state of the Moorish councils and armies. Thus, while the Gothic Christians, going on from conquest to conquest, succeeded in establishing a united and independent kingdom, and while Alphonso, triumphant at the very gates of Lisbon, dispatched part of the spoil of the Moors to Charlemagne, less indeed as a gift than as a proof of victory, and an inducement to cooperation, the monarch of the Franks used every means to retain the Saracen forces on the frontier, and promote the divisions which existed in their empire.

Many opportunities for effecting this purpose presented themselves. Abdallah, the exiled brother of Issem, sought the court of the Frankish sovereign, and, according to his own request, was sent back with honor to Spain, in order to head, the party of his adherents. Zatun, the Emir of Barcelona, soon forgetting his engagements with the Christians, returned to the domination of his former lord, and called back the Saracen power into the Spanish March. A new war instantly succeeded; and after a lingering siege of two years, Barcelona was recaptured by the Franks, and the defensive frontier of France, on the Spanish side of the Pyrenees, was restored to the state in which Charlemagne had left it. All these wars in the north of Spain acted as a continual drain upon the Moorish forces, and enabled Alphonso to contend with some degree of equality against their power. At the same time, the Spanish March was restored, and the passes of the Pyrenees were defended, by the care of Louis, with fortresses the remains of which, either real or imaginary, are shown to the present day.

These objects being attained, Charlemagne made no other effort on the side of Spain. It is true, he might have urged his conquest farther, and possibly, taking advantage of the weakness of all parties in the Peninsula, might have added that territory also to those which he already possessed. Some persons have censured him for not making the attempt; and indeed, had either conquest or conversion been his sole object in any of his enterprises, the situation of Spain would have invited his march. But in all his wars, either the security of himself or his allies had been an ingredient in his motives. Such inducements did not extent in the case of Spain: Alphonso was already well able to defend himself, especially after a vigorous diversion had given him the means of establishing his power on a firm basis; and the Pyrenees formed a sufficient frontier barrier for the French territory, as long as the Spanish March was preserved. No motive, therefore, but simple ambition could have carried Charlemagne back to Spain after these objects were accomplished; and the ambition of that great man was always mingled with something which elevated it far above the ordinary passion of vulgar conquerors.

Having, both in regard to the Saxons and the Saracens of Spain, violated the exact march of chronology for the sake of brevity and perspicuity, I may be permitted also to conclude the warfare with the Huns in this place, and to dispose of various other occurrences of minor consequence, in order that the more important events which were preparing in Italy may be noticed with separate distinctness.

The active hostilities which, from time to time, took place against the Avars, like those carried on with the Saracens, were no longer conducted by Charlemagne in person; and the annalists of the time, who principally directed their attention to the proceedings of the monarchy leave in very great obscurity both the motives for renewing the war and the circumstances which took place in its course. It is certain, however, that very shortly after the last victorious expedition of Pepin King of Italy, Thudun, the Hunnish chief, who had abandoned his religion and betrayed his country, unscrupulously violated the oaths which he had taken to

Charlemagne; and, probably, with a view to render himself master of the whole territory, took arms, and prepared to offer a more desperate resistance than the Franks had hitherto encountered. Two of Charlemagne's officers, one named Count Gerold, and the other Herric, Duke of Friuli, collected their forces with all speed, and being already posted on the frontier, hastened severally forward into Hungary, in hopes of suppressing the revolt before time and preparation had rendered it general and dangerous. It is probable that the desire of taking their enemy by surprise engendered some degree of negligence on the part of both the Frankish generals. Advancing from opposite sides of the country, the one, the Duke of Friuli, was led into an ambuscade and killed, with all his followers; while Count Gerold suddenly found himself in presence of a Hunnish army, and was slain as he was addressing his army, preparatory to a general battle, the event of which is doubtful.

From that period the course of the warfare against the Huns remains obscure; but that Charlemagne did not suffer the death of his generals to remain unavenged, nor the hostilities against the Avars to linger, is evident from various circumstances; and in the year 803 we find him at Ratisbon, writing for the return of his army from Hungary. That army returned completely victorious; and the Huns, now permanently subdued, embraced the Christian religion, and did general homage to the Frankish sovereign.

The fate of Thudun is not known. Some accounts declare that he was taken and executed for the breach of the vows which he had before lighted to the monarch of the Franks, but there is every reason to believe this statement to be perfectly erroneous; and, at the final subjection of his nation, we hear of a prince named Zudun, or Zodan, Duke of Panonia, who, with the rest of his countrymen, claimed and received the clemency of the king. That the individual who did so was the same who had before submitted in the year 795 is not only probable, but almost certain.

Although Charlemagne had to treat with the Hunnish people as a conqueror with the conquered; and although the state of weakness to which they had been reduced by the warfare they had themselves begun with the Franks left them no powers of resistance though their country was little better than an empty desert, and their armies scattered like dust before the wind, yet we do not find that the monarch took any base or unworthy advantage of their prostrate situation. He required some time to deliberate, we are told, upon the arrangements to be entered into with the vanquished people; but, at length, he dismissed those who had sought him at Ratisbon with kindness and honor. No precise information, indeed, exists in regard to the degree of submission which he demanded, or in respect to the influence he exercised in the government of the conquered country. But that he left the nation all their native laws and old forms of administration is clear; though we may infer, from the circumstance of his ratification having been afterward required for the nomination of a Chagan, that his assent was requisite on the elevation of any individual to the supreme dignity of the state. To spread the Christian religion universally among the people, and to ensure the purity of the doctrine taught, appears to have been the only interference which Charlemagne exercised in the domestic affairs of the Avars. But, at the same time, it would seem, that, in accordance with the advice of Alcuin, he exempted them from the payment of tithes to the priests whom he sent among them, and defended them with ready zeal from the attacks of external enemies.

For nearly thirty years Charles the Great had reigned over the Franks, seeing his dominions, his power, and his fame increase every hour. His court was not only the refuge of the unfortunate, but was the resort of ambassadors from all nations; and a history of the various embassies, and their causes, which from time to time reached his presence, would afford no incomplete picture of the general progress of the world during his life. Besides the envoys twice sent by Alphonso, the Gothic King of Spain, bearing rich presents, and instructed to call their monarch the faithful vassal of the French king, a number of other messengers presented themselves at his court during the years 797-8-9, the most important of whom were those either directly or indirectly, dispatched by the empire of the East.

IRENE, THE BYZANTINE EMPRESS, AND CHARLEMAGNE

For many years Irene, the beautiful Athenian girl who had been bestowed on Leo the Isaurian, had continued, after the death of her husband, to sway with delegated power the sceptre of the East, as the guardian of her son; but, after a time, her authority became irksome, both to the prince, whom she strove still to enthrall, after the period of pupilage was over, and to the people, from whom she exacted an undue submission. The Armenian guards of the emperor, the countrymen of the wife which she herself had given him, were the first to oppose her encroachments; the youthful Constantine seconded their efforts, resumed the power which had been entrusted to his mother, and consigned her once more to a private station. But power to man or woman is like blood to the lion—once tasted, it brings a consuming thirst for more. What Irene could not accomplish by boldness she undertook by art. She submitted with apparent resignation; and while she attempted by flattery and caresses to regain the affection of her son, she laid within the walls of his palace a deep intrigue for his destruction. One of the first steps of the young emperor, after he had taken the staff of rule into his own hands, was to seek the friendship of the great monarch of the Franks; and he transmitted to the patrician Nicetas, who then governed Sicily, an epistle, to be sent forward to Charlemagne, in order to bring about a closer alliance than had hitherto existed between the courts of France and Constantinople. In compliance with the emperor's commands, Nicetas instantly dispatched the letter by an envoy named Theoctistes, who found the monarch at Aix-la-Chapelle. He was immediately admitted to an audience, and acquitted himself of his charge; but his embassy proved fruitless; for, while still upon his journey, a change had taken place in the Eastern capital. The plots of Irene had been successful: Constantine VI indeed, suspecting some design against his liberty, had made his escape for a time from Constantinople; but his flight did not place him beyond the influence of his mother's cabals. His officers and attendants were the creatures of her will; and fears lest their treason should be betrayed by its instigator gave them courage to accomplish their crime. Constantine was carried back by force to his capital, to his palace, and to the chamber of his birth, wherein his own servants, by the commands of his own mother, deprived him for ever of the light of day.

When any singular natural phenomenon follows or precedes the great actions or mighty crimes of human beings, the superstitious vanity which teaches man to regard himself as the prime object of all creation easily points out a sympathy in the inanimate world with the interests of mankind. Thus, an extraordinary darkness which pervaded the mater part of Europe during seventeen days after the unnatural crime of Irene, was universally attributed, in those times, to her cruel ambition. Undaunted, however, by omens, the empress, now acknowledged sole ruler of the East, hastened to score her power as far as human cunning might prevail. To court the sovereigns around her to peace or alliance, till such time as her authority was established at home, was one great object; and the next ambassadors from Constantinople which appeared at the court of Charlemagne were Theophilus and Michel, surnamed Ganglianos, two men of high station and distinction, who came charged, apparently, with the unimportant task of soliciting the enlargement of Sisinius, an officer who had been captured in Italy, on the defeat of Adalgisus. He was, it is true, the brother of Tarasius, Patriarch of Constantinople, who had been the secretary and favorite of the empress; but the patrician Michel and his companion were entrusted, in reality, with a more important mission—that of communicating to the monarch of the Franks the cruel treason which had been perpetrated on the person of the unhappy Constantine, and of negotiating a peace between Constantinople and France.

The envoys stated, that the fallen emperor had been blinded by his attendants, on account of his depravities and tyranny; and Charlemagne, whether he believed the tale or not,—though it is probable, from his annals perpetuating the same story, that he did,—entered willingly into the alliance proposed by Irene; and, at her request, sent back to his native country the unfortunate Sisinius.

CHARLEMAGNE AND HAROUN AL RASCHID

About this time, which in the life of, Charlemagne was a period of negotiations; his first communication was opened with the great ruler of Asia. The throne of the caliphs had, sometime before, passed to the family of the Abbassides, and the mightiest of that family now governed the eastern continent. Haroun al Raschid, so well-known in both real and fabulous history, first signalized his arms against the empress of Constantinople, while yet she wielded the scepter in the name of her son. He also, at that period, acted only as deputy for his father Mohadi. But after having advanced to the shores of the Bosphorus, and having treated with Irene for the security of her territories, he retired on receiving seventy thousand dinars of gold; and assumed, soon afterward, the sovereign power, on the death of his father and his brother. Custom, with most of the oriental nations, is very readily fixed into a law, known among some of them by the name of *adeth*, or *canoun*; and, once established, is regarded as a kind of covenant, which is as binding as if written. Whether this understanding existed in the time of Haroun al Raschid or not, I do not know, but the seventy thousand dinars of gold, after having once been given, soon grew into an annual tribute, which the Greek empire found less expensive to pay than to neglect. Either by the conveyance of this tribute, or by the expeditions to which its occasional cessation gave rise, a constant intercourse of some kind was maintained between Constantinople and Bagdad. Various other means of communication also existed, both in the wanderings of the Jews, who were at this period spread over, and tolerated in all lands, and in the nascent efforts of commerce on the chores of the Mediterranean.

There were then but two great monarchs in the world; and the ears of the caliph were filled with the wars and enterprises of the sovereign of the Franks, who was either an open adversary or but a cold ally of the Greeks, on whom he himself trampled, and who was also the continual enemy of the Ommiads of Spain, whom the Abbassi contemned as heretics, and hated as rivals. The caliph beheld in the European king the same bold and daring spirit, the same rapid energy, the same indefatigable zeal, the same magnificent designs, by which he himself was animated, and similarity of mind, free from rivalry of interests, produced admiration, respect, and affection. The feelings were the same in the breast of Charlemagne; and reciprocal regard soon produced a more direct communion. At length, in 797, one of those wandering strangers who are so frequently to be found in the courts of monarchs undertook to conduct ambassadors from the French king to the presence of the caliph. Three envoys were accordingly sent under the conduct of Isaac the Hebrew, as he is called by the annalists; and were charged to offer the presents and the friendship of the French sovereign to the ruler of Asia. The Frankish ambassadors reached the court of the caliph in safety; and, having acquitted themselves of their mission, and received the gift of an elephant, which they had been instructed to request, prepared to return to Europe. The change of climate, however, proved fatal to the Franks; and Isaac the Jew, leaving the bones of his companions in Asia, returned alone, bringing with him the elephant and other presents from the oriental sovereign, together with the proud but flattering assurance from the mighty follower of Mohammed, that he regarded the friendship of Charlemagne more than that of all the monarchs of the universe.

Such were the feelings of Haroun al Raschid towards the sovereign of the Francs, and such was the state of intercourse between them when the patriarch of Jerusalem, moved by what circumstances we do not know, dispatched a monk of Mount Olivet to the court of France, bearing his benediction, and various relics from the holy places of the East, to the great promoter of Christianity in Europe.

Long prior to that period (about the year 637) Jerusalem had fallen under the yoke of the Saracens and the Christians of the Hebrew capital had been doomed for a long time to a general capitation-tax of two pieces of gold for each individual of the impoverished population. Three-fourths of the town also, had been usurped by the infidels; and whether the patriarch, in his embassy to Charlemagne, sought to mitigate the sufferings of his flock by securing intercession with the caliph, or was actuated solely by reverence for the many deeds of charity which the French monarch performed in favor of the pilgrims to the holy shrine, and the poor Christians of the African and Syrian coast, his conduct was at all events, attended with the most beneficial effects to the faithful inhabitants of the holy city.

The messenger of the patriarch was received with honor and kindness; and, anxious to spread comfort and consolation to every quarter of the world, Charlemagne suffered him not to depart without an effort to ameliorate the situation of the Asiatic Christians. Zacharias, one of the ecclesiastics of his palace, was ordered to accompany the Syrian monk to the presence of the caliph, and to use all the influence of the name of Charlemagne, in order to procure the favor of the Mohammedan monarch for his Christian subjects. At the same time, the sovereign of the Franks, sent innumerable rich offerings to the shrine of the holy sepulchre, together with alms for the consolation of pilgrims and travellers.

Charlemagne had not calculated wrongly on the magnanimity or the friendship of Haroun. The monarch of the East not only interposed from that moment the shield of his protection between the Christians of Jerusalem and the oppression of his vicegerents, but he placed it in the power of Charlemagne himself to provide for their wants, their safety, and their comfort.

In reply to the message of the French monarch, the caliph sent back the priests who had been dispatched to his court, bearing to Charlemagne the keys of the holy places, together with a standard, as the mark of sovereignty in Jerusalem.

Nor was this gift unimportant, either in the eyes of him who gave, or of him who received; for it must be remembered that the Mohammedans look upon the holy city with reverence little, if at all, inferior to that with which it is regarded by the Christians.

From that time forward, during the whole reign of Haroun al Raschid, the inhabitants of Jerusalem, to use the words of William of Tyre, seemed to live more under the domination of Charles than under that of their original sovereign. But Charlemagne made no vain, no ambitious, and no offensive use of the power with which the caliph entrusted him. He attempted to establish no claim of permanent domination—to revive no ancient pretensions to the city; he interfered not with the Moslem—he exercised no act of dominion, but for the consolation of the Christians of the place, and for the comfort and protection of the pilgrims to the holy shrine. For those objects, indeed, he spared neither care, nor trouble, nor expanse; and we find, that during his whole life, in the midst of a thousand other labours, and surrounded by anxieties without number, he never forgot or neglected his charitable exertions for the Christians of the East. Alms, assistance, and protection evinced his kindness and his zeal, during his life; and, long after his deaths a monastery, an hospital, and a library consoled the pilgrim, and perpetuated his bounty.

Haroun al Raschid esteemed the moderation as much as the talents of the French monarch; and the very temperate use of authority, which has caused the gift of the holy city to be, doubted by modem historians, secured him the regard of his great contemporary. Other embassies followed, from the Asiatic to the European court. A variety of magnificent presents attested the continued esteem of the caliph for his Christian friend; and unbroken amity and undiminished admiration reigned between the two greatest monarchs of the age, during the whole course of their mutual reign. The carriage of such objects as the presents sent from Bagdad to France was, of course, attended with no small inconvenience; and the neglected state of the science of navigation rendered the journeys of the ambassadors long and dangerous. Between three and four years were generally consumed in a mission from one capital to another and, indeed, it happened more than once that even after arriving within the dominions of the Frankish monarch, the envoys had still to seek him over a tract nearly as extensive as that which they had before crossed. Where a much greater degree of civilization exists in the monarch than in his subjects, where his mind must conceive every great undertaking, and his eye must see it executed, without relying on the inferior spirits that toil, with the pace of pigmies, after his giant footsteps, it is seldom, of course, that he can enjoy repose in any one place for a considerable length of time. But at the period in the life of Charlemagne which we are now considering, his journeys were more frequent, long and difficult than at any previous epoch.

Besides the unconcluded war which was still raging with the Saxons, and which, as we have seen, occupied so much of his attention, other dangers threatened his kingdom, in such a manner as to render the preparations necessary for defence more extensive and general than had hitherto been called for by any event of his reign. The same natural causes which had impelled the nations of the north, in succession, to invade the more fruitful and cultivated countries of the south of Europe, were now acting upon the Danes or Normans; and the same advantages of seacoast and easy ports, which had given a maritime character to the early expeditions of the Saxons, tended to lead this new horde of barbarians to carry on their warfare on the waves.

Long before the present period, the Normans had begun to essay their strength upon the sea; and in the absence of domestic arts, as the population of the country increased without the means of supply, the desire of wandering and the necessity of plunder drove them forth to seek in other lands the wealth they possessed not in their own.

Repelled in their first attempts upon Saxony by the Abrodites and other allies of France, which Charlemagne had placed on the borders of Germany, the Normans spread themselves over the ocean; and, by entering rapidly the mouths of the principal rivers, and making fierce and sudden descents upon the banks, they had now more than once carried terror and desolation into parts of France which had previously been exempt from the horrors of war.

Nothing was heard but complaints, and cries, and petitions for protection from the inhabitants of the coast; and the first moment that his presence could be spared by the armies warring in Saxony, Charlemagne hastened in person to examine the evil, and prepare a remedy. Scarcely had the spring of the year 800 appeared when the monarch set out from his palace at Aix-la-Chapelle, and, traversing the whole of France, followed the coast of the Bay of Biscay, which had been particularly infested by the Norman pirates; established fortresses and garrisons to defend the shore; and, causing an immense number of small vessels to be built, he stationed them well manned and armed, in the mouths of all the principal rivers of France and Germany. Thus, the Normans found themselves opposed at every point; and, in an extraordinary short space of time, the whole coast which had been subject to their depredations was in a complete state of defence. Driven back in every effort to land, they abandoned for the time their attempts upon the shores of France, and contented themselves with ravaging some of the small islands scattered on the borders of the German Sea. During this journey round the coast, Charlemagne is said to have arrived at one of the ports at the moment that the Norman pirates appeared. The invaders, however, learning the presence of the monarch, set all sail, and bore away; but Charlemagne remained gazing upon their departing vessels, while the tears were seen to roll over his cheeks. "I weep not, my friends", he said, turning to the nobles, who looked on in surprise, "because I fear myself those miserable savages; but I weep that they should dare to show themselves upon my coast while I am living; for I foresee the evils they will bring upon my people when I am dead".

Charlemagne, finding the entire success of the plan he had adopted against the Normans, pursued the same system in regard to Italy and to the French provinces on the shores of the Mediterranean. These were as much threatened and as often plundered by the Moors as the northern and western portions of his territory were by the Danes; and the same scheme of defence, adapted to both, produced equally happy effects. The mouths of the Rhone, the entrance of the Tiber, and all the ports of Provence and Italy were furnished with armed vessels, continually prepared to repel and to revenge invasion; and the Saracens, with the exception of the capture and pillage of Civita Vecchia, gained no further advantage on the shores of Italy.

As soon as he had concluded the preparations necessary to defend the coast of France, Charlemagne returned to the monastery of St. Richarius, near Abbeville, probably with the design of holding the general assembly of the nation, and proceeding immediately towards Rome. The illness of his queen, Luidgarde, however, opposed a temporary obstacle to the execution of this purpose. With that domestic tenderness which formed a fine and endearing point in the character of the great monarch, Charlemagne accompanied the dying queen to Tours; knelt with her at the shrine of the saint whose virtues she fancied might restore her to health; closed her eyes, after skill and prayers had proved impotent to save her, and rendered the last sad offices to the clay of her whom he had loved.

FROM CHARLEMAGNE'S LAST VISIT TO ROME TO HIS DEATH

800 TO 814.

While such had been the occupations of Charlemagne in France and Germany, Rome had been the theatre of events which strongly called for his presence in Italy. The hatred which Campulus and Paschal, the two disappointed aspirants to the papacy, had conceived against the more successful Leo had slumbered, but was not extinct; and towards the year 799 some circumstances which are not known seem to have roused it into new activity. The ecclesiastical situations held by the two factions Romans, and the favor with which they were regarded by the unsuspecting Leo himself, gave them many opportunities, we might imagine, for executing any project of revenue which went the length of assassination. It would appear, however, that Paschal and his fellow-conspirator, though determined to gratify their vengeance, and to open the way to their ambition, rendering the pope incapable of fulfilling the pontifical office, hoped, by a mixture of boldness and art, to escape the penal consequences of their crime, and to cover the mutilation they intended to perform under the hurry and confusion of a popular tumult.

The moment they chose for the perpetration of their design was while the pope, attended by all the clergy, and followed by all the populace, rode in state through a part of the city, performing what was called the Greater Litany. On the day appointed for the solemnity—the 25th of April—the ceremonies commenced without any appearance of danger, or any suspicion of treason. Paschal and Campulus were placed close to the person of the chief pontiff, and are said to have received from him some new mark of kindness on that very morning. All passed tranquilly till the line of the procession approached the monastery of St. Stephen and St. Sylvester; and even then the banners and crosses, the clerks and the chorists, which preceded the pope, were permitted to advance, till suddenly, as the higher clergy began to traverse the space before the building, armed men were seen mingling among the people. The march of the procession was obstructed a panic seized both the populace and the clergy. All fled but Campulus, Paschal, and their abettor; and Leo was left alone in the hands of the conspirators. The pontiff was immediately assailed and cast upon the ground; and, with eager but trembling hands,—for crime is generally fearful,—the traitors proceeded to attempt the extinction of his sight, and the mutilation of his tongue. It is probable that the struggles ot their unfortunate victim disappointed the strokes of the conspirators; and that his exhaustion from terror, exertion, and loss of blood deceived them into a belief that they had more than accomplished their purpose. Dispersing the moment the deed was committed, the chief conspirators left the apparently lifeless body of the prelate to be dragged into the monastery of St. Erasmus, which was done under the pretence of yielding him aid and succour, but in reality with the intention of retaining his person in captivity, if he survived the horrible infliction with which they had visited him. The news of the crime which had been committed spread like lightning, not only through Rome itself, but to the adjacent states, and soon reached the ears of Winegisus, Duke of Spoleto, who, though frequently opposed to the see of Rome, was on all occasions a frank and gallant enemy or a sincere and zealous friend. Without losing an instant, the Duke of Spoleto armed in favor of the pope, and, marching with all speed, encamped under the walls of Rome.

In the meanwhile, Leo had recovered from the first effect of his wounds, and was in a state to second the efforts which were made for his release by his friends and attendants. Albinus, his chamberlain, left no means untried to assist him; and cooperators having been found in the interior of the convent in which he was confined, he was lowered from the walls by ropes, and restored to his friends, who immediately conveyed him to the church of St, Peter. His recovery and escape struck the conspirators with astonishment and terror; and their suspicions instantly fixing upon the chamberlain as the person who had contrived his evasion and had given him refuge, they attacked that officer's house, which was speedily plundered and destroyed.

Before they could proceed, however, to further search, the arrival of the Duke of Spoleto with an overpowering force put a stop to their outrages; and the pope, placing himself under his protection, retired to Spoleto, while messengers were dispatched to Charlemagne to communicate the events and demand instructions. The news reached the monarch of the Franks as he was about to head one of his many expeditions into Saxony; and, without pausing on his march, he commanded Winegisus to send the Roman pontiff forward to Paderborn, with all the pomp and honor due to the successor of St. Peter.

His commands were immediately obeyed; and Leo was received at the military court of the monarch with distinction and kindness. Nevertheless, accusations were not wanting against the pontiff, and, though what the crimes were with which his enemies charged Leo cannot be discovered, it is sufficiently evident that Paschal and Campulus now attempted to justify what they could not conceal, by imputing atrocious vices to him whom they had attempted to destroy. The artifice was too apparent, and their own crime too glaring, for Charlemagne to give any credit to the charge, however boldly made, while it was unsupported by better evidence than their individual assertion.

Justice, nevertheless, required that examination and punishment should follow such accusations and such violence; and consequently, after entertaining the Roman prelate for some time at his court, Charlemagne sent him back to Rome, accompanied by nine commissioners, chosen from the highest and most incorruptible nobles of France, both clerical and secular, with orders to re-establish him in the apostolic chair; but, at the same time, to collect and investigate all the charges against him. The monarch's promise was likewise given to visit Italy himself and to judge between him and his accusers. Without any historical grounds for such a conjecture, a suspicion has been raised, and magnified into an assertion that Charlemagne, in saving that promise aimed at the assumption of the imperial dignity. The same populace which had fled terrified from the side of the pope when attacked by the conspirators received him with joy and acclamations on his return; while the presence of the Frankish commissioners, and the support of a Frankish army, gave dignity and security to the resumption of the pontifical office. The counts, bishops, and archbishops who had followed the prelate from France immediately proceeded to exercise the functions with which Charlemagne had invested them, by inquiring minutely into the assault that had been committed on the person of Leo himself, and by examining the charges which his enemies brought against him. What was the nature of the evidence given on this occasion does not appear; but the investigation ended by the arrest of Campulus, Paschal, and several other Romans, who were instantly dispatched as prisoners to France, to wait the promised journey of the monarch himself. By the various emergencies of state mentioned in the preceding book, that journey was delayed till late in the year 800; when at length Charlemagne, having convoked the general assembly of the nation, and announced the reasons which impelled him once more to journey into Italy, took his departure from Mayence, and, accompanied by an army marched on to Ravenna.

Various motives, besides the decision of the great cause between Leo and his enemies, combined to lead the monarch into Italy; and among these, one of the principal inducements was the desire of putting a termination to the war which had so long continued between his son Pepin and the young Duke of Beneventum. In this Charlemagne had hitherto taken no part, except by affording occasional advice and assistance to his son; but now, although he seems still to have determined upon refraining from personal hostilities, he came prepared to render more effectual support to Pepin than that prince had hitherto received.

Nevertheless, it is evident that the attention of Charlemagne was principally directed towards the reorganization of the deranged government of Rome. It cannot be doubted, indeed, that the defence and support of the Roman church was always an object of great—perhaps too great—

consideration with that monarch. But it must be remembered, at the same time, that in his days that church held out the only means within his reach of spreading the mild doctrines of Christianity, and thus afforded the only sure basis for civilization and improvement.

To guard and to maintain it, therefore, was one of the principal endeavors of his life; and, on the present occasion he did not show any relaxation of zeal in its defence. As soon as he had made all the necessary arrangements with his son Pepin, whom he sent at the head of the army he had brought from France to carry on the war against Beneventum, the monarch of the Franks quitted Ancona, to which place he had advanced, and then proceeded towards Rome. At Lamentana he was met by Leo, who was still received and treated with such marks of favor as showed no bad impression of his conduct; and on entering Rome the next day the monarch of the Franks met with the same enthusiastic reception which had welcomed him on his first visit to the eternal city.

After a repose of seven days, Charlemagne proceeded to the task which had brought him to Rome, and made every inquisition, we are told, in order to ascertain the truth or falsehood of the accusations which had been levelled at the pope. Every authority agrees in stating that these could not be to the slightest degree substantiated; but, at the same time, it is but fit to remark, that all the accounts which have reached us received their origin from either the adherents of the person who was acquitted, or of the judge who pronounced sentence in his favor. No reason, however, exists for supposing that the decision of Charlemagne was prejudiced or unjust. Nor did he solely rely upon his own judgment in a matter where, though he might feel sure of the equity of his intentions, he might doubt the impartiality of his affections. A synod, comprising all the higher clergy of Rome, was called; the evidence which had been procured was laid before it :

and the members of which it was composed were directed to pronounce between the head of their order and two of the most distinguished members of their own body.

Charlemagne, unbiased by the shrewd policy of ecclesiastical interests, sat as sovereign and judge to try the pontiff. He acted as the ruler that he felt himself to be; he used the authority he knew that he possessed; and only considered his capability of deciding justly without looking into the remote consequences of the proceeding in which he was engaged.

Not so the ecclesiastics whom he called to his aid. Each individual was a member of that mystic and indivisible whole—the Church of Rome, which, in the perpetuity of its own nature, communicated to all its parts that prescience and devotion to future interests that no temporal and transitory dynasty has ever been able to inculcate or enforce. To the synod, therefore, from whose wisdom and impartiality Charlemagne expected a verdict, the precedent of such a tribunal appeared most dangerous, especially while a lay monarch assumed to himself the privilege of presiding at its deliberations. To sanction it by any recorded sentence was painful to each of the members, while to oppose the will of the patrician, or to expose the motives which rendered the measure obnoxious, were equally impossible. One of those happy stratagems which have so often blessed the policy of the Vatican, and which was doubtless concerted between the chief pontiff and his prelates, delivered the assembly from the difficulty under which they labored.

No one appeared to accuse the pope, and each of the ecclesiastics declared his private opinion of his innocence; but, without at all imputing the right of Charlemagne to sit in judgment on the supreme pontiff, the assembled prelates severally declared that they could not, according to any of the rules of ecclesiastical discipline, pass sentence, whether of condemnation or acquittal, upon their general superior. In this dilemma, Leo himself proposed, that, according to a custom frequently resorted to under peculiar circumstances, he should purge himself, by a solemn oath, of the crimes of which he had been accused; and, mounting the pulpit of the church of St. Peter, he took the Book of Life in his hand, and with the most awful asseveration which can pass the lips of a Christian, declared, in the face of the assembled congregation, his perfect innocence of the charges which had been brought against him. Joy and festivity succeeded this termination of the trial; and the judgment to be passed on the assassins who had attempted the murder or mutilation of the pope was reserved for an after period.

THE CORONATION OF CHARLEMAGNE

A great epoch in the history of Europe was now approaching. We have seen that the Roman people, with their efforts directed and concentrated by their bishops had cast off the authority of the Eastern Empire on account of the iconoclastic heresy. They had not rendered their separation irreparable by electing a new Emperor of the West; but they had resumed some of the forms of the republic, and had named for themselves a patrician, who exercised in Rome the imperial power, without possessing the imperial name. That patrician had conquered for himself the kingdom of Lombardy, had claimed and received homage from Beneventum, had recovered a great part of the territories of ancient Rome in the West, and had acquired a vast extent of country that the empire, in her best days, had never been able to subdue. He had the power and the will to protect his subjects more than any other monarch in Europe; and he already possessed and exercised a degree of authority which no title could render greater.

At the same time, though the heresy of the East, which had caused the separation, was done away, the holy images restored to their places, and intemperate zeal displayed in their defence; yet the Patriarch of Constantinople was a dangerous rival to the pontiff of Rome; and the government of the emperors withheld from the pope many a rich diocese, and a profitable territory. The impotence of the court of Constantinople, either to defend or maintain the empire and its struggles with the Popes; and the natural predilection of the Byzantine monarchs for their eastern provinces had already proved the ruin and debasement of Italy.

To return, therefore, under the dominion of the East could never be contemplated either by the Romans or their pontiffs, while to render their separation eternal, by the election of a new Emperor of the West showed a prospect of many advantages, both direct and collateral. The orthodoxy of the French monarch, indeed, was more than doubtful in the eyes of the Roman church; but though his scribes had been zealous in their condemnation of the iconoclasts, even to ribaldry, the king himself had preserved a more temperate demeanor, and had bowed himself to the ancient proverb of following at Rome the usages of Rome. A thousand personal motives, also, conduced to close the eyes of the pope towards the heretical doctrines which had been honored by the name of Charlemagne. Gratitude for immense benefits conferred, and the prospect of rewards to follow, might act as a strong inducement in determining the restoration of the Western empire, and the election of Charlemagne. But there might be other and more powerful causes still, which operated in the mind of the pontiff to produce the same resolution. The general vassals of an emperor bore a much higher rank than the vassals of a foreign king. Italy, so long a dependent province, would at once take the first place, rise up from the ashes of four centuries and soar again into the blaze of empire; while the pontiff, whom a king had presumed to judge, would shake off the degradation of his submission, by rewarding his protector with an imperial crown. The distant prospect of future claims and encroachments, to be founded on that gift, might present itself vaguely to the eye of sacerdotal policy; and a basis for entire territorial independence and immense ecclesiastical dominion, might perhaps be seen by the pontiff, in his creation of an emperor, and nomination to dominion.

Such were probably the motives of Leo for the revival of the empire of the West in the person of Charlemagne. The motives of the French monarch for accepting it were as clear, but were not quite so unmixed with difficulties. The jealous enmity which must naturally arise in the bosoms of the Greek emperors would necessarily require opposition, either by arms or negotiations, in a moment when, surrounded on every side by enemies, all the energies of his own vast mind scarcely sufficed to meet the many dangers by which he was assailed. Nor could Charlemagne feel quite sure that the Franks would cordially accede to his deriving a higher title, and more unlimited authority, from another nation, than that which they conceded to their kings. All these matters required time for consideration; and, even when his resolution was fixed, time for preparation also. It is probable, that shortly after his arrival hi Italy, he received an intimation of the pope's intention to revive the empire of the West, and of the determination which had been formed, to elect him to the high station thus created; and it is probable also that he signified his disapprobation of the proposal in such terms as were intended not to crush the design, but to delay the execution.

The pope, however, impelled by much stronger motives, and withheld by no difficulties, having obtained the consent of the Roman people, and prepared all things for his purpose, determined not to lose the opportunity, or to suffer delay to bring forth obstacles to a transaction so advantageous to himself. It is not unlikely that some rumour of the preparations made by the pontiff might reach the ears of the French monarch, but that, always supposing he would be consulted before the ceremony actually took place, he felt sure of being able to delay it till such time as he himself had used every necessary precaution.

However that may be, on Christmas-day Charlemagne, with the rest of the Catholic world, presented himself in the church of St. Peter, to offer up his prayers with the multitude to the Giver of all dignities and debasements, the Ruler of kings and peasants. At the request of the pope, and to gratify the Roman people, he had laid aside the national dress which he usually wore on days of solemnity, and which consisted of a close tunic embroidered with gold, sandals laced with gold and studded with jewels, a mantle clasped with a golden *agraffe*, and a diadem shining with precious stones. He now appeared in the long robe of the patrician, and, as military governor of Rome, presented himself to the people as a Roman. The church was filled with the nobility of Italy and France; and all that they saw around, after they entered its vast walls, most have told them that some great ceremony was about to take place. At the high altar stood the head of the Christian church, surrounded by all the splendid clergy of Italy; and the monarch, approaching, knelt on the steps of the altar, and for some moments continued to offer up his prayers. As he was about to rise, Leo advanced, and, raising an imperial crown, he placed it suddenly on the brows of the monarch, while the imperial salutations burst in thunder from the people,—"Long life and victory to Charles Augustus, crowned by God great and pacific Emperor of the Romans!"

Whether the extraordinary preparations which he must have seen in the church had given Charlemagne any suspicion of the intentions of the pope, or whether the conduct of the pontiff really took him by surprise, must ever be a matter of doubt. At all events, the only alternative now left him was either to refuse the dignity for ever or to accept it at once; and though, in all probability, he would willingly have delayed the expression of his determination, he acquiesced in the proceeding of the pope when the ceremony had commenced. Daring the different intervals of the religious forms appropriate to the day, the supreme pontiff administered the oath which confirmed Charlemagne's acceptance of the title put upon him, anointed him from the head to the feet, in the manner practised on the coronation of the Jewish kings, and adored him according to the forms employed towards the Caesars. From that hour the titles both of king and of patrician were laid aside; and the monarch of the Franks became the Emperor of the Romans. Thenceforward his coins were inscribed with his new dignity, and his acts were dated from the years of his empire.

Magnificent presents, tables of silver, vases and chalices of pure gold, crowns and patenas enriched with gems, expressed the gratitude of the monarch for the zeal, if not for the service, of the pope; and though Charlemagne declared that he would not have visited the church that day if he had anticipated the event, he showed no anger at the officiousness of the prelate.

Shortly after his coronation, Charlemagne proceeded to the trial of the conspirators, whose brutal assault upon the sacred person of the supreme pontiff had been one of the principal causes of his journey to Rome. The accusations against the prelate, under cover of which they had attempted to shelter their own crime, remained, as I have before said, totally unproved, while the facts against themselves were susceptible of no evasion. Their trial was carried on in Rome according to the Roman law. Nothing was brought forward to palliate their offence, or to cast a doubt upon the charge; and, reproaching each other publicly for their mutual crime and common danger, they were silent in reply to the accusation and the evidence against them.

Their guilt being established beyond doubt, their condemnation followed; and the severest sentence of the law was pronounced against them by the emperor. But the object of their hatred and their violence became their intercessor with the monarch, and, by obtaining the pardon they little deserved, did more to prove his own innocence and their calumny than had been done by the synod of the prelates or the oath at the cathedral. Their lives were spared to the earnest prayer of Leo. Neither did they suffer that horrible infliction which they had attempted to execute upon the pontiff—the deprivation of sight, which was then a common punishment for criminals less guilty than themselves. Charlemagne, however, wisely removed them from the scene of their crime and their intrigues; and, by banishing them for ever, at once relieved the pope from their presence, and assigned them a degree of punishment, though most inadequate to their offence.

In the disposition and arrangement of the affairs of Italy the emperor passed the whole of the spring; and during his stay on this occasion, as well as on every former visit to Rome, he exercised an acknowledged power in ecclesiastical matters, which might have rendered the after claims of the clergy ridiculous, had they not been too successful. The conclusion of the war with Beneventum also occupied the monarch's attention; and, although he still refrained from mingling with it in person, the uncertain nature of his political relations with Constantinople made him far more anxious than he had ever hitherto been to conclude all domestic dissensions within the limits of Italy. The resistance, however, of Grimwald was obstinate, and often successful. Educated for some time under the eye of Charlemagne, his military talents had received a high degree of cultivation, while his bold and active disposition rendered him a dangerous rival for the young King of Italy. The war was thus protracted for many years; and the rapidity of the Beneventine prince often obtained for him considerable advantages over the superior strength of his adversary. These advantages he never used to a base or unworthy purpose; and though he resisted firmly the exactions of his benefactor's son,—exactions which, we have some reason to imagine, were severe in themselves, and haughtily supported,—yet, in military skill and generosity of demeanor, Grimwald approved himself a worthy follower of Charlemagne.

The greatest success he obtained during the whole course of his struggles against Pepin took place in 802, shortly after the emperor's last visit to Italy. Winegisus, Duke of Spoleto, who seems to have been entrusted by Pepin, at that period, with the chief command against the Beneventines, having captured and taken possession of Lucera, suddenly found himself invested in that city by the forces of Grimwald. Already weakened by disease, the Frankish commander was not equal to the task of resisting the young and active Beneventine; and after a brief but severe siege the town surrendered, and Winegisus fell into the hands of the enemy.

The fate awaiting a prisoner was in those days a very uncertain matter;

but the conduct of Grimwald to his fallen adversary was such as might have been expected from a prince who had followed for a length of time the camp of Charlemagne. The Duke of Spoleto was received with kindness; and, after having been entertained with honor during the winter, was set at liberty by his conqueror early in the following year. Very little of any interest or importance occurred afterward in the war of Beneventum. The resistance of Grimwald and the demands of Pepin still continued, till, in the year 806, the death of the Lombard prince made a change in the government of the province; and, shortly after, the Beneventines agreed to pay an annual tribute of twenty-five thousand solidi of gold, which put a termination to the war.

The prolongation of this struggle, however, weakened the forces of the young King of Italy by division, and prevented him from accomplishing many things which were necessary to the consolidation of the dominions entrusted to him by his father. On a minor scale, his contest with surrounding enemies resembled that which had occupied the whole life of the great monarch himself; and, continually opposed by the Venetians and the Beneventines in Italy, as well as frequently assailed by the Moors and by the Greeks from without, he showed courage, firmness, and activity, which justified the blood of Charlemagne.

Corsica, which had been bestowed by the emperor on the holy see, Pepin defended vigorously from the attacks of the Saracens; and, taught by his father's exertions on the coasts of France and Germany, he collected a navy round the Italian shores, which, under the command of the Constable Burchard, signally defeated the Moorish fleet in the Mediterranean.

Thus far the wars of Pepin were, in a manner, distinct and separate from the general progress of the empire of Charlemagne, and might properly be noticed apart; but the strife which took place between the young monarch and the Venetian republic, of which I shall soon have to speak more fully, is intimately connected with the revival of the Western empire, in the person of his father.

As king of Lombardy and patrician of Rome, the Frankish monarch had claimed all that portion of Italy which had been comprised in the dominion of the Lombard kings and the exarchs of Ravenna; but, as the emperor of the Romans, his wishes or his rights might extend his title to the whole of Italy, and comprehend, beyond the absolute limits of the peninsula, Sicily on the one side, with Croatia, Liburnia, and Dalmatia on the other.

But in assuming the title of emperor, Charlemagne had little desire to plunge himself in new wars; and if he ever did entertain the idea of invading Sicily, as Theophanes declares, he soon abandoned a project which, however successful, must have required blood, trouble, and fatigue, at a moment when his time and his forces were already fully employed.

An easy mode of reconciling the jarring interests of the East and the West was suggested to Charlemagne, either by his own political foresight, or by the officious zeal of the Roman pontiff. The ruler of the Eastern Empire, and the actual possessor of the disputed territories, was a woman, and a widow. Charlemagne himself, by the death of Luidgarde, had been left free to contract a new alliance; and the extinction of opposing claims, by the union of the opposite claimants, was soon agitated in the councils of the emperor. That the mutilator of her own son might, on occasion, easily become the assassin of her husband, was a consideration which did not deter Charlemagne from the proposed alliance; and the fact of his having demanded the hand of Irene in marriage, is perhaps the strongest instance on record of the personal courage for which he was famous.

Either before, or immediately after, his departure from Italy, messengers were sent to the court of Constantinople from Charlemagne, accompanied by legates from the pope, both charged with the formal annunciation of the revival of the Western empire, and with the more delicate commission of negotiating the union of the emperor and empress. The proposal was by no means disagreeable to Irene, who saw before her the prospect of terminating easily, by some method, those difficulties to which the occupation of the Western throne had given rise. It is not improbable, indeed, that she looked upon this alliance, also, as a means of gratifying, not only her vanity, but also her revenge upon those who had assailed or injured her. The power of the East, strengthened by the power of the West, might have conquered or overawed a world; and the young blood of the adolescent Franks, transfused into the veins of the ancient empire, might have given new vigor to the feeble frame of that decrepit monarchy, and raised it up once more to glory and to triumph. But whatever were the considerations which led the empress to desire the alliance proposed,—passion, vanity, policy, or ambition,—her inclinations were controlled by a domestic faction; and the eunuch Aetius, who had been raised by her to the highest stations of the empire, dared to oppose the will of his mistress. Supported by others equally indebted and ungrateful with himself, he compelled her to reject the hand of the monarch of the Franks, in the hopes of raising his brother to the imperial dignity, from which he was himself excluded by corporeal disabilities. The rejection, however, was accompanied by pacific proposals; and, in 802, an embassy reached the court of Charlemagne,—who had by this time returned to France,—in order to treat for a definitive arrangement of the claims of the two empires, and to determine the articles of a future peace.

Where such immense interests and extensive territories were involved, the negotiation, of course, offered many difficulties. However powerless might be Irene to enforce her claims, however moderate might be Charlemagne in his exactions, there were points to be considered, and obstacles to be removed, which required many conferences; and more than one doubt might naturally arise, which could only be solved by the court of Constantinople. Desirous that the transaction might be concluded with as much facility and speed as possible, the emperor committed the ultimate terms to which he would consent to Jesse, Bishop of Amiens, and Helingaud, one of the counts of his palace, who accompanied Leo, the ambassador of Irene, on his return to Constantinople.

On their arrival in that city, the negotiations were renewed; but, while still unconcluded, a revolution at the imperial court suddenly interrupted their progress. "The great treasurer Nicephorus was secretly invested with the purple, Irene's successor was introduced into the palace, and crowned at St. Sophia by the venal patriarch. In their first interview, she recapitulated with dignity the revolutions of her life, gently accused the perfidy of Nicephorus, insinuated that he owed his life to her unsuspecting clemency; and, for the throne and treasures which she resigned, solicited a decent and honorable retreat. His avarice refused this modest compensation; and, in her exile of the Isle of Lesbos, the empress earned a scanty subsistence by the labours of herdistaff".

In the midst of the confusion of a sudden change in the dynasty, it is not improbable that the ambassadors of the Emperor of the West were insulted by the populace of the Grecian capital. But no sooner was Nicephorus firmly seated on the throne which he had usurped from the usurper, than he hastened to conclude the peace which Irene had begun, and to send back with the Franks envoys on his own part to receive the ratification of the treaty from the hands of Charlemagne. The Greek ambassadors reached the monarch at Seltz; and the object of their coming was obtained without difficulty. The election of Charlemagne was recognized by the Emperor of the East; and his possession of Istria, Croatia, Liburnia, and Dalmatia was confirmed, as well as his title to Sardinia, Corsica, and Italy, as far as the limits of the inferior Calabria. Sicily and Naples remained in the hands of the Greeks; but the territories of Venice, it would appear, were left unmentioned in the document of partition.

Surrounded on every side by dominions possessed by Charlemagne, and forming an integral part of that territory which was now distinctly allotted to him, it is difficult to understand how the Venetians could wish or hope to remain attached to the Greek empire. Perhaps it might be the expectation of establishing their own independence, between the contending claims of the rival monarchs, which induced that people to waver between both; or perhaps it might merely be the vacillation of those factions which always arise in republics that alternately gave preponderance to the influence of France or Constantinople. Whatever was the origin of the disputes that followed, the minor facts are remote and obscure; and even the general question has been clouded by the national prejudices of critics and historians. That Charlemagne considered the Venetians as his subjects is evident; but it would seem that a strong party in Venice opposed that distribution of power which conveyed the sovereignty of their state to the monarch of the Franks. The chief of this faction was John, the doge, or duke, of the republic; but, at that period, the power of the chief magistrate was controlled or corrected by the authority of tribunes; and on the first manifestation of the leaning of the doge to Constantinople, in the appointment of a Greek to the bishopric of Olivola, one of the Venetian islands, his views were thwarted by the tribunes, who, heading the Frankish faction, prevailed on the patriarch of Grado to refuse consecration to the prelate-elect. The revenge of the duke, which could not overtake the tribunes, fell somewhat barbarously on the unhappy patriarch. In concert with his son, whom he had associated with himself in office, the Venetian chief led the fleet of the republic against Grado, captured the city, and precipitated the pontiff from the highest tower.

This criminal action instantly raised the voice of the whole Christian world against the perpetrators; and Paulinus, patriarch of Friuli, addressed an epistle to Charlemagne, demanding justice upon the duke, at the hand of his sovereign. At the same time, Fortunatus, said to be the nephew of the murdered prelate, sought refuge at the court of the Frankish monarch, and besought his aid against the assassins of his uncle.

What were the proceeding which took place upon this application is a question of much doubt; but the result is known. John and his son Maurice were deposed and banished; and the tribunes Obelerio and Beatus were raised to the ducal dignity together. The power of France was now for some time preponderant; and the sovereignty of the Emperor of the West appears to have been acknowledged by the voice of the friendly magistrates. At his desire, they visited his court and received his commands; and everything promised the tranquillity of the Venetian state, and the permanence of Charlemagne's authority.

The power of the monarch, however, was menaced from another quarter. Sigifrid, King of the Danes, or Normans, was now dead, and in his place had arisen one, whose powerful and comprehensive mind would in all probability have united the fierce nations of the north, and led them to sweep and desolate the south of Europe, had not Saxony been previously subdued. The junction of the Normans with the Saxons, inevitable if the latter had continued in their state of barbarism, would have created a force which Charlemagne himself could hardly have opposed. But at present, the German nations, if not so far civilized yet as to furnish a strong barrier against the Danish king, were so far subdued as to afford him no support, and Charlemagne had to contend with him only on his northern frontier. The first efforts of the French monarch were for peace; and it would appear that several years passed before the mind of Godfrey the Dane so completely lost the impression of the emperor's victories over the Saxons, as to dream of following the example of their incursions upon the Frankish territory. In the year 804, this impression was evidently but deeply fixed, although many bodies of his piratical subjects had ravaged the coast of France. In the great deportation of the Saxons which took place in that year, it would appear that some of the leaders had made their escape to Denmark, and the emperor immediately sent messengers to require that they should be given up. The Danish king neither absolutely conceded nor rejected the demand, but promised to come down to the frontiers of his own country, and confer with the Frankish monarch on a permanent treaty of peace between the two nations.

Charlemagne remained at Holdenstein, near the Elbe, in expectation of his arrival, and Godfrey advanced, with a fleet and army, as far as Schleswick, in South Jutland. There, however, the remonstrances of his court on the danger to which, it was supposed, he would expose himself if he proceeded any farther, succeeded in inspiring him with fears and doubts of the French monarch; and, pausing in his advance, he terminated the negotiations by acceding to the demands of the emperor through the intervention of ambassadors.

That these demands were conceived in the same spirit of moderation which was apparent in all the other actions of the Frankish monarch there can be no doubt; and indeed it would appear, that as years increased upon the head of Charlemagne he naturally became more desirous of that peace and quiet of which he had known so little during the course of a long life. The aspirations of ambition were gratified to the full; the impatient energy of youth had passed away; the vigor of manhood, though not lost, was easily governed; and that weariness of exertion, and desire of rest— which at the end of a short day may be relieved by a brief repose, but which towards the close of a long existence demands permanent tranquility— began to fall upon the hitherto indefatigable monarch of the Franks.

By unequalled efforts against a thousand enemies, he had now nearly conquered peace, and he sought to enjoy it; but, nevertheless, no desire of ease could prevent him from affording aid to such of his allies or dependants as required the support of military intervention. From the Elbe and the Danube to the Vistula and the Baltic extends a tract of country which was then occupied by various Slavonian tribes, some of which were strongly and permanently attached to the Frankish monarch; while others, retaining all the wild ferocity of their original state, willingly seized every opportunity of attacking whatever country acknowledged the dominion of a more civilized power. Among the latter were the Bohemians, who, lying on the frontiers of Pannonia and Hungary, took continual advantage of the depressed state to which long wars against the superior power of Charlemagne had reduced the Avars, and, by incessant and desolating incursions, gave that unhappy nation no time to recover vigor or to enjoy repose. The greater part of the people of Hungary had by this time embraced the Christian religion; and their monarch Theodore at length, in 805, undertook a journey to the court of Charlemagne, to beg that his nation might be allowed to abandon the country which they then held, and seek another less exposed to the attacks of the Bohemians.

The French monarch granted his request at once, and, with generous kindness, did all that he could to alleviate the sorrows of the Hunnish chief. Theodore, however, died soon after his return to Pannonia, and a new chagan being elected by the Avars, the consent of Charlemagne was solicited to his nomination. This was not only immediately given, but, before permitting the Hunnish tribes to execute their purpose of emigration, the emperor commanded his eldest son Charles to lead an army into Bohemia, and endeavor by chastisement to restrain the Slavonians within their own bounds.

The will of the monarch was instantly accomplished by his son, who seems to have possessed much of his father's military talents and rapid activity. Before the year was concluded, the Frankish forces had been lead into Bohemia; a battle had been fought and won; Lecho, the Bohemian duke, had been slain,—it is said, by the hand of Charles himself; and the prince, leading back his victorious troops, met his two brothers Louis and Pepin at the palace of the emperor near Thionville.

The union of his children around the emperor's person was not without an object. Already considerably past the age which his father and his grand-father had attained, Charlemagne, notwithstanding the great degree of corporeal vigor that he still enjoyed, and the robust constitution which promised many years of health, determined to prepare against the approach of death, and to provide, as much as human foresight could, against those dissensions among his children which had caused the difficulties and cares of his own early reign, which might destroy the empire he had acquired, and sweep away the institutions he had founded.

He accordingly determined to remove all future cause of dispute, by himself allotting, among his sons, the territories which they were to possess at his death, and by gaining the solemn and irrevocable consent, both of his people and his children, to the charter of division he was about to trace out. The character of Charlemagne has been assailed by some, his virtues depreciated, his motives misconstrued, his actions misstated, and his laws reproached; but the enthusiasm of his people when danger menaced his person, their devoted zeal in seconding all his efforts, and the boundless confidence with which they adopted all his views, have left a glorious testimony in favor of his wisdom and his virtue deep written on the page of history, which neither malignity can efface nor hypothesis obscure. His children at once gave their consent to that distribution of his dominions which he thought fit to provide against the period of his death, and the general assembly of the nation sanctioned it without hesitation. The princes and the nobles swore to observe the partition; and a copy of the document was transmitted to the head of the Christian church, that the authenticity of the deed might be preserved undoubted, by a transcript, attested by the supreme pontiff himself, remaining in the archives of the church.

The division of the empire among the children of the monarch had been a principle admitted with the Franks from the earliest ages, although the equality of partition, and even the admission of all the heirs, had by no means been strictly enforced. If ever extent of dominion could render such a division necessary, it was in the case of the territory agglomerated by Charlemagne, which, in addition to the difficulty of consolidation, implied by extreme bulk, presented other inconveniences of a more insurmountable nature, from the composition of its various parts. The acquisitions of ancient Rome had been gradual, and in comparison slow. Step by step each province had in general been fully incorporated with the empire before other conquests were achieved; and but a small district added to the dominions of Rome was enough for the glory and triumph of a life. But, warring upon every frontier at once, Charlemagne had added to his native kingdom, in the short space of one man's existence, as much as would have cost two centuries of Roman conquest to acquire. No time had been given to blend the separate nations into one; they remained still discrepant, inharmonious, and requiring the same great mind which had conquered and united them to hold them in subjection and assimilate them together.

Such considerations may have been among the motives which combined to reconcile Charlemagne to the division of the empire; but probably the most powerful of all was the fact of its beings the custom, if not the law, of his nation. A sound and judicious policy might, and probably would, have induced the monarch to abrogate that law if his dominions had been small; but the extent of territory to be divided took from the custom its strongest objection, and in the act of partition itself we have a singular instance of the deference of the monarch to the privileges and institutions of hia country.

We have already seen several examples of the strong influence attributed to the popular voice in the election, or rather succession, of the Frankish monarchs. Eginhard states that the Franks were accustomed *to choose their kings from the Merovingian race*; and the supreme pontiff, in crowning Pepin, threatens with the thunders of the church such persons as should attempt *to elect a monarch from any other family than the Carolingian*. Charlemagne, more expressly still, points at the same active power in the people, and declares by his will, that if any of the three kings among whom he divides the realm shall in dying leave a son, and his people choose to elect that son in the place of his father, that portion of the empire shall descend to him, without claim or molestation on the part of his uncles.

The further dispositions of the monarch are directed to keep peace and amity among his children, and so to provide for all cases, that no disputes may arise, either between the monarchs themselves in regard to the territories allotted to each, or between them and their people in regard to the jurisdiction under which each individual subject is placed. Even while dividing his dominions, Charlemagne also strongly enjoins that mutual support and cooperation which would give to the several kingdoms the same strength as if still united in one empire; and he points out the path by which each prince may lead his armies to the support of his brothers. No precaution is wanting on the part of the monarch to secure the future concord of his sons; and, under the warrant of the oath which they mutually took to obey his will, he commands them, in case of any dispute in regard to their territories, to abstain from arms, and to have recourse to the judgment of the cross,—a judgment which, like every other sort of ordeal, supposed the active interposition of God to establish an earthly right. Even had this injunction not referred to one of the firm-rooted superstitions of the day, the command of Charlemagne would have still been wise, as, by subjecting every matter of doubt to a certain and indisputable method of decision, it guarded against the most remote chance of those bloody contentions which had desolated the realm under the Merovingian kings. Had he directed them to draw lots, the same purpose would have been answered; but, in the mode of judgment to which he now commanded them to apply, the religious feelings of the people, and even of the princes themselves, operated in support of the award.

Such was the charter of division conceived by Charlemagne; and certainly the clearness of his judgment and the benignity of his heart were never more fully displayed than in that document. It was destined, it is true, to have no effect; but it remains a striking proof of the power which a great mind has to employ the very prejudices and superstitions of his age for the best and noblest of purposes.

END OF ALL THE WARS OF CHARLEMAGNE

Soon after the deed had been received and ratified by all whose interests were implicated, the three princes quitted the court of their father, and betook themselves to the several occupations which had been assigned to them. Charles, the eldest, once more turned his steps towards the north, where the Bohemians, having been joined by another predatory tribe of Slavonians, were ravaging with fire and sword the frontiers of Bavaria and Hungary. The measures taken against them, however, were prompt and effectual. Charles himself led one body of troops against the Slavonians on the banks of the Sale and the Elbe, defeated them completely, slew their chief in battle, and, after guarding the frontier by the construction of two fortresses, returned to join his father on the banks of the Meuse. At the same time, a triple army from Germany, Bavaria, and Hungary entered the country of the Bohemians, and by laying waste the border territory, punished their aggression on the Hungarian provinces, and put a stop to their future incursions.

This campaign terminated the Bohemian war, and left the frontiers of Bavaria and Pannonia in security and peace. But Charlemagne was still destined to encounter hostilities on the northern verge of his territories, where Godfrey King of Denmark was daily increasing in power and in confidence. The peace which had been concluded with him, soon shared the fate of all treaties entered into with barbarous nations, and was broken as soon as the Northman king found it convenient to ravage the coast of France and Germany. He still covered his breach of faith with some degree of decency; and a renewal of individual acts of piracy on the shores of Charlemagne's dominions first announced the frail nature of the Dane's engagements. The next mark of hostility, though more glaring, was not directed against the emperor personally, but took the shape of an incursion into the territories of the Abodrites, those faithful allies on whose vigilance and courage Charlemagne greatly depended for the security of Saxony. The northern chief did not undertake this enterprise, however, without the certainty of some support; and, in the Welatabes, the Winidi, and the Smaldingi, a congregation of wild Slavonic tribes inhabiting the country between the Oder and the Vistula, and covering the whole of modem Pomerania, he found willing allies against their more civilized neighbors. To these were added the Linones, on the southern bank of the Oder; and instead of passing at once from Denmark by land into the territory of the Abodrites, which was probably guarded on that frontier from the anticipation of hostilities, he transported his troops into Wenedonia, or Pomerania, and thence marched upon that point of the destined territory where his prey was least prepared to oppose him.

The excursion of Godfrey was rapid and terrible. Attacked by so many of the Slavonian tribes, as well as the Danes, the unfortunate Abodrites were conquered before any assistance could reach them; and when Charles, dispatched by his father to their aid, arrived with his army on the banks of the Elbe, he found that their duke, Thrasicon, had been expelled from his country, and that the whole land had been pillaged and subdued. This, it is true, was not effected by the Danes without great loss on their own part.

The nephew of the king himself fell in battle—the best of their army perished; and, in no condition to resist the force they knew to be advancing against them from France, they once more retired into Pomerania, took ship, and set sail for Denmark. Apparently fearful of pursuit by sea the Danish monarch, before his departure, destroyed the port from which he embarked, and carried away the merchants into Denmark. Charles did not reach the scene of action till the Danes were gone; and no trace of them was left but in their ravages. The tribes who had aided them in their expedition, however, still remained; and throwing a bridge over the Elbe, the Franks poured into the territory of the inimical Slavonians, and took severe vengeance for the injuries inflicted on the Abodrites.

In the meantime, Godfrey, warned of the proximity of the Frankish army, and remembering the bitter and never-failing punishment which had overtaken the similar irruptions of the Saxons, hastened to add to the means of defence which his country already possessed. The narrow neck of land between the duchy of Holstein and the province of South Jutland offered every facility for the formation of such a fortified boundary as he proposed to construct. His arrival at the port of Schleswick brought him on the very spot suitable to his purpose; and he instantly began the erection of a defensible wall, running across the isthmus, from the estuary on which that town is situated to the mouth of the Eyder and the German ocean.

While this great work was in progress, the Danish monarch found it necessary to temporize with the emperor; and accordingly, sent ambassadors to the court of France, in order to justify his aggression on the allies of the Franks; and to demand a congress of deputies from both nations, in order to consider and determine all matters in dispute. This was immediately granted; but the negotiations produced no effect; and the Danish king prepared to renew the war against the Franks themselves.

The multitude of his Slavonian allies rendered the power of Godfrey formidable even to Charlemagne; and, had the Saxons been still inclined, even in their state of depression, to join with the Normans, the whole of Europe, as I have before observed, would most probably have been once more plunged in blood and darkness. But the Saxons, now beginning to appreciate the benefits of civilization, were the first to aid in repelling the advances of their barbarous neighbors. Thrasicon, Duke of the Abodrites, was soon restored to his country; and, being supported by a large Saxon force, while the Danish king swept over the seas and made a terrible descent upon the German coast, he entered the territories of that monarch's Slavonian allies, and with fire and sword retaliated the injuries they had inflicted on his nation.

The Frisons, also, so long the implacable enemies of the Franks, were now the first safeguards of their shores. Though, after three rapid and bloody combats with the Danes upon the German coast, they were at length obliged to buy the invaders' absence with a hundred pounds of silver, yet the smallness of the sum demanded by Godfrey, and the speed of his retreat, evinces how steady had been the resistance of the Frisons, and how dearly purchased had been the victory he gained.

His landing, however, and his persevering contest with the inhabitants of the coast, had spread consternation into the heart of France. He had been heard boldly to declare, that he would carry his arms to Aix-la-Chapelle; and that he would make the attempt, was universally believed. But, though now in his seventieth year, Charlemagne forgot the load of age, started from the repose in which he had indulged, and once more hastened to the field. No mark of time's enfeebling power was to be found in the movements of the great monarch; and all the active energy of his brightest days reappeared on the approach of danger. Messengers were sent in every direction to gather together his troops; and, while land forces were assembling, he hastened, without loss of a moment, to inspect in person the state of the fleet in the mouth of the Rhine, and prepared to contend with the Norman on his own element. No sooner were his commands given, and the means of war in readiness in that direction, than, forgetful of all personal fatigue, the emperor hastened back to the head of his army; crossed the Rhine at Lippenheim; and, after forming his junction with other forces, which were marching up to support him, advanced as far as the confluence of the Aller and the Weiser, in order to give battle to the Danes.

At that spot, news of a varied complexion reached him, which rendered his further march unnecessary. Thrasicon, Duke of the Abodrites, while pursuing hit success against the Slavonians, had been assassinated by emissaries of the Danish king. But, at the same time, Godfrey himself had quitted in haste the shores of the Frisons, in order to return to Denmark, and the tidings almost immediately followed of his own death, by the same treacherous steel he had used against others. He had been slain by one of his followers,—whether instigated by personal revenge or kindred ambition, does not appear. A more pacific sovereign, however, succeeded. A truce was concluded between the Danes and Franks; a congress was held; and with little difficulty a peace was agreed upon, which terminated the Norman war during the life of Charlemagne.

In the northern campaigns, the principal active agent on the part of Charlemagne had been Charles, his eldest son; but, in the south, Pepin, King of Italy, had been in no degree unoccupied since the partition charter, for the purpose of acknowledging which he had been called to France. Scarcely had he returned to Italy, when he found that Nicephorus, now firmly seated on the throne of Constantinople, began to regret the concessions which he had made in the first dangers of usurpation, and to seek the recovery of those territories, which he had too hastily suffered to be alienated from the Greek empire. His first efforts were directed against Dalmatia, the seaports of which, commanding the whole commerce of the Adriatic, were of infinite importance to the Greeks. In the year 806, we accordingly find the patrician Nicetas, accompanied by a large fleet, sailing with the express purpose of recovering Dalmatia. It would appear, that his expedition ended without any great military effort; and, probably, the success of the Frankish armaments against the Moors, who were about the same time signally defeated on the coast of Corsica, determined the Greek commander to bring the incipient war to a speedy termination.

He accordingly hastened to conclude a fresh treaty of peace with the young King of Italy; and withdrew his fleet from their station in the Adriatic. It appears not unlikely, indeed, that at this time, by the commands of his father, Pepin yielded to the Greeks the sovereignty of the Dalmatian ports, while the rest of that province was reserved to the Franks. That such a transaction ultimately took place we know from the account of Eginhard; but the period is left in doubt.

The state of Venice also, about this time, is very obscure. The very same year in which we find the duke, or doge, and his coadjutor at the court of Charlemagne, submitting to his will as to that of their sovereign, we are told that Nicetas, coming avowedly with hostile intentions towards the dominions of the Western emperor, remained with tranquil security in the Venetian ports. Nevertheless, through all the contradictory events which now took place in regard to Venice, the effort is still apparent, of a weak state struggling to gain independence among the contending claims of two more powerful countries; and possibly it was a part of the policy of the Venetians to cast as much obscurity as possible on the degree of submission they were forced to yield to either empire.

The peace concluded between Pepin and Nicetas was not of long continuance; for either the emperor Nicephorus was dissatisfied with the terms granted and hoped, by a renewal of warfare, to obtain more, or some new cause of hostility immediately arose. The patrician withdrew his fleet from Venice in August of the year 807; and before the winter of the following year, another Greek armament appeared in the Adriatic. The commander Paul, prefect of Cephalonia, was still charged to negotiate with the King of Italy; but he seems to have imagined that some military success would prove a good prelude to the demands he might be instructed to make; and, accordingly, he landed a part of his forces at Commachio, then garrisoned by the Franks. The Greeks, ever unsuccessful in their contests with the Franks, found fortune still unfavorable to their efforts; and, after suffering a shameful defeat at Commachio, they made all sail for the port of Venice.

Peace was here once more proposed; and it appears that both Pepin and the Greek commander were desirous of obtaining it but such a consummation did not accord with the policy of the Venetians; and they contrived to break off the negotiations before they were half-concluded. Their treachery, however, was not long in reaching the ears of Pepin; and probably this instance of duplicity opened his eyes to much more of the same double and perfidious policy. An injury is always a thousand-fold aggravated when united to the insult of deceit; and the King of Italy, with natural indignation, proceeded to take vengeance on the Venetians. Their territories were immediately attacked both by land and sea; but the degree of success which attended the arms of Pepin has been for years a matter of national dispute. That he was successful to a certain point is proved by the French, and admitted by the Venetians; but in determining the extent of his conquest, if we suppose it a little more than Venice will allow, and a little less than France exacts, we shall probably be very nearly correct. That he subdued all their continental possessions is clear; for from that day the Venetians paid some kind of tribute for their lands on terra firma. But it would appear, that though he conquered most of the islands which composed the Venetian state, he was repulsed from Rialto, not so much by the courage of the inhabitants, as through the difficulty of access, and the unwieldy nature of the vessels he employed. Probably the sight of his partial success, and the menace of pursuing his advantage, induced the Venetian government to submit, when they found that easy terms would be imposed, in return for the doubtful conquest.

Pepin willingly desisted from an enterprise which had offered many difficulties, and dispatched the fleet, for which he had no longer any occupation at Venice, to ravage the coasts of Dalmatia, which had been resign to the ungrateful Greeks. The appearance, however, of the patrician Paul, with a superior force, obliged the Frankish armament to retire; and not long after, the Venetian states were formally ceded by Charlemagne to the desires of the Eastern emperor.

Such was the end of the struggles which the empire of the East made to recover from Charlemagne some portion of that territory which Nicephorus, in the lavish timidity of unconfirmed authority, had deemed a trifling sacrifice for the enjoyment of unmolested dominion. As he grew old in empire, his native covetousness resumed its power over his mind; but before he could proceed to exact more from the generous moderation of the Frankish monarch, the steel of the Bulgarians had terminated the life of the avaricious usurper. Stauracius, who succeeded, devoted his short reign of six months to render himself hated and contemned at home; and Michael I, who followed Stauracius, was too eager to seek the friendship of Charlemagne, either to impugn his title to empire, or to strive for the dismemberment of his dominions.

Those dominions were now as extensive as the proudest ambition could well desire to possess, or the mightiest genius could pretend to govern. The whole of France and Belgium, with their natural boundaries of the Alps, the Pyrenees, the ocean, the Mediterranean, and the Rhine, formed no inconsiderable empire. But to these possessions were added, to the south, all that part of Spain comprised between the Ebro and the Pyrenees, and to the north, the whole of Germany, to the banks of the Elbe. Italy, as far as the Lower Calabria, was either governed by his son or tributary to his crown; and Dalmatia, Croatia, Liburnia, and Istria, with the exception of the maritime cities, were joined to the conquered territories of Hungary and Bohemia. As far as the conflux of the Danube with the Teyss and the Save, the east of Europe acknowledged the power of the Frankish monarch. Most of the Slavonian tribes, between the Elbe and the Vistula, paid tribute and professed obedience; and Corsica, Sardinia, and the Balearic Isles were dependent on the emperor's possessions in Italy and Spain.

Such were the dominions of Charlemagne at the conclusion of the Venetian war in 810; and such were the dominions which he proposed to leave divided among his sons. The fatigue and difficulty which he felt in governing and restraining this vast empire himself doubtless rendered him the more willing to see it parted among his children, whose powers of command he could not but perceive were far inferior to his own. Yet probably paternal tenderness and affectionate equity might combine with his other motives for the equal allotment of his territories; as we know that a private station, where all the softer sympathies of domestic life are fostered by every means of reciprocation, never produced a tenderer parent than the monarch of that mighty empire.

This division, as I have already stated, was destined never to take place. That prolongation of existence, to which human nature clings with so much fond tenacity, brought with it to Charlemagne many of those concomitant sorrows attendant ever on old age. He saw his friends and his children die around him. The companions of his dangers and his glory, the participators of his labors and their success, in general sank into the grave, ere the great spirit which had called forth, directed, and combined their efforts was separated from its human dust. Alcuin had died some time before; but the severer stroke still awaited Charlemagne of seeing the order of nature reversed, and the children of his love fall before the parent who had given them birth.

His first loss was that of his eldest daughter Rotruda; and though the irregular conduct of the female part of his family had caused him frequent pain and continual anxiety, he felt her early fate with all the poignancy of a father's grief, and forgot her weakness in her death. Scarcely had the news of his son's victories over the Venetians reached the ears of the emperor, when it was followed by the tidings of his decease; and scarcely had the monarch secured to the son of Pepin the kingdom which he had formerly assigned to the father, ere Charles, for whom the imperial throne had been reserved, was also called to the tomb. Honor, and glory, and strife, and labor, and victory, and success, had not been able to extinguish one spark of those warm affections with which Charlemagne had been endowed by nature; nor had a long life of prosperity, dominion, and absolute command been sufficient to weaken one of those gentler feelings, which united the great monarch so endearingly with his fellow- creatures. Charlemagne wept the loss of his children, and the broken ties of kindred affection, with as bitter, as human a sorrow as if he had been the tenant of a cottage, instead of being the emperor of one-half the world; nor can his preservation of domestic attachments surely be looked upon as a weakness when they interfered with no public duty, and served only to soften his private character.

Of the emperor's three sons, none now remained but Louis, King of Aquitaine, and in him centred all the affection of the monarch. After the death of his brothers, a feeling of diffidence and modesty withheld him for some time from his father's court, lest he should appear too eagerly to covet the dominion which, in the course of nature, would soon fall into his hands. But Charlemagne was incapable of being jealous of his son; and, as soon as he had terminated the various negotiations which the loss of Pepin and Charles left entirely to his own exertions, he dispatched messengers into Aquitaine to call Louis to his presence.

Although the death of his two elder sons had abrogated the charter of division, and though the emperor had provided for Bernard the son of Pepin, by confirming him in the government of Italy, so that the succession of Louis to the imperial throne, with all the territories attached to it in France and Germany, was not to be doubted, yet Charlemagne resolved, by a solemn act of association, to secure the empire more firmly to his surviving son, and to guard against the intrigues of faction and the efforts of ambition.

As soon after the arrival of Louis as possible, the emperor called the general assembly of his people to meet at Aix-la-Chapelle; and there, in an eloquent speech, he alluded to the probability of his own death before many years could pass, and exhorted the nation to be faithful and obedient to his successor, as they had been to himself. He then demanded the consent of each individual present to the nomination of Louis as heir to his empire, and required the promise of their allegiance to that prince. The assent of the nobles was unanimous; and on the Sunday that followed, the emperor marked, with solemn ceremony, the ratification of his own purpose by the voice of his subjects.

The immense church which he himself had built at Aix-la-Chapelle was prepared for the occasion, and, a little before the morning service began, the monarch proceeded to that building, which was already filled with the nobles of all the different nations he united under his sway. His usual simple garments were laid aside, and, robed with imperial splendor, and surrounded by imperial pomp, he advanced to the high altar of the church, leaning on the shoulder of the King of Aquitaine. The father and the son knelt together, and continued for some time in prayer, beseeching the blessing of Heaven upon their designs. At length the emperor rose, and addressed his son in the presence of the whole multitude. He exhorted him, above all things, to fear and love God, and to follow his law; to govern carefully the church, and to protect it against its enemies; to show kindness and endurance towards all his relations; to honor the clergy as fathers, and to love the people as his children; to force the proud and corrupt to turn to a better path; and to be himself the friend of the faithful and the poor. He prayed him also to choose his ministers from those who were known to be trustworthy, filled with the fear of God, and the enemies of unjust partiality; to deprive no man of his property without full cause; and to keep himself irreproachable in the sight of God and of his people.

After having addressed him for a length of time with great power and eloquence, he demanded if he were willing to follow those precepts for the government of his people; and on Louis's reply in the affirmative, he directed him to raise, with his own hands, a crown which had been laid purposely on the altar, and place it on his own head, as "a gift which he held from God, his father, and the nation". Louis complied, and the ceremony ended with the usual solemn service of the day.

Not long after this event the King of Aquitaine returned to his government, and Charlemagne, embarrassed by no hostile movements, except some slight disturbances among the Slavonian tribes, dedicated the rest of his days to the general organization of his dominions, and to preparation for that interminable future towards whose awful barrier he was fast approaching. His external relations I have already traced; and the internal regulations attributable to this period of his reign afford no cause to alter the opinion before expressed, that if they were not the best which could be formed on abstract principles, they were the best that could be adapted to the circumstances of his age and nation.

Notwithstanding the weight of seventy years, the Latin emperor had yet lost but little of his personal energy; and the reconstruction of the ancient light-house near Boulogne, the long and fatiguing journeys he took to inspect the state of the fleets destined to protect the coast, and the design of a that bridge at Mayence, which he proposed to build in stone, after the destruction of the former wooden structure by fire, evince the incessant activity of his mind, and its fertility in projects for the protection and improvement of his dominions.

Notwithstanding frequent attacks of the gout, and a degree of lameness which that disease had left, he still followed the chase, in which he had always delighted, with unabated ardor, and still enjoyed the bath, wherein he had so long been accustomed to exercise himself in swimming. It was one day after he had been using the thermal waters of Aix-la-

Chapelle, that he felt the first attack of that malady which terminated his life. He was suddenly seized with a violent pain in the side, which was soon proved to proceed from pleurisy. In common with all men who during a long life have possessed robust health, Charlemagne despised and rejected the aid of medicine, and, imagining that abstinence was the sole remedy for all sorts of sickness, he refused food of every kind, and only allayed his feverish thirst with small quantities of water. The violence of his disease required more active means of cure; these were not employed, and at length, after a few days' illness, on the 28th of January, in the year 814, Charles the Great expired, in the seventy-second year of his age, and the forty-seventh of his reign.

The character of Charlemagne can alone be appreciated by comparing it with the barbarism of the times from which he emerged; nor do his virtues or his talents acquire any fictitious grandeur from opposition with the objects around; for, though "the ruins of Palmyra derive a casual splendor from the nakedness of the surrounding desert", his excellence lay not alone in adorning, but in cultivating the waste. His military successes were prepared by the wars and victories both of Pepin and Charles Martel; but one proof of the vast comprehensiveness of his mind is to be found in the immense undertakings which he accomplished with the same means which two great monarchs had employed on very inferior enterprises. The dazzling rapidity with which each individual expedition was executed was perhaps less wonderful than the clear precision with which each was designed, and the continuous, persevering, unconquerable determination wherewith each general élan was pursued to its close. The materials for is wars,—the brave, the active, and the hardy soldiers,—had been formed by his father and by nature; but when those troops were to be led through desert and unknown countries, into which Pepin had never dreamed of penetrating, and in an age when geography was hardly known—when they were to be sup- plied at a distance from all their resources, in a land where roads were unheard of, and provisions too scanty for the inhabitants themselves—the success was attributable to Charlemagne, and the honor is his due. His predecessors had contented themselves with leading an army at once against the point they intended to assail, or against the host they proposed to combat; but Charlemagne was the first in modem Europe who introduced the great improvement in the art of war of pouring large bodies of men, by different roads, into the hostile country; of teaching them to co-operate though separate, to concentrate when required, and of combining their efforts and their movements for a general purpose on a preconcerted plan.

In a life like his, which was a life of improvement on all that immediately preceded him, it is wonderful that he did not meet with repeated disappointments and disasters, from the many hazardous experiments he was obliged to make, and from the insecurity attending many of his conquests, on account of the very rapidity with which they were accomplished. This will appear the more extraordinary when it is remembered that, in addition to the fierce savages of the north, he had to contend with the civilized and warlike Saracens, with the veteran Lombards, whose whole history was warfare, and with the cunning Greeks, who supplied by art much that they wanted in vigor. The native energy, activity, and strength of the Franks, indeed, gave him advantages and facilities in all his struggles; but had he not, as a leader and a king, possessed energy, activity, and strength in a far greater proportion than all, the very qualities in his subjects which he used as implements in his own great designs would have been employed by them against himself; and, instead of combating and conquering a thousand foreign enemies at once, he would have had, like many who preceded him, to strive through life with unwilling vassals, for a precarious throne.

War was a necessity of the time and the country; and the Franks could not have been governed without war. Charlemagne, happily for himself and for his people, brought with him to the throne warlike talents, and a warlike disposition; and, happily for the world, possessed likewise the spirit of civilization and improvement.

Notwithstanding one instance of terrible severity,—which, however erroneously, he judged necessary to strike terror into a fierce and lawless people, and to stop the further desolation of both nations,—he was the most clement of kings, and the least selfish of conquerors. After his victories, he imposed a benefit and not a yoke, and raised instead of degraded the people who became his subjects.

His great success in civilization was all his own. Nothing had been done by those who went before, scarcely a germ, scarcely a seed had been left him. He took possession of a kingdom torn by factions, surrounded by enemies, desolated by long wars, disorganized by intestine strife, and as profoundly ignorant as the absence of all letters could make it. By the continual and indefatigable exertion of mental and corporeal powers, such as probably were never united but in himself, he restored order and harmony, brought back internal tranquillity, secured individual safety, raised up sciences and arts; and so convinced a barbarous nation of the excellence of his own ameliorating spirit, that on their consent and approbation he founded all his efforts, and sought no support in his mighty undertaking but the love and confidence of his people.

Of his many conquests, the long and persevering wars which he waged with the barbarians of the north have been, in their success, the most advantageous to Europe; for as civilization advanced step by step with victory, and as he snatched from darkness all the lands he conquered, he may be said to have added the whole of Germany to the world. Italy fell into greater disorders than before; France underwent another age of darkness; but from the Rhine to the Elbe, and from the Danube to the ocean, received light which has continued unextinguished to the present day.

In domestic life, Charlemagne was too indulgent a father, and perhaps too indulgent a husband; and the consequences of this weakness often gave him pain. Nevertheless, the monarch could hardly reproach his daughters for passions which they inherited from himself, nor for yielding to those passions when he set them the example. The private vices or follies of any man can only become legitimate matter for history when they have had an effect upon society in general; but it may be observed, without entering deeply into any unpleasant details, that Charlemagne scarcely could expect the morality he inculcated to be very strictly observed, when his own incontinence was great and notorious.

This, however, is the only vice which history has recorded of Charlemagne, among a thousand splendid qualities. He was ambitious, it is true; but his ambition was of the noblest kind. He was generous, magnanimous, liberal, humane, and brave; but he was frugal, simple, moderate, just, and prudent. Though easily appeased in his enmities, his friendships were deep and permanent; and, though hasty and severe to avenge his friends, he was merciful and placable when personally injured. In mind he was blessed with all those happy facilities which were necessary to success in the great enterprises which he undertook. His eloquence was strong, abundant, and clear; and a great talent for acquiring foreign tongues added to his powers of expression. The same quickness of comprehension rendered every other study light, though undertaken in the midst of a thousand varied occupations, and at an age to which great capabilities of acquisition are not in general extended. His person was handsome and striking. His countenance was fine, open, and bland, his features high, and his eyes large and sparkling. His figure was remarkable for its fine proportions; and though somewhat inclined to obesity in his later years, we are told, that, whether sitting or standing, there was always something in his appearance which breathed of dignity, and inspired respect. He was sober and abstemious in his food, and simple to an extreme in his garments. Passionately fond of robust exercises, they formed his great relaxation and amusement; but he never neglected the business of the public for his private pleasure, nor yielded one moment to repose or enjoyment which could be more profitably employed. His activity, his quickness, and his indefatigable energy in conducting the affairs of state having already been spoken of at large, it only remains to be said, that in private life he was gentle, cheerful, affectionate, and kind; and that—with his dignity guarded by virtues, talents, and mighty renown—he frequently laid aside the pomp of empire, and the sternness of command.

No man, perhaps, that ever lived, combined in so high a degree those qualities which rule men and direct events, with those which endear the possessor and attach his contemporaries. No man was ever more trusted and loved by his people, more respected and feared by other kings, more esteemed in his lifetime, or more regretted at his death.

.

Printed in Great Britain
by Amazon